CODE RED

Michele Crawford
Rob Nicholas
Stuart Cochrane

B2

Student's Book

MACMILLAN

Contents

Theme	Reading	Grammar
1 Person to person Communication Relationships *page 6*	FCE Reading Part 3 Mobile phones • scanning B2 Exam Practice Tuareg marriage customs	• present simple • present continuous • state verbs • present perfect simple • present perfect continuous **FCE Use of English Part 4:** transformations
2 24/7 Jobs Services Daily life *page 18*	FCE Reading Part 1 Busking B2 Exam Practice Job advertisements	• past simple • past continuous • *used to* and *would* • past perfect simple • past perfect continuous **FCE Use of English Part 2:** open cloze

Review 1   *page 30*

Theme	Reading	Grammar
3 Open your mind! Education Learning *page 32*	FCE Reading Part 2 First day B2 Exam Practice University brochure	• comparatives and superlatives • gradable and non-gradable adjectives • question forms • question tags **FCE Use of English Part 4:** transformations
4 Changes Science Technology Social change Crime *page 44*	FCE Reading Part 3 Crime in the 21st century B2 Exam Practice Bill Gates	• infinitive and *-ing* forms • future forms • time clauses in the future **FCE Use of English Part 2:** open cloze

Review 2   *page 56*

Theme	Reading	Grammar
5 Movement Travel Transport *page 58*	FCE Reading Part 2 I get around B2 Exam Practice Outdoor activities	• modal verbs (1) • *so* and *such* • *too* and *enough* **FCE Use of English Part 4:** transformations

Vocabulary	Listening	Speaking	Writing
• communication • phrasal verbs • *say*, *tell* and *speak* • character adjectives • word partners • prefixes and suffixes **FCE Use of English Part 3:** word formation	**FCE Listening Part 1** multiple choice	**FCE Speaking Part 1** • expressing likes and dislikes • talking about ambitions • syllable stress	**FCE Writing Part 2** non-transactional letter (job application) • topic vocabulary • paragraphing
• shops and services • phrasal verbs • *do* and *make* • work and jobs • adjective endings • easily confused words **FCE Use of English Part 1:** multiple choice cloze	**FCE Listening Part 2** sentence completion	**FCE Speaking Part 2** • *-ing* and *-ed* adjectives • comparing • pronunciation of *-ed* endings	**FCE Writing Part 2** story • setting the scene • describing action • commenting on events • adverb formation
• education and learning • easily confused words • phrasal verbs • noun suffixes • word patterns with *get* and *take* • expressions with *set* **FCE Use of English Part 3:** word formation	**FCE Listening Part 3** multiple matching	**FCE Speaking Part 3** • making suggestions • pronunciation	**FCE Writing Part 2** article • making a statement • expressing point of view
• technology • society and crime • word partners • prepositions • phrasal verbs **FCE Use of English Part 1:** multiple choice cloze	**FCE Listening Part 4** multiple choice	**FCE Speaking Part 4** • expanding on answers • conversation fillers	**FCE Writing Part 1** transactional letter • formal and informal register • expanding on notes • opening and closing • making suggestions
• means of transport • easily confused words • word partners • prepositions • travel • phrasal verbs **FCE Use of English Part 3:** word formation	**FCE Listening Part 1** multiple choice	**FCE Speaking Complete test**	**FCE Writing Part 2** essay • listing points • giving explanations • giving examples • making suggestions

Theme	Reading	Grammar
6 Mother Nature Environment Food *page 70*	FCE Reading Part 1 School dinners B2 Exam Practice Yellowstone National Park	• passive voice • articles • countable and uncountable nouns FCE Use of English Part 2: open cloze

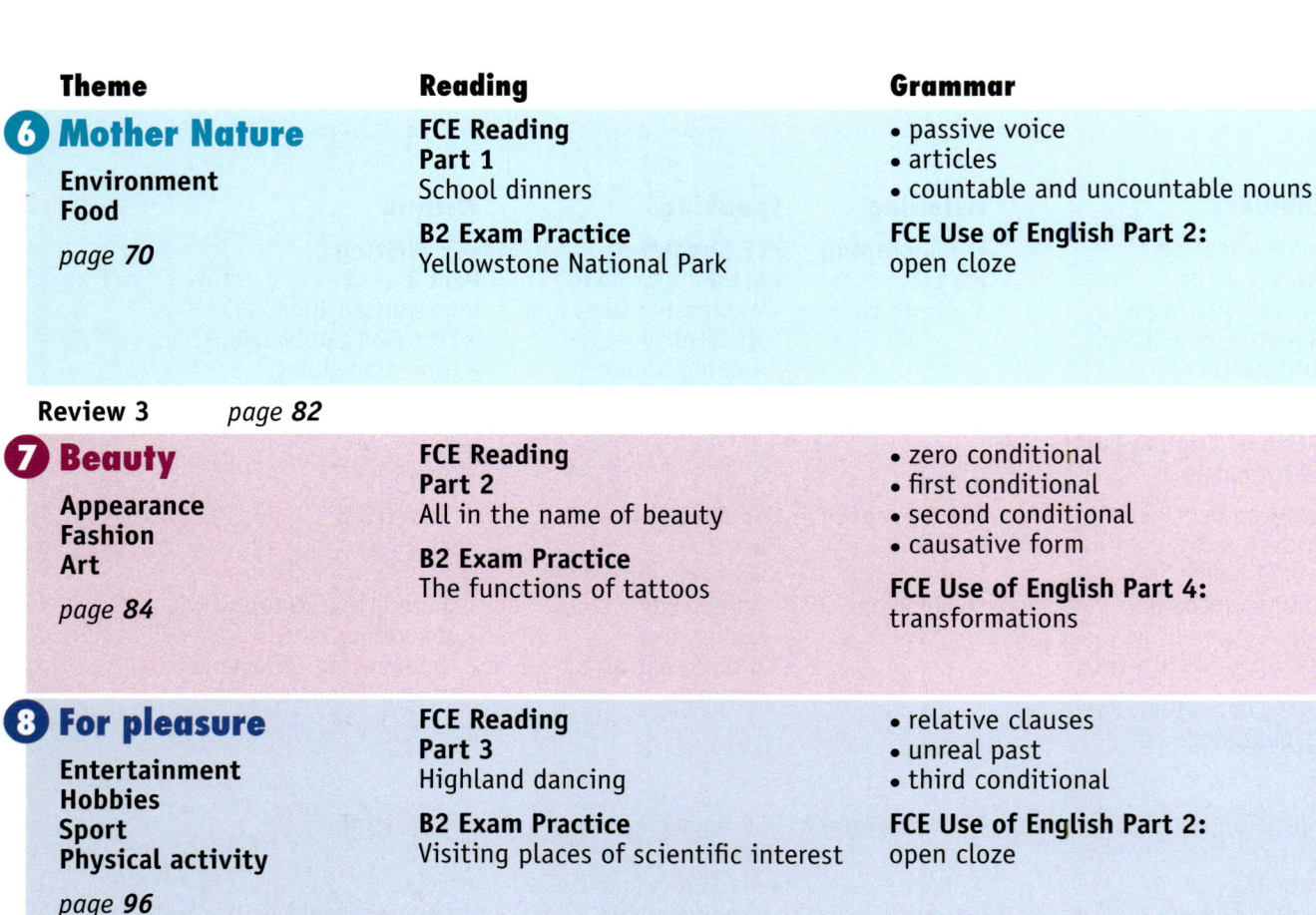

Review 3   *page 82*

Theme	Reading	Grammar
7 Beauty Appearance Fashion Art *page 84*	FCE Reading Part 2 All in the name of beauty B2 Exam Practice The functions of tattoos	• zero conditional • first conditional • second conditional • causative form FCE Use of English Part 4: transformations
8 For pleasure Entertainment Hobbies Sport Physical activity *page 96*	FCE Reading Part 3 Highland dancing B2 Exam Practice Visiting places of scientific interest	• relative clauses • unreal past • third conditional FCE Use of English Part 2: open cloze

Review 4   *page 108*

Theme	Reading	Grammar
9 Words Media Advertising *page 110*	FCE Reading Part 1 Word-of-mouth advertising B2 Exam Practice Printing museum brochure	• reported speech • reported questions FCE Use of English Part 4: transformations
10 Different places Cultures Nationalities *page 122*	FCE Reading Part 2 Culture shock B2 Exam Practice Foreign food restaurant guide	• modal verbs (2) • inversion FCE Use of English Part 2: open cloze

Review 5   *page 134*

Pair work   *page 136*
Grammar reference   *page 138*
Vocabulary file   *page 150*
Writing bank   *page 160*
Speaking bank   *page 168*

Vocabulary	Listening	Speaking	Writing
• health and diet • phrasal verbs • word partners • cooking and eating • the natural world • prepositions **FCE Use of English Part 1:** multiple choice cloze	**FCE Listening Part 2** sentence completion	**FCE Speaking Parts 1 and 2** • talking about yourself • expanding on answers • describing people's feelings • commonly made mistakes	**FCE Writing Part 2** Report • analyzing the task • using headings • explaining the purpose of writing • making recommendations • speaking in general • concluding
• appearance and fashion • word partners • phrasal verbs • *match, suit, fit, go with* • art • word formation **FCE Use of English Part 3:** word formation	**FCE Listening Part 3** multiple matching	**FCE Speaking Parts 3 and 4** • keeping the conversation going	**FCE Writing Part 2** article • writing about what people do • linking words and phrases • expressing preferences
• sports, hobbies and pastimes • sports equipment • phrasal verbs • entertainment • word partners • easily confused words **FCE Use of English Part 1:** multiple choice cloze	**FCE Listening Part 4** multiple choice	**FCE Speaking Parts 1 and 2** • talking about your interests • describing objects and places • silent letters	**FCE Writing Part 2** essay • participle clauses • introducing arguments • giving reasons • describing results/effects
• radio and television • phrasal verbs • newspapers • word formation • advertising **FCE Use of English Part 3:** word formation	**FCE Listening Part 2** sentence completion	**FCE Speaking Parts 3 and 4** • responding to comments • pronunciation	**FCE Writing Part 2** review • paragraphing • using adjectives • introducing the subject • explaining what it is about • saying what you liked about it • making recommendations
• buildings • adjectives • places • prepositions • easily confused words • phrasal verbs **FCE Use of English Part 1:** multiple choice cloze	**FCE Listening Part 4** multiple choice	**FCE Speaking** Complete test	**FCE Writing Part 1** transactional email • editing your work • expanding notes • answering questions • reminding and reassuring

1 Person to person

A Which of the different means of communication would you choose for:
- arranging to meet a friend for a coffee?
- keeping in touch with a relative who lives abroad?
- sending a document to someone?
- communicating with a group of people?
- sending a photo to someone?

email • text message • fax • phone call • online chat
conference call • letter • voicemail

What could the others be used for?

Reading 1

B Do the Communications Quiz!

1 What do the letters SMS stand for?
  a Silent Method of Speaking   b Speedy Mini Speeches   c Short Message Service

2 What can an attachment be part of?
  a a letter   b an email   c a phone call

3 When you are on the internet, you are … .
  a ongoing   b online   c onboard

4 What do we call the device that lets you talk on a mobile phone without holding it?
  a hands off   b hands away   c hands free

5 What is the symbol @ always part of?
  a a website address   b an email address   c a fax

6 When you finish a phone call, you … .
  a hang up   b hang on   c hang down

B2 Exam Practice

You will be given a text which is divided into several parts. You will have to match the parts of the text with 15 answer choices.

Steps to success
- Don't read the paragraphs in detail — just scan them to find the answers to the questions.
- When you find the information that answers the question, underline it.

A Allie, 14

I mostly use my mobile for sending text messages — I probably send about 20 a day! It's much cheaper than talking, so my parents don't moan about the bill. They like me having a phone so that they can keep tabs on me, which is a bit annoying sometimes. I take my phone to school with me, but we have to switch them off during lessons. They threatened to ban them completely a couple of months ago when they caught a pupil using his phone to cheat during an exam. He was in serious trouble! Since then we've had to be more careful about when and where we use our phones at school.

B Edith, 78

I never wanted to have a mobile phone. I didn't see the point at my age and I thought they would be really complicated to use. Then my daughter bought me one for my birthday last year and now I use it all the time. Having it with me makes me feel safe. It's useful too — if, for example, I want my daughter to give me a lift home from the supermarket, I just give her a buzz. She also knows she can contact me at any time, which stops her worrying about me! Obviously I could live without a mobile phone if I had to, but it certainly makes life a lot easier.

C You are going to read a magazine article about mobile phones. Find the answers to questions 1-15 as quickly as possible, underlining where you found the answer in the text.

Which person:

wasn't keen on having a mobile at first? **1**

doesn't make calls on their mobile very often? **2**

was given a mobile as a present? **3**

mentions how mobiles can be used for dishonest purposes? **4**

Mobile phones

C Helen, 48

I'm a mobile phone addict, I'm afraid. I'm one of those irritating people who uses their phone everywhere — on public transport, walking along the street and when I'm out having dinner at a restaurant! The thing is I'm a very busy person and my mobile is invaluable because it allows me to do more than one thing at the same time. I can talk to my bank manager while I'm shopping or text my husband while I'm in a meeting at work. I probably spend at least an hour a day on my mobile and I do sometimes worry about the health risks, but I just couldn't do without it now.

D John, 37

I'm in a minority, I know, because I don't possess a mobile phone. I've actually made a conscious decision not to get one, which most people find strange, but I've never been the kind of person who follows trends. Call me old-fashioned, but I don't want people to be able to contact me whenever they want, night or day. There's a time and a place for everything and I like to have phone calls in private in the comfort of my own home. It really gets on my nerves when people talk loudly on their mobile in public places and I could never be so inconsiderate. The only times it might be useful to have a mobile phone are when I'm travelling and I need to check train times or let someone know what time I'm arriving somewhere. I just have to be a bit more organized and make sure I've got some change on me for the payphone!

E Ben, 11

My mum and dad won't buy me a mobile phone because they say I'm too young to have one. They think I would use it to ring my friends all the time and then they'd have to pay the bill. My parents also think mobile phones are unhealthy, so neither of them has got one. I don't think it's fair, though. All my friends have got them and I feel a bit left out when they text each other or play games on their phones. I'd like to get one of those phones with lots of different gadgets on them, one that can send pictures as well as messages. I'm saving up for one at the moment, and hoping my parents will change their minds!

Exam alert

There will always be some words and expressions that are new to you in a reading text, but don't panic! Use the context to help you work out their meaning.

Work it out!

D Find words in the text that mean:

1 complain (A) ....
2 not allow (A) ....
3 difficult (B) ....
4 communicate with (B) .... , ...
5 extremely useful (C) ....
6 dangers (C) ....
7 fashions (D) ....
8 annoys me (D) ....
9 useful devices (E) ....
10 collecting money (E) ....

* The letters in brackets refer to the paragraphs in the text.

---

finds mobile phones annoying? **5** ☐
thinks mobile phones might be harmful? **6** ☐
wants to buy a mobile phone? **7** ☐
thinks that mobile phones save time? **8** ☐
isn't free to use their mobile whenever they want? **9** ☐
would like a particular type of mobile? **10** ☐
doesn't like being checked up on by other people? **11** ☐
doesn't mind not having a mobile phone? **12** ☐
is considered unusual by others? **13** ☐
thinks their mobile phone is essential? **14** ☐
has changed their opinion about mobiles? **15** ☐

Quick chat

When and where do teenagers use mobile phones the most? Why do you think texting is so popular with teenagers? When is talking better than texting?

Grammar 1

✓ Check present simple and present continuous

See page 138 for information about the present simple and the present continuous tenses.

Match the uses with the sentences.

Present simple
1 a habit
2 a permanent situation
3 a future event that happens regularly at the same time
4 a fact/truth about life in general

Present continuous
5 something happening at this moment
6 something happening during this period
7 a plan for the future
8 a complaint

a Jack's getting a new laptop next week.
b Human beings communicate via language.
c I send about ten text messages per day.
d The internet café closes at midnight on Friday.
e We live near the post office.
f Carl is going out with Lucy.
g 'Are you paying attention?'
h You're always telling lies!

A Complete the dialogue with the present simple or present continuous form of the verbs in brackets.

Mum: What (1) .... you two .... (do)?
Bob: Er, Tim (2) .... (help) me with my homework.
Mum: Why (3) .... you .... (play) computer games, then? You (4) .... (spend) far too much time on that computer!
Tim: Well, actually, we (5) .... (do) a project about computer games at school. This (6) .... (be) research.
Mum: Really? You (7) .... (get) interesting homework at your school! Why (8) .... you .... (do) it together, though?
Bob: Well, Tim's computer (9) .... (not work) so he (10) .... (use) mine.
Tim: Yes. I (11) .... (always have) problems with my computer. It (12) .... (be) really old. My parents (13) .... (buy) me a new one for my birthday.
Mum: Good. Then you'll be able to do your next computer game 'project' on your own!

✓ Check state verbs

See page 138 for information about state verbs.

Complete the sentences with the correct form of the verbs given. What do all the verbs have in common?

1 I .... (not understand) this word!
2 She .... (seem) a bit upset.
3 .... (you / believe) what Andy said?
4 My mum .... (love) her new mobile phone!

B Circle the correct word or phrase.

I (1) **read / am reading** a really interesting book at the moment. It (2) **says / is saying** that our personalities (3) **depend / are depending** on our birth order, that is, our position in relation to our brothers and sisters. For example, according to this book, the eldest child in a family (4) **usually likes / is usually liking** to be the leader. Now I (5) **know / am knowing** why my older sister (6) **bosses always / is always bossing** me and my brother around! I (7) **am / am being** the youngest child in our family and, apparently, youngest children (8) **usually get / are usually getting** on well with everyone. I (9) **think / am thinking** it's true, but things might change because my mum (10) **has / is having** another baby next month!

Vocabulary 1
Communication

A Match the actions with when you do them.

1 wave
2 frown
3 shake your head
4 nod
5 raise your eyebrows
6 sniff
7 sigh
8 yawn

a to show surprise
b to say 'no'
c when you've got a cold
d when you're tired or bored
e to say hello or goodbye
f to say 'yes'
g when you're annoyed
h when you're sad

Key phrasal verbs

B Match the phrasal verbs with their meanings.

1 I don't want to go out with Dan. How can I **get** the message **across** without hurting his feelings?
2 What do the letters BA **stand for**?
3 Don't **make up** excuses. Tell me the truth!
4 Sue **comes out with** the strangest comments!
5 Why did he **bring up** the subject of exams?
6 I managed to **talk** my mum **into** letting me go camping with my friends.

a invent
b say suddenly
c persuade
d communicate
e represent
f introduce

C Complete the sentences with phrasal verbs from Exercise B in the correct form.

1 I believe Tim. He never .... things ....
2 When Jenny .... the correct answer to his question, the teacher was speechless!
3 Hugh didn't want to have a tattoo, but his friends .... him .... it.
4 Our teacher .... the subject of cheating.
5 Do you know what the letters PS .... ?
6 Teachers have to be able to .... their ideas .... to other people.

Word patterns: *say, tell, speak*

Be quiet!
I'm speaking! ✔
I'm telling! ✘
I'm saying! ✘

I spoke to him about the problem. ✔
I spoke to him for the problem. ✘

I told Liz the news. ✔
I said Liz the news. ✘
I told to Liz the news. ✘

The man didn't say anything. ✔
The man didn't tell anything. ✘

D Write *say*, *tell* or *speak*.

1 .... the time
2 .... someone off
3 .... sorry
4 .... a language
5 .... a lie
6 .... a prayer
7 .... what you think
8 .... a story
9 .... your mind
10 .... the truth
11 .... up
12 .... a joke

E Complete the text with the correct form of *say, tell* or *speak*.

How to spot a liar!

How do you know when someone is (1) .... a lie? According to experts, there are some signs you can look out for. When someone (2) .... something without looking you in the eye, this is the first clue that they aren't (3) .... you the truth. Other signs include looking uncomfortable, blushing or fiddling with something while they're (4) .... Of course, really good liars have learnt how to cover up these signs and (5) .... stories in such a way that they resemble the truth. Whatever they (6) .... , they manage to be convincing! In cases like this, a lie detector is the only answer!

Listening

B2 Exam Practice

You will hear eight short monologues or dialogues. There will be a multiple choice question based on each one. You will hear each extract TWICE.

Steps to success
- Read the questions and answer options carefully.
- Decide what the key words are and underline them.
- When listening, pay attention to anything that could be related to these words.

A 🎧 Look at this question and the answer options. Some key words are highlighted. Now listen and answer the question.

Listen to this girl talking to her friend. **Why doesn't** her friend **want to borrow** the **magazine**?

A She's **already read it**.
B It **isn't serious** enough.
C She **doesn't like** Robbie Williams.

B Look at the questions and answer choices below. Underline the key words in each one.

1 What does the boy think of Sean?
A He likes being alone.
B He's only interested in himself.
C He isn't very confident.

2 Listen to this message on a mobile phone answering machine. Who is James Duffy?
A a writer
B a singer
C a film star

3 What does the boy want to do in Spain?
A Take Spanish lessons.
B Practise speaking Spanish.
C Go to a place where English is spoken.

4 Who wrote the book the girl has just read?
A a Japanese woman
B a foreign woman who lived in Japan
C an American man

5 You overhear this conversation on a bus. What does the man think of mobile phones?
A They save time.
B They aren't very useful.
C He wishes he had a better one.

6 Listen to this man talking on the radio. What is the programme about?
A Bulgarian culture
B foreign languages
C body language

7 You hear someone talking on the phone. Who is she talking to?
A a hotel receptionist
B a bank clerk
C a hospital employee

🎧 Listen and choose the best answer (A, B or C).

Speaking

B2 Exam Practice
You will have to answer questions about yourself and your life.

Steps to success
- Listen very carefully to the examiner's questions.
- Avoid giving one-word answers!

A Look at these common questions and tick the answer(s) which would be correct. Sometimes more than one is correct.

1 Where are you from?
2 How long have you been studying English?
3 How many people are there in your family?
4 How often do you go to the cinema?
5 Have you got any ambitions for the future?
6 Do you prefer being on your own or spending time with friends?

1
a I'm coming from Patras.
b I come from Patras.
c I'm from Patras.

2
a About eight years.
b I'm studying English for about eight years.
c I've been studying English for about eight years.

3
a Four.
b Four – my mum, my dad, my brother and me.
c We are four.

4
a About once a month.
b I'm going to the cinema once a month.
c I go about once a month.

5
a Yes. I'm thinking to be a journalist.
b Yes. I like being a journalist.
c Yes. I'd like to be a journalist.

6
a Being on my own.
b I'd prefer being on my own than spending time with friends.
c I prefer spending time with friends to being on my own.

B Ask and answer the same questions with a partner. Use the Language chunks to help you.

Language chunks

Likes and dislikes
I like/don't like/love/hate + ...-ing
I prefer ...-ing to ...-ing
I'm keen on ...-ing

I'd like/love to ...
I wouldn't like to ...
I'd hate to ...
I'd prefer to ... than (to) ...

Talking about ambitions
I'm hoping to ...
I'm looking forward to ...
I'm thinking about ...

C Follow the instructions below.

Student A: Use the prompts below to form questions and interview your partner.

what / you like / do / free time?
which country / you like / visit?
what job / you / like / do / in the future?
you prefer / spend time / with family or with friends?
you / have got / any ambitions?

Student B: Answer your partner's questions, using the Language chunks to help you.

Student B: Now use the prompts below to form questions and interview your partner.

where / you / like / go / on holiday?
you / have got / any hobbies?
what kind / books / you / like?
you prefer / newspapers or magazines?
what / your favourite subject / at school?

Student A: Answer your partner's questions, using the Language chunks to help you.

Say it right!

D Read these words aloud and underline the stressed syllable in each.

1 ambition
2 cinema
3 magazine
4 holiday
5 information
6 reliable
7 journalist
8 apologize
9 advertisement
10 capable

E Now listen to see if you were right.

1

A Which of the following customs exist in your country?

- Parents decide who their children will marry.
- During the wedding ceremony, the guests shower the couple with rice.
- The bride must promise to obey her husband.
- The groom leads the bride as they walk in a circle.
- The bride and groom take turns feeding each other.
- The couple goes on a honeymoon after getting married.

What other wedding customs exist in your country?

Reading 2

B Choose the word that best completes each sentence.

1 A .... is what a man or a woman makes when they ask someone to marry them.
a proposal   c penalty
b partnership   d proposition

2 Before they get married, a couple gets ....
a engaged   c encountered
b encouraged   d enormous

3 The men who take part in a wedding ceremony normally wear smart ....
a customs   c suites
b costumes   d suits

4 At a wedding reception, tables are often decorated with flower ....
a arrangements   c bunches
b patterns   d beds

5 Most marriages take place during a special ....
a display   c ceremony
b reception   d congregation

6 One year after their wedding the happy couple celebrates their first wedding ....
a day   c anniversary
b memorial   d date

B2 Exam Practice

You will read a text based on factual information, and have to answer six multiple choice questions.

Steps to success
- Read the text carefully.
- Quickly read through the questions and then read the text again underlining ideas that relate to the questions.

C Read the following passage about certain marriage customs among the Tuareg in Africa and then answer the questions.

Marriage in the dunes

The people known as the Tuareg, who have lived in Africa's Sahara region for centuries, have their own marriage traditions. A Tuareg wedding will only take place if both sets of parents agree and, if the groom has an elder brother, he also must consent. The families are also involved in arranging the bride-wealth. When a man gets married, it is usually his father who gives the necessary number of cattle to the bride's family. The tent, mats and cooking utensils for the married couple are the obligation of the bride's family.

During the day before the wedding ceremony the bride and the groom are kept apart from each other at opposite sides of the camp and their faces are covered with thick veils. These are only removed when the two meet at midnight at the specially prepared wedding place close to the tents of the bride's family. Once they are married, Tuareg women are prohibited from calling their husbands by their usual names and they must not talk too much to them.

Tuareg society also has strict customs about which people the newly-weds should avoid. For instance, after getting married a husband should not talk to his mother-in-law or eat in her presence and he should not sleep in a tent which is close to hers.

1 What must happen before the wedding ceremony?
a The bride only must remove her veil.
b The bride's parents must give their permission.
c The groom must build the tent.
d The bride must prepare the feast.

2 Where do the couple stay just before the wedding ceremony?
a with the groom's family
b with the bride's family
c in separate tents
d in one large tent

3 Where do Tuareg wedding ceremonies take place?
a in the tent of the bride's family
b in the tent of the groom's family
c in a special wooden building
d near to where the bride's family live

4 What should Tuareg wives never do?
a talk to their husbands
b call their husbands by their names
c speak to their mothers
d take off their veils

5 Who should not sleep in a tent close to the bride's mother's tent?
a her parents
b an unmarried brother
c her ex-husband
d her son-in-law

6 Which of the following statements best expresses the main idea of this passage?
a Tuareg wedding ceremonies are very long.
b Tuaregs follow very strict rules concerning marriage.
c Tuaregs have very close relationships.
d Tuareg brides must obey their husbands.

D Choose the correct meaning for these words from the text.

1 consent (1)
a express his opinion
b give his permission

2 bride-wealth (1)
a money that is given to the bride's family
b property that is given to the bride's family

3 cattle (1)
a farm animals
b a kind of tent

4 utensils (1)
a customs
b tools

5 obligation (1)
a duty
b permission

6 apart (2)
a in pieces
b at a distance

7 once (2)
a the first time
b when

8 prohibited (2)
a allowed
b not allowed

E Complete the text with the words in the box.

arrangements • best man • custom • engaged
reception • suit • toast • wedding

At the wedding (1) .... the groom, who was wearing a very smart (2) .... , was standing at the top table. Both he and the (3) .... gave speeches, which is a local (4) .... The tables had been decorated with beautiful flower (5) .... The bride looked fabulous in her gorgeous (6) .... dress. The couple, who had fallen in love so quickly and had only been (7) .... for six months, looked like the hero and heroine from a fairy tale. Once the speeches were over, everyone raised their glasses as the best man proposed a(n) (8) ....

Quick chat

What are the differences between a traditional wedding in your country and a Tuareg wedding?

Grammar 2

✓ Check present perfect simple

See page 138 for information about the present perfect simple.

Which of the following does the present perfect simple not describe? What tense is used instead?

1 actions in the recent past
2 actions at specified times in the past
3 actions that began in the past and continue into the present
4 actions that happened in the past, but we don't know when

✓ Check present perfect continuous

See page 139 for information about the present perfect continuous.

Look at these examples of the present perfect simple and continuous tenses and complete the sentences below.

Rob **has been trying** to find a job since April. **He's** already **had** 15 interviews.

I**'ve been looking** for my purse for ages. I think someone**'s stolen** it.

We use the .... to describe a recent action that is repeated or continued over a period of time.

We use the .... to describe a recent completed action.

A Some of the sentences below contain verbs that should be in the present perfect simple tense. Rewrite them correctly.

1 My cousin only lives in New York for a few months, so she's still getting used to it.
2 We're seeing this film before. Isn't there anything else on TV?
3 Did you like fairy tales when you were younger?
4 Jane loves magazines, but she never read a book in her life!
5 How long do you know your best friend?
6 Harry's information technology course started in January and it finishes in September.

B Which sentence (a or b) follows on most naturally from the first sentence?

1 Let's wake Jerry up.
a He's slept all day.
b He's been sleeping all day.

2 I'm exhausted.
a I've run around all day.
b I've been running around all day.

3 I wish I hadn't gone shopping with Rachel.
a I've spent too much money!
b I've been spending too much money!

4 Oh, no!
a Are you sure you've lost your keys?
b Are you sure you've been losing your keys?

C Complete the second sentence so that it has a similar meaning to the first sentence, using the word given.

1 Is Philip Scottish?   **from**
  Does .... Scotland?

2 This is Kate's first time on TV.   **never**
  Kate .... on TV before.

3 This is my mobile phone.   **to**
  This mobile phone .... me.

4 Chris moved to Moscow when he was ten. **lived**
  Chris .... he was ten.

B2 Exam Practice

You will have to re-express sentences using a given word. You mustn't change the word given and your answer must be no more than five words long.

Steps to success

- Consider tenses. You may have to use a different tense from the one in the original sentence.
- Check that your verb endings agree with the subject.

5 I last saw Angela in 1996.   **for**
  I .... a long time.

6 Jenny gossips about people all the time! **is**
  Jenny .... about people!

Vocabulary 2
Character adjectives

A Match the words with the synonyms. Then, use some of the words to describe the girls in the pictures.

1 outgoing — a chatty
2 talkative — b dependable
3 rude — c sociable
4 shy — d quiet
5 sympathetic — e understanding
6 reliable — f impolite
7 punctual — g on time

Word partners

B The highlighted words are in the wrong pairs. Change them around to make correct pairs.

1 best **grandmother** ....
2 next door **friend** ....
3 brother **neighbour** ....
4 only **in-law** ....
5 twin **family** ....
6 great **sister** ....
7 single **child** ....
8 extended **parent** ....

Negative prefixes

C Form opposites by using *un-*, *in-*, *im-*, *mis-* or *dis-*. Then, write *n* for noun, *v* for verb or *a* for adjective in the brackets.

1 ....understand ( ), ...understanding ( )
2 ....suitable ( ), ...suitability ( )
3 ....able ( ), ...ability ( )
4 ....satisfaction ( ), ...satisfied ( )
5 ....believable ( ), ...belief ( )
6 ....possible ( ), ...possibility ( )
7 ....agree ( ), ...agreement ( )
8 ....tolerant ( ), ...tolerance ( )
9 ....certain ( ), ...certainty ( )
10 ....politeness ( ), ...polite ( )
11 ....treat ( ), ...treatment ( )
12 ....capable ( ), ...capability ( )

Negative suffixes

D Which suffix can you add to these words to form negative adjectives?

help • hope • meaning • pain • sense • worth

B2 Exam Practice

You will have to form words to fill the gaps in a text. You will be given a word and you must change its form to make it fit correctly in the text.

Steps to success
- You might have to add a prefix or suffix to the word given, or sometimes both.
- Look carefully at the sentence to decide if a negative word or plural is needed.

E For questions 1–10, read the text below. Use the word given in capitals at the end of the lines to form a word that fits in the gap in the same line. Write your answers in CAPITAL LETTERS.

Good neighbours

According to a recent survey, most people are (**1**) .... with their neighbours and think they deserve better! It's not that they want to have a close (**2**) .... with them, but they would like them to be more (**3**) .... The ideal neighbour is apparently 'friendly, but not too (**4**) ...., easygoing and dependable.' Noise is one of the biggest problems, with loud music and barking dogs at the top of the list. (**5**) .... between neighbours are becoming more and more common. Take the recent case of a man in the United Kingdom who was (**6**) .... to control his fury when his neighbour started mowing his lawn at seven o'clock one Sunday morning. Still dressed in his pyjamas, the man climbed over the garden fence and grabbed the lawnmower. Then, while his neighbour watched in (**7**) ...., he threw the lawnmower into the garden pond! 'I'm usually a (**8**) .... person,' the man later said. 'The (**9**) .... is I was tired and I wanted to have a lie-in.' Fortunately, most people don't go to these extremes, even if they aren't always in (**10**) .... with their neighbours about everything!

SATISFY
RELATION
CONSIDER
CHAT
UNDERSTAND
ABLE
BELIEF
TOLERATE
TRUE
AGREE

Writing: letter

B2 Exam Practice

You might be asked to write a letter applying for a job. You must write between 120 and 180 words.

Steps to success
- Take three minutes before you start writing to make a quick PLAN.
- You can MAKE IT UP – change your age, qualifications, experience and interests.
- Use the correct BEGINNINGS and ENDINGS, eg *Dear Mrs .../Dear Sir or Madam, Yours sincerely/faithfully.*
- Lay out your letter in short, clear PARAGRAPHS with an opening and closing.
- Use a FORMAL style of writing (avoid short forms like *I'm* and other chatty language).

A Read the advertisement and look at the profiles of three applicants below. Who would be most suitable for the position and why?

Magazine Work Experience

We are offering a student aged 14 to 18 the **opportunity** to spend six weeks this summer working as a **trainee journalist** in the offices of *Crush!*, the best-selling **magazine** for teenagers. The work is unpaid, but you will have the chance to develop your writing and reporting skills, working alongside professional journalists. Applicants should have a good knowledge of pop music and fashion and be friendly and outgoing. If you are **interested** in applying, write a letter to the Editor, including details of your **experience** and interests, and saying why you believe you are suitable for the position.

Mike, 16
likes: *writing poetry and songs*
looking for: *a month's work during the summer*

Claire, 17
likes: *all kinds of music, writing stories*
looking for: *something interesting to do in the holidays*

Jake, 15
likes: *new challenges, meeting people*
looking for: *part-time holiday job where he can earn some money*

B Read one of the applicants' letters and fill in the gaps using the highlighted words from the advertisement.

Dear Sir or Madam,

1 I am writing in response to your advertisement for a (1) .... which appeared in *The Daily Star* last Tuesday. I am interested in applying for this position.

2 I am a 17-year-old student and am hoping to go to university to study journalism next year. I am very (2) .... in fashion and also have a good knowledge of music. I recently interviewed a local band for my school (3) .... and I have written several other articles too. I am also hardworking, confident, and I get on well with people.

3 This position would help me gain valuable (4) .... in journalism, which would be very useful for my future career. It would be a great (5) .... for me to learn about different aspects of running a magazine and to work with experienced journalists.

4 I am available from the beginning of July until the end of August and would be happy to attend an interview at any time convenient to you.
I look forward to hearing from you.
Yours faithfully,
Claire Jones

C Write the paragraph number next to these things that Claire does in her letter.
She:
says when she's free for work ....
gives some background information about herself (interests, experience, etc) ....
says how the job would benefit her ....
says why she's writing ....
says when and where she saw the advertisement ....

D Find formal words and expressions in the model letter that mean the same as those below.
1 to answer ....
2 job ....
3 lots of ....
4 get ....
5 free ....
6 come for ....

E You are going to write a letter of application in reply to this advertisement. Make very brief notes for each of the points in the plan – you have three minutes!

Assistant wanted for internet cafe

Bill's Internet Cafe is looking for a temporary assistant to help out over the summer period. Duties will include serving drinks and helping with technical problems. Hours: Monday – Friday, 9 am – 5 pm. Would suit a student with a good knowledge of computers, who is friendly and enthusiastic. Anyone interested should write to Bill Jones with details of their experience and interests, saying why they think they are suitable for the job.

3-minute plan!

Paragraph 1
Say why you are writing ....
Say when and where you saw the job advert
....

Hint: Make up the name of a newspaper and the day/date you saw the advert.

Paragraph 2
Give a couple of facts about yourself
....
Say what your interests and experience are
....

Hint: Invent some things about yourself that make you sound suitable for the job.

Paragraph 3
Say how the job would benefit you
....

Hint: Say how the job relates to your interests/ future studies/future career.

Paragraph 4
Say when you're free for work
....

F Now write your letter in 120–180 words using your notes and some of the Language chunks to help you. Lay out your letter like the model in Exercise B.

Language chunks

Letters of application
I am writing in response to …
I am interested in …
I have a good knowledge of …
I am good at …
I feel I am suitable for this position because …
It would give me the opportunity/chance to …
I am available from … to …
I look forward to hearing from you.

2 24/7

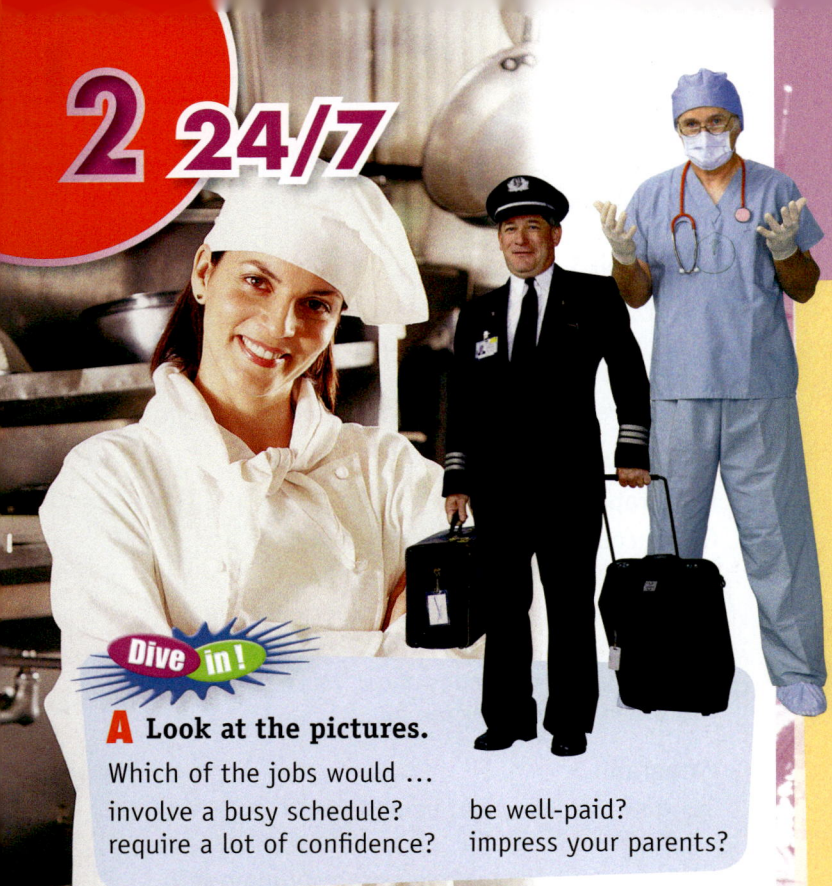

A Look at the pictures.
Which of the jobs would …
involve a busy schedule?
require a lot of confidence?
be well-paid?
impress your parents?

Reading 1

B2 Exam Practice
You will have to answer multiple choice questions about a text.

Steps to success
- Read the passage quickly before looking at the questions to get an idea of what it's about.
- Read the questions. Do not look at the answer choices because they might confuse you.
- Find the answer in the text, underline it and read it carefully.
- Read the options (A, B, C, D) and choose the correct answer based on what you underlined.

B You are going to read an article from a magazine. Read it quickly and decide which of these titles is the most suitable.
1 Fame Story
2 Life on the Metro
3 Underground Entertainers

Exam alert
- Avoid options which sound logical, but are not mentioned in the text.
- Avoid options which include a word or phrase from the text, but refer to something different.
- Be careful with options that generalize by using words like *always, never, all* and *every*.

Buskers have been entertaining passengers on the Paris Metro for years, but recently their profession has become a whole lot more respectable. Only the most talented performers now have the right to play in the French capital's vast underground network. For some, who were used to living off bits of **change** from passersby, it has even led to fame and fortune.

It all started in 1997. That's when it was decided to introduce licences for any entertainer wishing to perform in one of the Metro's 297 underground stations. Would-be buskers now have to go for an **audition** in order to be considered for one of the licences, of which there is a limited number. Unlicensed buskers still play on the metro, but if they are caught, they have to pay a **fine** of 40 euros.

Twice a year talented individuals from all over the world crowd into the office where the auditions take place. Only about 300 artists a year are chosen from a total of about 800. Today's busy schedule includes a classical violinist from Japan, a group of drummers from the West Indies and a South American flamenco dancer. In order to get this far, they have already gone through a **lengthy** application procedure, but this is the nerve-racking part. Each of them has just ten minutes in which to impress the panel of judges and the atmosphere is **tense**.

It's hardly surprising that there's so much competition to become a licensed metro performer. After all, playing in this unusual **venue** has been the start of a brilliant career for many. Charlie Morton from England arrived in Paris in 1998 and started playing his guitar at St Paul station, where many other musicians used to

C For questions 1-8 choose the answer which you think fits best according to the text.

1 What has changed about busking in the Paris Metro?
A It is better paid than it used to be.
B Only certain people are allowed to be buskers.
C It guarantees a successful future career.
D Only professional entertainers now busk there.

2 Busking licences are
A in demand.
B 40 euros each.
C given to anyone who applies for one.
D held by all performers on the Paris Metro.

gather. 'On a good day, I would make 100 francs (about 15 euros), just enough to live on,' he says. He was one of the first to audition successfully for a licence, which was 'a great boost to my confidence'.

While he was playing, Charlie met the man who got him a **lucrative** recording deal and is now his manager. Since he recorded his bestselling album, Charlie hasn't looked back, but he still likes to play in the Metro now and then. 'The atmosphere there is unique. It's the best concert hall in the world,' he says. 'And when you're famous, they don't make you audition for a licence!'

Not everyone is interested in becoming a star, however. Jean Hubert, a skilled accordion-player, has been busking in the Metro for over 30 years. 'Music brings a touch of magic into people's lives,' he says. 'If through my music I can make someone happy, even for a moment, then this is my reward.' He believes that the introduction of busking licences was a good thing because it keeps the standard of playing high. 'Now there are fewer of us, but the quality is better than in the past. I think people appreciate that,' he says.

Inspired by the success of the Paris Metro's musical experiment, many other countries have decided to introduce similar schemes. Barcelona, London and Tokyo have all made busking **official**. The London Underground has even released a CD called 'Sounds of the Underground' featuring metro musicians which rivals the Paris Metro's earlier release, 'Correspondances'.

3 What is meant by 'nerve-racking' in the third paragraph?
A enjoyable
B stressful
C complicated
D important

4 What do we learn about the auditions in the third paragraph?
A The people who take part are all musicians.
B There are three per day.
C They are judged by more than one person.
D They are the first stage in applying for a licence.

5 What effect did getting a busking licence have on Charlie Morton?
A It decreased his income.
B It allowed him to play with other musicians.
C It made him feel more positive about himself.
D It encouraged him to learn to play the guitar.

6 Why does Charlie Morton still play in the Metro?
A to make money
B to advertise his album
C in the hope of becoming famous
D because he enjoys it

7 How does Jean Hubert feel about busking licences?
A They aren't a good idea.
B They have raised the performing standards.
C There aren't enough of them.
D They have made buskers happier.

8 The 'Sounds of the Underground' CD
A came out after 'Correspondances'.
B was made by musicians from the Paris Metro.
C was recorded for buskers.
D was copied by musicians in Barcelona and Tokyo.

Work it out!

D Match the words in bold from the text with their meanings.
1 where performances take place ....
2 allowed by the law ....
3 which makes lots of money ....
4 performance to judge if you are good enough ....
5 which takes a long time to do ....
6 not relaxed ....
7 coins ....
8 money paid as a punishment ....

Quick chat

What do you want from your future job? Number these things in order of preference then discuss your reasons with your partner.
- to feel useful ☐
- to travel ☐
- to be well paid ☐
- to be respected ☐
- to be the boss ☐
- to be famous ☐
- to be creative ☐
- to be challenged ☐

Grammar 1

✓ Check past simple and past continuous

See page 139 for information about the past simple and past continuous tenses.

Write PS (past simple) or PC (past continuous) next to the rules and complete the examples.

Use	Tense
1 completed actions in the past	
I .... (write) the letter and .... (post) it this morning.	
2 past states	
Helen .... (not be) very happy in her previous job.	
3 past habits	
Bob .... (ride) his bike to work. Then he got a car.	
4 actions in progress at a particular moment in the past	
What .... you .... (do) this time last week?	
5 actions that were interrupted by another event	
I .... (shop) this morning when I bumped into Daisy.	

A Complete the text with the past simple or past continuous form of the verbs given.

Have you ever had one of those days when everything goes wrong? Well, I (**1**) .... (have) one yesterday! First of all my alarm clock (**2**) .... (not go) off for some reason and I (**3**) .... (not have) time to have any breakfast. Then, when I (**4**) .... (look) out of the window, I (**5**) .... (notice) it (**6**) .... (rain). That (**7**) .... (put) me in a really bad mood! While I (**8**) .... (cycle) to school, my bike (**9**) .... (have) a puncture. By then it (**10**) .... (pour) down, so I (**11**) .... (get) really wet and of course I (**12**) .... (be) late for school!

When I (**13**) .... (arrive), I (**14**) .... (hang) my bag over the back of my chair. My teacher, Mrs Jones, (**15**) .... (walk) past my chair when she (**16**) .... (knock) my bag onto the floor by mistake. While she (**17**) .... (pick) it up, a fluffy pink teddy bear (**18**) .... (fall) out. 'Is this yours, Andrew?' she asked. 'No, Miss. It belongs to my baby sister,' I replied and all the other kids (**19**) .... (start) laughing. I was so embarrassed that my face (**20**) .... (turn) bright red! That's the last time I let my baby sister play with my things!

✓ Check used to and would

See page 139 for information about *used to* and *would*.

Which one of these sentences is incorrect? Why is it incorrect?

1 We **lived** in a suburb of Leeds when I was a baby.
2 We **used to live** in a suburb of Leeds when I was a baby.
3 We **would live** in a suburb of Leeds when I was a baby.

B Tick the sentences in which the highlighted verbs can be replaced by *used to* and rewrite them. In which sentence could you replace the verb with *would* + the bare infinitive?

1 Most women **didn't have** a career 50 years ago.
2 I like your new trainers. Where **did** you **get** them?
3 Until recently, supermarkets **weren't** open 24 hours a day.
4 Sean **wanted** to be a magician, but he actually became a dentist!
5 In my job in the sweet shop, I **gave** free sweets to some of the kids.
6 **Was** the way of life very different 50 years ago?

Vocabulary 1

Shops and services

A In which of the places in the box could you …

1 have a cut and blow-dry?
2 borrow a book?
3 buy lots of different things?
4 take a prescription for some medicine?
5 buy old and valuable furniture?
6 have your car serviced?
7 arrange to buy a house?
8 wash and dry your clothes?
9 send an email?
10 buy a magazine and some sweets?
11 see an exhibition?
12 send a bouquet of flowers to someone?
13 buy some second-hand clothes?

> antique shop • art gallery • charity shop • chemist's
> department store • estate agency • florist's
> garage • hairdresser's • internet café • launderette
> library • newsagent's

Key phrasal verbs

B Complete the sentences with these phrasal verbs in the correct form.

> **bring out** – produce a new product and start to sell it
> **sell out** – sell everything there is of something
> **try on** – wear to see if something fits
> **set up** – start a business
> **run out of** – not have any more of
> **look round** – look at the things in a shop

1 'Hello. Can I help you?'
  'No, thanks. I'm just ……………………… .'
2 'Oh, no, we've ……………………… coffee!'
  'I'll pop over to the corner shop and get some.'
3 'Have you got this shirt in any other colour?'
  'No, sorry. We did have some blue ones, but we've completely ……………………… now.'
4 'Can I ……………………… these jeans, please?'
  'Yes, of course. The changing room's over there.'
5 'Why do you need a bank loan?'
  'Because I want to ……………………… my own catering business.'
6 'When did they ……………………… the new iPod?'
  'Oh, ages ago! I got mine last year.'

Word patterns

C Complete with *do* or *make*.

1 ……………………… homework
2 ……………………… dinner
3 ……………………… a job
4 ……………………… housework
5 ……………………… a living
6 ……………………… money
7 ……………………… one's best
8 ……………………… the ironing
9 ……………………… the most of (something)
10 ……………………… an offer
11 ……………………… (someone) a favour
12 ……………………… an effort
13 ……………………… up one's mind
14 ……………………… damage (to something)

D Rewrite the sentences, replacing the highlighted words with phrases from Exercise C.

1 I know you'll **try as hard as possible** at the interview.

2 Sid and Nancy **earn enough to live on** by selling the vegetables they grow.

3 I've **decided**! I'm going to give up my job and travel round the world by motorbike!

4 We always **clean our house** on Saturday morning.

5 Ben works long hours in the week, so he really **tries to enjoy** his weekends.

6 Helen doesn't **try** to dress smartly for work because she's a plumber.

7 Heavy snow can **ruin** farmers' crops.

8 Mum's really tired. I'm going to **help her** by cooking dinner.

2

Listening

A Which of the following jobs are often done in shifts?

- school teacher
- plumber
- office worker
- taxi driver
- waiter
- civil servant
- nurse
- bank employee

Can you think of any others?

B Imagine you are a shift worker. How would your working hours affect your life? Discuss the following aspects:

time spent with family   health
social life   hobbies and interests

B2 Exam Practice

You will hear a monologue or conversation between different speakers. You will be given some sentences based on what you hear with gaps for you to complete with words and phrases.

Steps to success
- First, read all of the notes to find out what the recording is about.
- Try to predict the words that might be missing.
- Remember that the sentences will express the ideas you hear in different words.

C What kind of word is missing from the sentence (eg noun, adjective, number)?

It's possible to shop at the ……………………… at night.

D 🎧 Listen to the first part of a radio talk about the body clock and write down the exact phrases that you hear which mean the following:
1 available ………………………
2 work from midnight to morning ………………………

E What kind of word or phrase is missing in each of the sentences below?
1 Employees in hospitals and ……………………… are used to working at night.
2 Over ……………………… per cent of people now work shifts.
3 The body produces the hormone melatonin when it's ……………………… .
4 A lot of ……………………… have occurred during night shifts.
5 It is usually ……………………… before the body adapts to being in a new time zone.
6 There is a time difference of ……………………… between London and Johannesburg.
7 Jet lag can be treated with ……………………… .
8 Shift workers find it hard to ……………………… .
9 ……………………… people have a similar problem to shift workers.
10 Taking doses of melatonin might not be good for the ……………………… .

🎧 Now listen to the complete talk. For questions 1–10, complete the sentences. You will need to write a word or short phrase in each gap.

Speaking

B2 Exam Practice
You will be given two photos to talk about on your own for a minute. You will have to compare the photos and answer a general question about them.

Steps to success
- After comparing the photos, remember to answer the question about them.
- Say as much as you can in one minute, as the examiner will then stop you.

Language chunks

Comparing
The office looks very ... whereas the plane looks ...
The plane looks more/ ...-er ... than the office.
One thing they've got in common is that ...
Both the office and the plane seem ...
Compared with the office, the plane is ...

A Look at this example of an exam question.
Compare the photographs.

What's it like to work in places like these?

D Circle the correct adjectives.
1 It would be **excited / exciting** to work on a plane.
2 Office work would get a bit **bored / boring**.
3 It would be **scared / scary** to do that job.
4 It's probably quite **relaxed / relaxing** to work in that kind of office.
5 I bet that job's really **tired / tiring**.

Make sentences with the remaining adjectives. Can you think of any other pairs like these?

E Compare the photographs. Use the Language chunks and your own ideas.

Whose job is more enjoyable?

What do you have to do?
a Describe the office where your mother works.
b Discuss working in the two places.
c Say why you would like to be an air steward.

B Look at the photos and consider the question *What's it like to work in places like these?* How could you begin your answer?

a I'd like to become a doctor and work in a children's hospital.
b There are a lot of office buildings in the city centre.
c Working on a plane must be very interesting.

Say it right!

F Read these past participles aloud and write the number of syllables they have.

1 wanted ....
2 worked ....
3 cried ....
4 painted ....
5 helped ....
6 needed ....
7 missed ....
8 fitted ....
9 wished ....
10 added ....

C Talk about the two photos using the Language chunks to help you.

G 🎧 Now listen to see if you were right. What is the rule about the pronunciation of the final 'ed'?

2

A Which of the following part-time jobs would you like to do? What qualities would someone need in order to do these jobs?

- dog walker
- sales assistant
- camp counsellor
- museum volunteer
- waiter/waitress
- babysitter

Reading 2

B2 Exam Practice

You will be given a number of short texts on a connected topic. You must answer questions about the texts and in some cases find things they have in common.

Steps to success
- Go through each question and underline the key words.
- Skim the advertisements listed in the four answer choices to find the information.

B Read the six advertisements for job vacancies. Use the information in the advertisements to answer the questions.

1. Your friend wants a job that gives employees reductions on its goods. Which job should she apply for?
   a 1   **b** 2   **c** 3   **d** 5

2. You want a job that provides training. Which two should you consider?
   a 1 and 3   **b** 1 and 4   **c** 4 and 5   **d** 2 and 6

3. You prefer to work alone. Which would be the best jobs?
   a 2 and 5   **b** 1 and 4   **c** 1 and 6   **d** 3 and 6

Animal lovers wanted ❶

Bow Wow Wow is an established pet sitting and dog walking company. We are seeking exceptional carers to add to our great staff. If you love dogs, feel comfortable walking dogs of all sizes, and are available Monday to Friday, this could be the job for you. Ideal position for responsible teenager. Good pay.

Please apply by email and tell us the days/hours you are available and where you are located.
info@bow_wow_wow.co.uk

The best music store in town! ❷

Family-owned business seeks an energetic, easygoing, part-time sales assistant. Your duties will include stocking the shelves, working the cash register and helping customers. Ideally you'll be available Friday 5-9pm and Saturday 9am-5pm, with extra work during the summer and Christmas holidays. Prior experience is not required, but you should be a fast learner, have basic computer skills and love music. The hourly pay is €12. Good staff discounts!

Interested applicants should phone **Mr Cole on 301-546-5216** to arrange an interview.

Summer fun ❸

We are looking for a counsellor to be responsible for the care of a small group of children at summer camp. If you enjoy travelling, meeting new people, sports and activities in a fun environment, this job is ideal. Applicants will need to have some childcare experience, the right attitude and the enthusiasm to work with children of all ages. In addition, you must be 18 years old by July 1st and be available on August 1st for a minimum of four weeks.

application@campsummer.co

History Museum

Our museum's volunteers greet visitors and show them around the museum. Each volunteer must work one four-hour shift (mornings or afternoons) every week or one six-hour shift every other weekend. Basic training of the museum's exhibitions is provided. You must have excellent communication skills, the ability to speak a foreign language and enjoy working as a member of a team. This position would suit anyone interested in history.

For more information, call the History Museum on 653-896-2344.

❹

Time Out Café

★ Have you got great interpersonal skills and an excellent attitude to customer service?
★ Are you a nice, respectful, optimistic person who enjoys working with the public?
★ Are you well presented, hard-working and willing to learn new skills?

If so, we'd like to talk to you about weekend work at our café.
Full training will be provided on the job.
Knowledge of Spanish is essential.
Pay rate: $7 per hour, plus tips.
Minimum age requirement is 16.

★ Apply in person at Time Out Café, 234 Lexington Street.

❺

Babysitter required

We have a four-year-old daughter and are seeking a babysitter for the occasional night out. We are willing to negotiate a fair hourly rate if we are lucky enough to find the right person! The babysitter must be female and experienced in caring for a young child. Responsible teenagers are welcome to apply, but you must be at least 15 years old and live locally. You must also provide references.

If you are interested, please contact us on 212-566-8931, and ask for Rachel or Matthew.

❻

---

4 Your British friend can't speak a foreign language. Which jobs is he not qualified for?
   a 4 and 5   b 1 and 3   c 2 and 6   d 4 and 6

5 Which companies allow you to apply online?
   a 1 and 3   b 2 and 4   c 3 and 6   d 4 and 5

6 You don't have any computer skills. Which job are you not qualified for?
   a 1   b 2   c 4   d 6

7 You are 14 years old. Which jobs can't you apply for?
   a 2, 3 and 4   b 2, 4 and 6   c 3, 4 and 6   d 3, 5 and 6

8 You want a job working outdoors. Which jobs are suitable?
   a 2 and 3   b 4 and 6   c 1 and 3   d 2 and 5

9 Which job doesn't provide any payment?
   a 1   b 2   c 4   d 6

10 You don't want a job during the school year. Which one should you apply for?
   a 2   b 3   c 4   d 5

11 Your friend is a boy. Which job can't he apply for?
   a 1   b 3   c 4   d 6

12 Which job will provide you with more money than the standard hourly rate?
   a 2   b 4   c 5   d 6

C Complete the sentences with the words in the box.

> easygoing • energetic • exceptional • hard-working
> optimistic • respectful • responsible • well presented

1 Kurt had been accepted into medical school, so he was very .... about his future.
2 We had put Jilly in charge of the shop while we were away – she's very ....
3 Don't wear your scruffy jeans today! You should be .... at a job interview.
4 Jim gets on well with everyone as he's a very .... person.
5 The latest Jason Bourne film isn't just good; it's .... !
6 You can't accuse Tania of being lazy. She's very ....
7 If you are .... of your colleagues, they will treat you well too.
8 My grandfather is surprisingly .... for a man of his age.

Quick chat

Do you or any of your friends have a part-time job? Is it enjoyable? Does it interfere with your schoolwork?

Grammar 2

✓ Check past perfect simple and past perfect continuous

See page 139 for information about the past perfect simple and past perfect continuous tenses.

Complete the sentences with the correct form of the verbs given, then label the tenses correctly.

Past perfect ....
Mum was annoyed because we .... (watch) DVDs all day.

Past perfect ....
Eleanor was very upset because she .... (fail) her exams.

B2 Exam Practice
You have to complete each of the gaps in a text with one word.

Steps to success
- Read the whole text first to understand the gist and to see how the sentences relate to each other.
- Work out what part of speech (preposition, verb, noun, etc) is needed in the gap.
- Check verb endings for tense and subject agreement.

A Complete the text with the past perfect simple or past perfect continuous form of the verbs in brackets.

Tania **(1)** .... (wait) for the letter for weeks before it finally arrived. Two months earlier she **(2)** .... (go) for an audition at the Royal Academy of Drama and the Performing Arts in London. She **(3)** .... (want) to be a singer ever since she was a little girl and she **(4)** .... (have) singing lessons for the last three years. The audition **(5)** .... (be) tough, but she **(6)** .... (do) her best. Now the moment **(7)** .... (come) to find out whether all her hard work **(8)** .... (be) worthwhile! The white envelope had the words *Royal Academy* across the top and her own name and address clearly printed underneath. She **(9)** .... (look) at the envelope for a full five minutes when her mother came into the kitchen. 'The letter's come,' she told her mother. 'Open it!' said her mother excitedly. With trembling fingers, Tania tore open the envelope. 'I've passed!' she shouted. Her dream **(10)** .... (come) true at last!

B For questions 1–12, read the text below and think of the word which best fits each gap. Use only one word in each gap.

I've **(1)** .... working in a bank for several years now, but I haven't always **(2)** .... such a normal job. **(3)** .... I was 18, I **(4)** .... in the laboratory of a company that produced hair growth treatments for men who **(5)** .... lost their hair. I had **(6)** .... looking for a temporary summer job when I came across the advert for the job in the local paper. They probably didn't have many applicants because they **(7)** .... me the job straight away! My duties were simple. Every morning the first lot of clients **(8)** .... arrive. All I had to do was apply a chemical solution to their heads, wait for 15 minutes and then wash it off. I **(9)** .... this several times a day.
Some of the clients were quite interesting and I **(10)** .... to enjoy talking to them. They didn't seem to mind the fact that the treatments never worked! Once I was **(11)** .... such an interesting conversation with one man that I left the chemical on his head for too long and it turned his head blue! Although he forgave me, my boss didn't and I got the sack. I **(12)** .... often laughed about what happened, but at the time I was really upset!

Vocabulary 2
Work and jobs

A Match the jobs with the areas. Which area would you like to work in?

> bank manager • travel agent • surgeon
> ballet dancer • midwife • architect • reporter
> solicitor • civil engineer • holiday rep • judge
> scriptwriter • TV presenter • accountant

1 the media ....
2 tourism ....
3 construction ....
4 medicine ....
5 finance ....
6 law ....
7 the arts ....

B Add the suffixes to the words to form adjectives, making any other spelling changes neccessary: -ous, -ive, -ful, -ic, -d, -able, -ing.

1 create ....
2 energy ....
3 organize ....
4 communicate ....
5 like ....
6 charm ....
7 enthusiasm ....
8 ambition ....
9 sympathy ....
10 care ....
11 adapt ....
12 tact ....
13 persuade ....
14 determine ....

Easily confused words

C Explain the difference between:

1 an **employer** and a **manager**
2 a **job** and a **profession**
3 a **friend** and a **colleague**
4 a **wage** and a **salary**
5 a **part-time** job and a **full-time** job
6 working **nine to five** and working **shifts**
7 working for a **company** and working **freelance**
8 being **unemployed** and being **on strike**
9 **resigning** and **retiring**
10 **winning** money and **earning** money
11 one's **income** and one's **expenses**
12 **being made redundant** and **getting the sack**

B2 Exam Practice
You have to choose the correct words to complete a text.
Steps to success
- Read the whole text through once quickly before you begin.
- Look at the whole sentence when trying to find the answer that fits.
- Remember that some words in English are followed by certain other words (eg prepositions).

D For questions 1–12, read the email below and decide which answer (A, B, C or D) best fits each gap.

Dear Annabel,

My mum and dad are really getting on my nerves at the moment. We've been discussing my future and as usual we can't agree about anything! They want me to go into the medical (1) .... like them, but I don't want to be a(n) (2) .... ! They think that a big (3) .... is really important, but I'm not interested in (4) .... money. Anyway, I've already made up my (5) .... that I want to be an actress! I know a lot of actors are (6) .... of work for long periods, but I think I'm (7) .... enough to be successful. Everyone has to make the most (8) .... their abilities, don't they?

I'd better finish my homework now or I'll be in (9) .... with Mum and Dad again. (10) .... the way, Adam's having a party on Friday and you're invited. I know you're busy at the moment, but do your (11) .... to come!

Love,
Stacey

PS Can you do me a(n) (12) .... ? I don't know what to wear to the party. Can you lend me your black top?

	A	B	C	D
1	job	employment	profession	career
2	architect	surgeon	civil engineer	solicitor
3	salary	wage	pay	earning
4	winning	doing	making	creating
5	wish	decision	brain	mind
6	off	out	under	by
7	adaptable	talented	tactful	assertive
8	in	at	with	of
9	trouble	fights	arguments	problems
10	On	In	With	By
11	good	better	best	most
12	favour	offer	effort	job

2

Writing: story

B2 Exam Practice

You might be asked to write a story. You will usually be given a sentence to use at the beginning or end of your story. You must write between 120 and 180 words.

Steps to success
- Think of an IDEA for your story before you start writing and make sure it fits in with the sentence you've been given.
- ORGANIZE your story. It should have a beginning, a middle and an end.
- Pay attention to verb TENSES. You will need to use mainly past tenses (past simple and continuous, past perfect simple and continuous, *used to, would*, etc) to tell your story.
- Use DIRECT SPEECH to make your story livelier.
- Use a VARIETY of words and expressions.

A Look at this question and two possible ideas for the story. Which idea is better? Why?

You have been asked to write a story for your school magazine beginning with these words:
Sam's day started badly, but fortunately it turned out OK.

Idea 1
Sam found some money in the street and spent it on some CDs, which he left on the bus by mistake.

Idea 2
It was Sam's birthday. He thought everyone had forgotten, but they had organized a surprise party for him.

B Now read an answer to the question based on a different idea (ignoring the gaps). Does the first sentence fit in with the rest of the story?

C Fill in the gaps in the story with three phrases from the list below.

beforehand • suddenly • in the end • at first • on the way

D Complete the sentences about the story, paying attention to the highlighted words and phrases.

1 **After** Sam got up, he ....

2 The dog ran away **while** Sam ....

3 The girl felt sorry for Sam **so** ....

4 **Although** they searched for hours, they ....

5 **As soon as** they got back to Sam's house, ...

E *Sam's day started badly ...* . Find four more examples in the story of phrases containing adverbs and underline them. Write them below.

Sam's day started badly, but fortunately it turned out OK. He was bored because all his friends were away on holiday. When he went downstairs, he found a note from his mum. 'Don't forget to take the dog for a walk!' it said. The dog was wagging his tail happily. 'OK, Bertie, let's go to the park,' Sam said. (1) ...., Sam stopped at the newsagent's to buy some chewing gum and left Bertie outside. To his surprise, when he came out of the shop, Bertie wasn't there! 'Excuse me,' he said anxiously to a girl who was walking past. 'Have you seen a big, black dog?' 'No, I haven't' she replied, 'But I'll help you look for him.'

Sam and the girl looked everywhere, but they couldn't find Bertie. (2) ...., they gave up and walked slowly back to Sam's house. Sam couldn't believe his eyes when he saw Bertie waiting outside the front door! 'Clever dog!' said the girl. 'My name's Anna, by the way,' she added. Sam smiled at her. (3) .... things didn't seem so bad after all.

F Complete the sentences with adverbs formed from the adjectives in the box.

> angry • desperate • excited • lazy • sad

1 Kim stretched .... and wished she didn't have to get up.
2 The two girls were chatting .... about their holidays.
3 The teacher shouted .... at the boy, who started running in the opposite direction.
4 Daniel held on .... to the rope, hoping it wouldn't break.
5 Lydia stared .... out of the window with tears in her eyes.

G Now look at this question.

Write a story beginning with the words:
I thought it was going to be an ordinary day, but I was wrong.

Think of an idea for your story and complete the plan below.

3-minute plan!

First paragraph: set the scene
Where were you? ....
Who were you with? ....
How did you feel? ....
What were your plans? ....

Middle paragraph(s): describe the main event
How did the unexpected event happen? ....

What happened exactly? ....

What was the effect on you/other people? ....

Final paragraph: comment on what happened
What happened in the end? ....

Was it a good or bad experience? ....

H Now write your story in 120–180 words using the model, your notes and some of the Language chunks to help you.

Language chunks

Setting the scene
The wind was blowing and it was pouring with rain.
I've never believed in ghosts, but …
He thought it was going to be a boring day because …

Describing the action
I couldn't believe my eyes!
She had a shock when …
To his surprise, …
We had no idea where/what/how …
I breathed a sigh of relief.

Commenting on events
Everything had turned out all right in the end.
Suddenly, things didn't seem so bad, after all.
The funniest/best/most annoying thing was that …
It was the strangest/most frightening/most exciting experience I've ever had!

Review 1

A Read the text and choose the best answer, A, B, C or D.

Starting young

Danny Rowler grew up as a(n) (1) .... child with busy parents. He (2) .... spend a lot of his time (3) .... online or communicating with friends by email. He realized from surfing the internet that there were very few teen-friendly websites with interesting content about real teenage issues. Most of the websites presented (4) .... information about celebrities and pop stars. He became (5) .... to create something that would satisfy real teenage needs. A place where teenagers could (6) .... their minds.
It was a(n) (7) .... plan, but Danny was optimistic that he could find teenage (8) ....
to write interesting material. He (9) .... all his friends and persuaded them to send in articles. He had soon collected enough articles to (10) .... the first issue of the online magazine.
Danny emailed the first issue to all the teenagers he knew and encouraged people to send in their own articles. Five years later, Danny (11) .... receiving thousands of articles and teenagers were paying to subscribe to the magazine. What had started as a fun part-time job, had become a full-time profession.
Now Danny sells his magazine to schools and libraries. What does Danny say about his life? 'When I was 16, I hadn't (12) .... up my mind about what I wanted. Choosing the right job is complicated. It's not just about earning money. It's about doing something that feels right.'

1　A single　　　　C only
　　B favourite　　D individual
2　A would　　　　C did
　　B used　　　　D had
3　A saying　　　　C calling
　　B chatting　　　D writing
4　A careless　　　C meaningless
　　B helpless　　　D hopeless
5　A determined　　C organized
　　B enthusiastic　 D interested
6　A talk　　　　　C make
　　B say　　　　　D speak
7　A likable　　　　C lucrative
　　B ambitious　　D responsible
8　A colleagues　　C companies
　　B employers　　D volunteers
9　A impressed　　C treated
　　B contacted　　D wrote
10　A set up　　　　C bring up
　　 B bring out　　　D make up
11　A had been　　　C has been
　　 B was　　　　　D is
12　A set　　　　　C made
　　 B done　　　　D given

B Complete the text with ONE word that best fits each gap. Write your answers in CAPITAL LETTERS.

Communicating successfully

Have you (1) .... asked yourself if you are a good communicator? That doesn't mean being good (2) .... telling jokes or (3) .... other languages. It means being able to (4) .... what you think clearly and effectively.
However, that isn't all. What about listening? Ask yourself if you really pay attention to what other people say, even if they're getting on your (5) .... Try to (6) .... an effort to listen to other people. Don't you find it rude when people (7) .... in agreement, but you know they're not really hearing your words?
Also, you should do your (8) .... to look at people when they are talking. (9) .... shows that you are interested and also helps avoid unnecessary misunderstandings. Remember, a big part of communication is non-verbal. Someone might sound angry, but when you actually look at their face they aren't (10) .... , they're smiling.
Another tip (11) .... to ask lots of questions. Don't be afraid to show tactful interest in other people. And it isn't wrong to say that you don't understand. Nobody knows everything, so speaking (12) .... and asking for clarification is a good thing.

C Complete the text with the correct form of the words in capitals. Write your answers in CAPITAL LETTERS.

Mobiles in the classroom

The number one gadget for most teenagers today is the mobile phone. They seem to get enormous (1) .... from comparing new models, and their (2) .... to send text messages at the speed of light is amazing. But most teachers are totally (3) .... of mobile phone use in the classroom. Text messaging is completely (4) .... and mobiles should be firmly switched off. This approach gets across the message that students need to concentrate. However, it shows that many schools (5) .... the full (6) .... of the mobile phone. After all, a mobile phone is just like a mini computer, with full access to the web. There are many (7) .... ways in which a mobile phone can be used for (8) .... Teachers have over the past few years, slowly (9) .... to using computers and whiteboards in the classroom. Perhaps they will soon realize that mobiles can be a(n) (10) .... tool, too.

SATISFY
ABLE
TOLERATE

BAN

UNDERSTAND
CAPABLE

CREATE
LEARN
ADAPT

VALUE

D Rewrite the sentences using the words in capitals. Use between two and five words, including the word given. Write only the missing words in CAPITAL LETTERS.

1 Sally and Jim plan to marry next year.
ARE
Sally and Jim .... next year.

2 The teacher tells me off all the time!
IS
The teacher .... off.

3 We first met each other three years ago.
KNOWN
We .... three years.

4 Veronica started dancing when she was 15.
SINCE
Veronica .... she was 15.

5 Until quite recently people didn't have computers in their homes.
USE
People .... computers in their homes.

6 I sent the email before I sent the text message.
ALREADY
I .... when I sent the text message.

7 Martin was working at the time of the accident.
BEEN
Martin .... when the accident occurred.

8 I don't normally tell stories. It's unusual for me.
TO
I'm not .... stories.

3 Open your mind!

Dive in!

A What do you like best about school? What are some of the problems children have at school?

B Put these subjects in order of preference (1 = your favourite, 10 = your least favourite).

- [ ] chemistry
- [ ] maths
- [ ] English
- [ ] computer studies
- [ ] history
- [ ] art
- [ ] physics
- [ ] geography
- [ ] biology
- [ ] PE

C What other things do you think you should learn at school?

(eg cookery, money management, job interview skills)

D Which sentence (a or b) follows on most naturally from the first sentence?

1 They say that schooldays are the best days of your life.
a It was good most of the time, but not always.
b I, however, didn't find this to be true.

2 A boy in my class called Darren Blake used to pick on me whenever he got the chance.
a He was about twice my size and I was too scared to stand up to him.
b Fortunately, he never bothered me again.

3 The only thing Helen was good at was art.
a Painting seemed to come naturally to her.
b She dreaded every lesson.

4 Julian and I had one thing in common.
a I used to help him with his homework after school.
b We both hated physical exercise and would do anything to avoid it.

5 Teachers nowadays are much more humane than they were when I was at school.
a In those days, we were terrified of them.
b I was never afraid to ask questions in class, for example.

Reading 1

B2 Exam Practice

You will be given a text that has had some sentences taken out of it. You have to decide where the missing sentences fit in the text.

Steps to success

- Look very carefully at the sentences that come before and after the gap.
- Look for clues within the missing sentences/ paragraphs as to where they go, eg
  → reference words (*this, that*, etc)
  → pronouns (*it, she, they*, etc)
  → function words and expressions (*however, although, for example, also*, etc)
  → verb tenses
  → names

E Seven sentences have been removed from the story. Choose from the sentences A–H the one which best fits each gap (1–7). There is one extra sentence which you do not need to use.

First day

On a crisp, sunny morning in September 1978 I started at Chelmsford Secondary School. I arrived with butterflies in my stomach. I was **convinced** that I would never be able to find my way around the huge building, with its never ending corridors, flights of stairs and grey, **identical** classrooms. My old junior school, with its yellow walls and wooden desks, seemed a million miles away. I was alone in the big, wide world now.

I had spent hours getting ready that morning. I was wearing my brand new navy blue uniform, crisp white blouse and the Chelmsford blue and gold striped tie. On a recent shopping trip with my mum, we had also **purchased** a shiny brown leather satchel. (**1**) .... I couldn't wait to fill it with books.

I lined up in the playground with all the other new first years and waited for my name to be called out to find out whose class I was in. (**2**) .... She must have been fresh out of university and didn't look much older than some of the sixth formers. I breathed a sigh of relief. I'd been **dreading** that I'd get Mr Taylor, whose nickname was 'The Dictator'. Apparently, he gave detention if you were even a minute late for school. (**3**) ....

We followed her through the main entrance and down endless corridors until we reached our classroom. There, in a trembling voice, she told us to sit down and started taking the register. I took a seat on the front row and another girl sat down next to me. My heart sank when I realized it was Amanda East. Amanda had been the most popular girl at my junior school. (**4**) .... I had never been one of her gang and in ordinary circumstances she would have **ignored** me. Now, without her usual crowd of admirers, she looked almost pleased to see me. 'Hey, Smithie, mind if I sit here?' she said, pretending to smile. 'Or are only swots allowed on the front row?'

Amanda wasn't well known for her academic abilities. Her only talent was for sports and she had often made fun of my athletic shortcomings. In every other subject, she managed by cheating in tests and using other people's homework as a study aid. Indeed, 'borrowing' from other people came so naturally to her that she automatically started copying my timetable down. When I pointed out that hers was different from mine, her mouth dropped open. 'So we're not going to be in the same class for everything?' she asked, then added with a **fake** smile. 'That's a pity, Smithie. (**5**) ....'

That was the last thing I wanted, but my thoughts were interrupted by a bell ringing. This was the signal for us all to go and begin the first lesson of the day. (**6**) .... 9–11 am: double geography, room 17B, it said. This time I would make sure I got as far away from Amanda East as possible – but first I had to find the right room. After getting hopelessly lost several times, I finally managed to **track down** my geography class. (**7**) .... I scanned the sea of faces before me, hoping to spot a friendly one. Then I heard a **familiar** voice say, 'There's a spare seat over here, Smithie'. The voice was coming from the back row and I knew exactly who it belonged to.

A She was both pretty and good at sport, things which counted for a lot at the age of 11.
B My form teacher turned out to be Miss Hare.
C I looked at my timetable.
D By the time I got there, however, nearly every seat had been taken.
E Miss Hare was equally scary.
F Just carrying it made me feel sophisticated and mature.
G I was hoping we could stick together.
H Miss Hare, on the contrary, seemed more afraid of us than we were of her.

Work it Out!

F Match the words in bold from the text with their meanings.

1 .... exactly the same
2 .... known
3 .... sure
4 .... find
5 .... taken no notice of
6 .... false/not sincere
7 .... bought
8 .... expecting (something bad)

G Match the pictures with the words.

1 register ....   4 playing field ....
2 satchel ....   5 detention ....
3 uniform ....

Quick chat

How did you feel on your first day at secondary school?

Grammar 1

✓ Check comparatives and superlatives

See pages 139-140 for information about comparatives and superlatives.

Circle the correct word or phrase.
1 This exercise is **more / most** difficult **than / from** the last one.
2 This is the **better / best** grade I've ever had for maths!
3 Mrs Bellows is the **most strict / strictest** teacher at our school.
4 Biology isn't as difficult **as / than** physics.
5 Joanna works more **slower / slowly** than her sister.

A Find seven mistakes with comparatives and superlatives and correct them.

Everyone knows that the better way to learn a foreign language is to live in the country where it's spoken. If you can't do that, though, there are other most practical solutions!

Talking with native speakers is the more effective way to improve your speaking skills. So if you're learning Spanish, for example, try to make friends with someone Spanish living in your town. You'll soon be speaking the more fluently.

On the other hand, it might be more easier to find a Spanish pen friend, who you can write to and email in Spanish. It won't be as good than having face-to-face conversations, but your written language will improve more quicker than you expect. And if you're lucky, they might even invite you to their country for a holiday!

Quick chat
Talk about your school subjects using comparatives and superlatives and the adjectives below. Explain why you think so.

boring • complicated • enjoyable • hard • simple • useful

Maths is more useful than art because you need to use numbers every day. However, I think art is more enjoyable because it's fun to create new things.

✓ Check gradable and non-gradable adjectives

See page 140 for information about gradable and non-gradable adjectives.

Tick the correct sentences.
1 I think this is an extremely difficult exercise.
2 It was very freezing this morning when I got up.
3 That action film was completely fantastic.
4 We were absolutely delighted to see them again.
5 Don't you think that lecture was completely interesting?

B Circle the gradable adjectives and underline the non-gradable adjectives. Then, find the synonymous pairs.

angry • boiling • cold • difficult • ecstatic freezing • furious • happy • hot • hungry • impossible ridiculous • scared • silly • starving • terrified

C Choose the word that best completes each sentence.
1 I haven't eaten all day. I'm absolutely .... (hungry, starving)
2 The child was .... scared of the dark. (completely, very)
3 Dad was extremely .... when I broke the window. (angry, furious)
4 I'm .... sad today. (a bit, totally)
5 That hat you're wearing is very .... (ridiculous, silly)

D Use the following adverbs and adjectives to write your own sentences.

a bit • very • absolutely   fantastic • annoyed • cold

1 ....
2 ....
3 ....

Vocabulary 1
Education and learning

A Match the places of learning with the ages at which you attend them. Which one are you at now?

1 secondary school   a 2–5 years old
2 nursery school   b 5–11 years old
3 university   c 11–16 years old
4 primary/junior school   d 16–18 years old
5 sixth form college   e 18–21 years old

B Explain the difference between

1 **exams** and **continuous assessment**
2 a **state school** and a **private school**
3 a **compulsory** lesson and an **optional** lesson
4 a **desk** and an **office**
5 a **class** and a **classroom**
6 an **academic** subject and a **practical** subject
7 a school **timetable** and a school **report**

C Some of the definitions below are in the wrong place. Tick the correct ones and put the others in the correct place.

1 a playground = an area next to a school where children play
2 a library = a room where experiments are done
3 a staff room = a place where teachers and students/pupils eat
4 a hall of residence = a room for teachers only
5 a laboratory = a place where you can borrow books
6 a lecture theatre = a large room where university students have classes
7 a canteen = a place where university students live

Easily confused words

D Complete the sentences with the correct word from each pair or group.

1 **degree, certificate**
a Matt is studying for a .... in law at Glasgow University.
b At the end of the cookery course, we all got a .... of attendance.

2 **pass, take**
a Whenever I .... exams, I get really nervous beforehand.
b If I .... my driving test, I'm going to save up and buy a second-hand car.

3 **tutor, instructor, professor**
a I'm hopeless at maths so I'm going to have some lessons with a private ....
b Phil works as a ski .... every winter.
c My dad is a(n) .... at Cardiff University.

4 **pupil, student**
a Heather is a .... at university.
b My mum was a .... at Greenwood School years ago.

5 **subjects, lesson, course**
a I dread every chemistry .... because I never understand anything!
b Katie's got exams in two .... today.
c My grandma is doing a .... in computer skills for beginners.

6 **reading, revising**
a Timothy's .... for his exam tomorrow.
b I'm .... a really good book at the moment. I'll lend it to you when I've finished it.

Key phrasal verbs

E Match the two halves of the sentences.

1 Nick's parents were disappointed when he
2 I've been trying to do this question for ages, but I still haven't
3 It's time you stopped talking and
4 We've been living in Holland for three years now and I still haven't
5 My first French teacher always
6 I've just heard that I've

a **got into** Oxford University!
b **worked out** the answer.
c **picked up** Dutch.
d **got on with** your work.
e **dropped out of** college after a few months.
f **pointed out** my mistakes without making me feel bad.

F Now match the phrasal verbs (1–6) with their meanings (a–f).

1 get into
2 work out
3 point out
4 pick up
5 get on with
6 drop out (of)

a concentrate on doing
b calculate
c leave an educational institute (without completing course)
d be accepted at an educational institute
e draw attention to something
f learn (a language or skill)

Listening

B2 Exam Practice

You will hear five different people talking about a subject. You have to match the speakers with what they say.

Steps to success
- Listen to **everything** the speakers say before you make your choice.
- Don't expect speakers to always state their opinions directly.

A 🎧 Listen to five short conversations and tick the correct sentences (a or b).

1
a He went to university.
b He didn't go to university.

2
a She wanted to leave home.
b She didn't want to leave home.

3
a The university flat is luxurious.
b The university flat isn't luxurious.

4
a She's surprised Steve failed his exams.
b She isn't surprised Steve failed his exams.

5
a He thinks he's going to pass his driving test.
b He doesn't think he's going to pass his driving test.

B 🎧 Listen again and make a list of some of the phrases that helped you decide.

....
....
....
....

Quick chat
What would you like to do after secondary school? Would you prefer to get a job or go to university?

C Look at the photos and discuss what aspects of life at university they show.

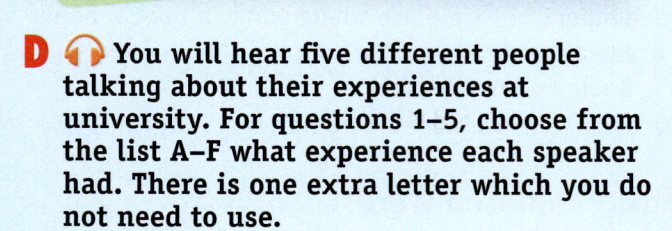

D 🎧 You will hear five different people talking about their experiences at university. For questions 1–5, choose from the list A–F what experience each speaker had. There is one extra letter which you do not need to use.

A She worked very hard.
B He was asked to leave.
C It didn't make much difference to her future career.
D He didn't finish his course.
E He had expected it to be better.
F He met someone there who is important to him.

Speaker 1 ☐
Speaker 2 ☐
Speaker 3 ☐
Speaker 4 ☐
Speaker 5 ☐

Speaking

B2 Exam Practice
You will be asked to do a task with the other candidate. You'll be given one or more pictures that show a situation and asked to make a decision or solve a problem.

Steps to success
- Listen carefully to what the examiner asks you to do.
- Don't just describe the picture(s), talk about them in relation to the task.
- Talk to the other candidate, not the examiner.

A Read the situations below and then discuss them with a partner. Give reasons for your ideas. Use the Language chunks.

1 Your teacher is leaving and your class has collected 50 euros to buy her a present. What do you think you should buy for her?
2 Your best friend already speaks English, but wants to learn another foreign language. Which language do you think he should choose?
3 Your mum has got some free time and wants to learn a new skill. What should she learn?

Language chunks

Making suggestions
What about + -ing … ?
How about + -ing … ?
What do you think about + -ing … ?
Maybe/I think we should …
It would be a good idea to … because …

Quick chat
What changes would you like to make to your school? If you could study any language, which would you choose?

B Now do this task with a partner.
Someone has donated 10,000 euros to your school. These pictures show different things the money could be spent on. Talk about the advantages and disadvantages of each one and then suggest what the best way to spend the money is.

What are the advantages and disadvantages of each one?
What is the best way to spend the money?

Say it right!

C 🎧 Listen and circle the word you hear in each pair.

1 filled / field
2 sit / seat
3 still / steal
4 chip / cheap
5 live / leave
6 hall / whole
7 law / low
8 caught / coat
9 walk / woke
10 floor / flow

3

Dive in!

A What famous universities can you name?

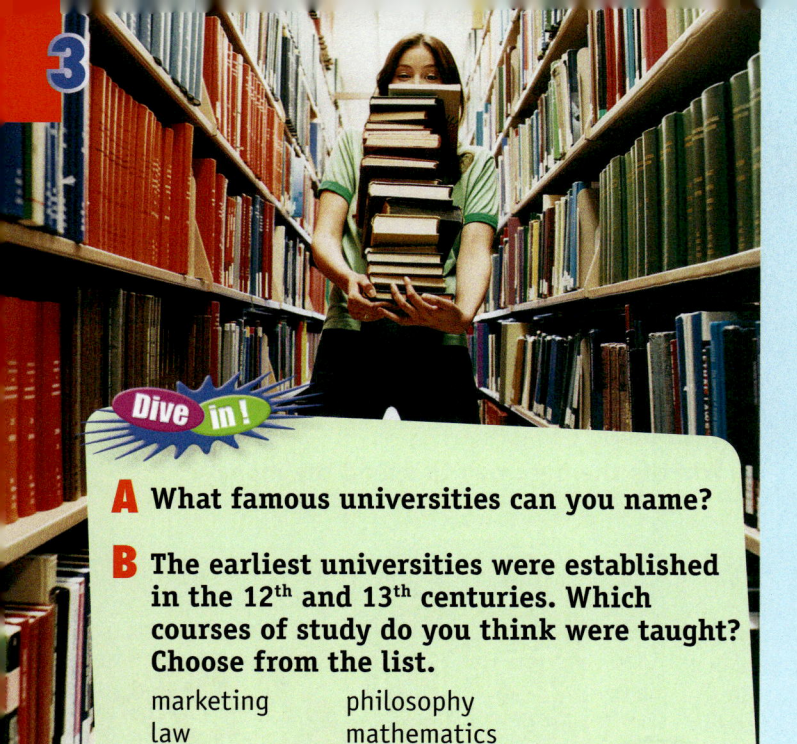

B The earliest universities were established in the 12th and 13th centuries. Which courses of study do you think were taught? Choose from the list.

marketing   philosophy
law   mathematics
business   astronomy
medicine   environmental studies
theology

Reading 2

C Complete the sentences with the words provided.

1 **public / private**

You have to pay to attend a .... school.

.... schools are funded by the government.

2 **undergraduate / graduate**

.... students are still attending university for their first degree.

.... students have got their first degree and are studying for a more advanced degree in their field.

3 **bachelor's / master's**

After receiving his .... degree with honours, he was confident of successfully completing his ....

B2 Exam Practice

You will be given an article or leaflet describing a place. You will then need to answer multiple choice questions about the information provided.

Steps to success
- Skim the different sections of the text before looking at the questions.
- Use the headings to help you locate information relevant to each question.

D Use the information in the leaflet about Harvard University to answer the questions that follow.

1 Who made a donation to the university?
a Charles W. Eliot
b Barack Obama
c John Harvard
d Tommy Lee Jones

2 In what way was Tommy Lee Jones different to Obama and Portman?
a He earned a bachelor's degree.
b He was not involved with journals.
c He became an actor.
d He was a Harvard graduate.

3 When were many more schools set up?
a about 100-150 years ago
b in the 1930s
c in the 21st century
d in the 17th century

4 When were the first doctors trained at Harvard?
a in 1909
b when Eliot was president
c after the course was offered at Oxford
d before the law school was founded

5 According to the text, what is one reason why Harvard is the world's top university?
a It has the most members of staff.
b It gets the best students.
c It offers the most courses.
d It conducts the best research.

6 What is unique about Harvard?
a It has produced the most presidents.
b It has a House Plan.
c It was established before any other US university.
d It gives the most scholarships.

7 According to the text, what is notable about Radcliffe?
a It was a part of Harvard.
b It agreed with Harvard.
c It offered accommodation.
d It allowed women to study.

Harvard University

Harvard University is a private university in Cambridge, Massachusetts, USA.
Eight Presidents of the United States have graduated from Harvard University, including Barack Obama.

Which is the oldest university in the United States? Harvard.

Important Events

1636 Founded and initially called New College

1639 Named Harvard College

1643 First scholarship granted

1653 First Native American begins studying at Harvard

1780 Harvard officially recognized as a university

1782 Harvard Medical School founded

1817 Harvard Law School founded (oldest in the United States)

1879 Affiliated college for women opens (Radcliffe College)

Early History

The university has grown from nine students with one master to more than 18,000 degree candidates, including undergraduates and graduate students. Over 14,000 people work at Harvard, including more than 2,000 faculty members. Harvard was established in 1636 and was named after John Harvard, who left his library and half his estate to the new learning institution when he died. During its early years, Harvard offered courses similar to those of the English universities, particularly Oxford and Cambridge.

Later History

As the university grew in the 18th and 19th centuries, so did the **curriculum**, particularly in the sciences. Charles W. Eliot, who was university president from 1869 to 1909, changed Harvard from a small provincial institution into an impressive modern university. During his presidency, the graduate schools of Business, Dental Medicine, and Arts and Sciences were established. Enrollment rose from 1,000 to 3,000 students, and the faculty grew from 49 to 278 members.
By the 1930s, the House Plan had been established. This provides a small college atmosphere within the larger university. After their first year, students go to one of 12 **campus** Houses and live there for the remainder of their undergraduate courses. Each House has a master and teaching staff, as well as a dining room and library, and offers a large range of athletic, social and cultural events.

Recent History

In the 20th century, the quality of undergraduate and graduate education at Harvard continued to improve. The university – keen to make higher education available to everyone – provided more and more **scholarships** to poorer students. In 1943, Harvard and Radcliffe signed an agreement which allowed Radcliffe's women students into Harvard classrooms. At this time, the university also firmly established its role as an outstanding **research** institution.
Harvard's excellence has continued into the 21st century. It is consistently the number one university in the world in international college and university rankings. The university makes every effort to ensure it attracts the best teaching staff, and the strongest students regardless of **financial** circumstances.

Famous Harvard Graduates

US President Barack Obama is a graduate of Harvard Law School. While there, he was president of the Harvard Law Review – a legal **journal** published by students at Harvard Law School. In fact, he was the Review's first African-American president.

Tommy Lee Jones, an Academy Award-winning actor, attended Harvard on a scholarship, was roommates with future US Vice President Al Gore, and played for the university football team. He graduated with a degree in English.

Actress Natalie Portman graduated from Harvard with a bachelor's degree in psychology. While there she was a research assistant in a psychology lab and she co-authored two research papers which were published in scientific journals.

E Use the words highlighted in the text to complete the sentences below.

1 Physicists carry out scientific ....
2 .... pay for some students' studies.
3 At university, you can live on ....
4 This .... is in the science library.
5 The university can help students who have .... problems.
6 Biology, physics and chemistry make up the science .... at my school.

Quick chat
Would you like to go to university? What do you think university life would be like? What would you enjoy the most?

Grammar 2

✓ Check question forms

See pages 140 and 141 for information about question forms.

Put the words in the correct order to form questions.

Direct questions
1 school / you / which / to / go / do / ?
....
2 was / the maths test / how / ?
....

Indirect questions
3 who / I / took / wonder / it /
....
4 me / this / you / could / tell / if / is / correct / ?
....

✓ Check question tags

See page 141 for information about question tags.

Complete the sentences and fill in the table.
1 They don't like chemistry, ... ?
2 You can't study in front of the TV, ... ?
3 She has finished her homework, ... ?
4 The lecture will be about art, ... ?
5 We must hand in our essays today, ... ?
6 They shouldn't be here, ... ?

A positive statement is followed by a .... question tag.
A negative statement is followed by a .... question tag.

A Rewrite the questions correctly.
1 You are studying or watching *X Factor*?
2 Mark and Anthony, do they go to a private school?
3 What means this word?
4 How went your exam yesterday?
5 Could you tell me if has started the film?
6 I wonder what is the time.

B Complete the second sentence so that it means the same as the first.
1 Where's my rubber?
  Could you tell me .... ?
2 Are we having a vocabulary test today?
  I'd like to know ....
3 Has Jim taught his parrot to talk?
  I wonder ....
4 What time is it?
  We want to know ....
5 Does Maggie speak Japanese?
  Do you know .... ?

B2 Exam Practice
You have to rewrite a sentence using a given word.
Steps to success
- Do not change the word you are given in any way.
- Your answer mustn't be more than five words long.

C Choose the correct question tag.
1 You'd better leave now, **shouldn't you/wouldn't you/hadn't you**?
2 The train will be on time, **doesn't it/is it/won't it**?
3 Get a haircut, **will you/don't you/do you**?
4 Nowhere is safe nowadays, **are they/is it/isn't it**?
5 You have to study, **haven't you/don't you/will you**?

D Complete the second sentence so that it has a similar meaning to the first sentence, using the word given.
1 My dog is more intelligent than yours.   **as**
  Your dog .... mine.
2 I've never seen a worse film before.   **the**
  This is .... I have ever seen.
3 Where does Nigel live now?   **lives**
  Do you know .... now?
4 There isn't a better university than this in the country.   **the**
  This .... in the country.
5 John, do you agree that it's nice here?   **it**
  It's nice here, ..., John?
6 We didn't realize how far the school was.   **than**
  The school was .... we thought.

Vocabulary 2
Noun suffixes

A Add these suffixes to form nouns making any spelling changes necessary: -ure, -ion, -ment, -ness, -ity, -ance.

1 depress ....
2 improve ....
3 attend ....
4 press ....
5 entertain ....
6 real ....
7 able ....
8 populate ....
9 fail ....
10 determine ....
11 sad ....
12 perform ....
13 develop ....
14 qualify ....
15 achieve ....
16 willing ....
17 disappoint ....
18 happy ....
19 enter ....
20 popular ....

C Find the one word that can complete all of the sentences. Then, match each use with the correct definition a–d.

1 Have they .... a date for their wedding?
2 The film *300* is .... in the year 480 BC.
3 Our teachers usually .... a lot of homework for the weekend.
4 I always .... my alarm clock for 7.30am.

a to make a piece of equipment start at a particular time
b to decide where or when something will happen
c to give something to someone to do
d to put a story in a particular time or place

The correct word above has more definitions than any other word in the English language. In fact, it has 464 different definitions!

B2 Exam Practice
You will have to form words to complete the gaps in a text.

Steps to success
- Read the whole text first.
- Work out what part of speech is missing (adjective, noun, verb, etc) by looking at the rest of the sentence.
- Remember, you might have to make some nouns plural.

Word patterns

B Complete the text with the correct form of *get* or *take*.

Hi Ollie,
How are you? How did your exams go? Don't worry – you always (1) .... good marks! Did I tell you that your old teacher, Mr Hopps, is (2) .... us for maths now? The other day when he was (3) .... the register, he asked me if I was your sister. Anyway, he seems OK – I just wish we didn't (4) .... so much homework!
Don't forget that I'm coming to stay with you next weekend. I (5) .... there at eight o' clock on Friday night. I can't wait! I hope you're going to (6) .... me out and introduce me to all your friends! Mum's worried about me coming on my own, but I've told her that you'll (7) .... care of me! She and Dad (8) .... on my nerves as usual!
I'm dying to hear your news, so email me when you (9) .... the chance.
Lots of love,
Becky

D For questions 1–10, read the text below. Use the word given in capitals at the end of the lines to form a word that fits in the gap in the same line. Write your answers in CAPITAL LETTERS.

Brain power

Nowadays there is more (**1**) .... than ever to stay young. **PRESS**
This may explain the popularity of a computer game which claims
to improve the brain's (**2**) ....! **PERFORM**
Each (**3**) .... in Brain Age, which includes lots of puzzles and **ACTIVE**
mathematical problems, has been specially designed to stop mental
(**4**) .... deteriorating. After playing the game, you are told **ABLE**
what your 'brain age' is. A 30-year-old man or woman might be
(**5**) .... to find they have the brain age of a 50-year-old, for **SURPRISE**
example. (**6**) .... is possible, however! The makers of the **IMPROVE**
game, designed by a Japanese (**7**) .... , say that playing it **PROFESS**
will make your brain 'younger'. A combination of (**8**) .... and **ENTERTAIN**
mental stimulation for the older generation, it has already become
a great (**9**) .... in Japan, where an amazing fifth of the total **SUCCEED**
(**10**) .... is over 65 years old. So if your grandma or grandad **POPULATE**
is starting to get a bit forgetful, maybe it's time you introduced
them to computer games!

Writing: article

B2 Exam Practice
You might be asked to write an article. You must write between 120 and 180 words.

Steps to success
- Give your article a TITLE.
- Write about a subject that is RELEVANT to the question or title.
- Organize your article in PARAGRAPHS.
- Give REASONS and SUGGESTIONS related to the subject.
- Give your POINT OF VIEW.
- Check the LENGTH.

A Look at the task below and read two different answers to it. Which article would get a higher mark?

Your school magazine is asking for articles with the following title:
What's wrong with school today?
The best articles will be published in the magazine. Write your article in 120–180 words.

Article 1

What's wrong with school today?

Although many children dislike school, it isn't so bad. Everybody needs an education in order to find a job later. That's why we should see its good side.

School offers many positive things. It gives children knowledge which will be useful to them in the future. They study a wide range of subjects and some are very interesting. It's a good place to meet your friends too.

In conclusion, there are some things wrong with school, but we shouldn't criticize it too much. There are lots of good things about it too.

Article 2

What's wrong with school today?

Although some children don't like school, the fact is that education is extremely important. It's true that there are problems in schools, but a few simple changes would help to improve pupils' lives.

In my opinion, the most difficult thing for school pupils is the amount of homework they get. We spend most of the day at school and then we have to study for hours at home. Teenagers need time to do other activities, such as sports and hobbies. Teachers should limit the amount of homework they set so that pupils have time to develop other interests.

Another problem is school exams. Many children get very nervous before exams and this can have a bad effect on their health. Personally, I think that a system of continuous assessment would be much better. I believe that if pupils didn't have to take so many exams every year, they would be less stressed and they would get better results.

Although school will never suit everyone, these improvements would make a big difference to many pupils' lives. With less homework and fewer exams they would be healthier and happier people.

B Look at this list of points about a good article. Write *Yes* or *No* next to each point for the two articles you read opposite.

	Article 1	Article 2
a It is relevant to the question/title.		
b It is organized into paragraphs.		
c It gives reasons and suggestions.		
d It gives the writer's point of view.		
e It is long enough to fully answer the question.		

C Look at this task. Discuss the question with your partner, using the pictures to help you, and write down two or three ideas you could use in your article.

Your school magazine is asking for articles with the following title:
What can we do to make school more enjoyable?
The best ones will be published in the magazine. Write your article in 120–180 words.

D Complete the sentences with your own ideas.
1 The fact is that many classrooms are not …
2 We often get two or three hours' homework a night. Personally, I think …
3 Don't forget that the purpose of school is to …
4 As far as I'm concerned, art and drama lessons are …

E Now write your article in 120–180 words using the model and some of the Language chunks to help you. When you've written it, check that it does everything in the list in Exercise B.

Language chunks

Writing an article

Making a statement
The fact is …
It's true that …
Don't forget that …

Expressing your point of view
In my opinion, …
Personally, I (don't) think …
I believe that …
As far as I'm concerned, …

4 Changes

A Which of these predictions about the future do you think will come true in your lifetime?

- 'Plastic money' will replace real money.
- People will have silicon chips implanted in their bodies so they can communicate directly with computers.
- Scientists will discover life on another planet.
- Parents will be able to choose the sex and appearance of their babies.
- It will be legal to clone human beings.

Reading 1

B2 Exam Practice

You will be given a text made up of different parts. One question may require two answers.

Steps to success
- Quickly read through the whole text.
- Go through the text again scanning for information which is similar, in order to locate the answer(s) to the question.

B Quickly read all the paragraphs (A, B, C and D), and underline any sections in them to do with personal information being used illegally.

C In which of the paragraphs (A, B, C and D) did you underline words or phrases?

Paragraph A ☐   Paragraph C ☐
Paragraph B ☐   Paragraph D ☐

The two paragraphs which you ticked above are the answers to questions 1 and 2. Use the underlining technique to answer the remaining questions in Exercise D.

D For questions 1–15, choose from the people (A–D). The people may be chosen more than once.

Which person or people

mention how personal information can be used illegally?	**1**☐	**2**☐
mention places where large amounts of personal information are kept?	**3**☐	**4**☐
mention devices for finding where people are?	**5**☐	**6**☐
think that we will be better protected from crime in the future?	**7**☐	**8**☐
says that making payments can be dangerous?	**9**☐	
say that more crimes are committed nowadays?	**10**☐	**11**☐
thinks that crime is going to become less violent?	**12**☐	
give examples of crimes that have happened?	**13**☐	**14**☐
says that people felt safer in the past?	**15**☐	

Crime in the 21st century

A The Computer Expert

Technology is going to make it easier for people to commit crimes in the future. Advances in computer technology mean that crimes using computers will become more common. Robbing a bank in person will become a thing of the past. As we've already seen, computer hackers can break into a bank's security system from their own computer and transfer millions of dollars into an account. There's the internet too, which has led to new kinds of crime. There are some websites where you can find out whatever you want about someone — their address, telephone number, everything. These details can be sold to other people or used for criminal purposes. Emails can also be used to trick people into giving out confidential facts about themselves. For example, you might get a message, supposedly from your bank, asking you to give details of your bank account. In reality, of course, banks never ask you to send this kind of information by email.

B The Police Officer

According to statistics the crime rate is going up. Fortunately, though, it's becoming easier for us to detect crimes and catch those responsible. For example, we're already using electronic tagging to keep an eye on ex-prisoners who have just been released. This means we know all their movements, which prevents them from committing further crimes. They say that ten years from now, we'll have a national database of DNA profiles for every member of the public. People don't like the idea because it sounds like something out of a science fiction film, but it will make our job a lot easier. OK, so people will have less privacy, but isn't it worth it if it makes them feel more secure? When they first put cameras in public places, everyone complained about that too, but they soon got used to it. I believe the measures we're taking will help make the world a less dangerous place to live in.

C The Scientist

Methods of fighting crime are becoming more and more advanced. For example, at the moment we're working on a method of tracking criminals using smell. Each of us has our own particular odour, which is different to anyone else's. We hope that one day we'll be able to use odour recognition to help identify suspects. Another future development which will make everyone feel safer will be the introduction of emergency panic buttons. The idea is that everyone will have one of these buttons, which they'll press if someone attacks them. These will be linked to global positioning satellite (GPS) receivers, which can find someone's location within seconds. Advances in technology will obviously affect the way crimes are committed too. CS gas sprays and stun guns are already being used by some criminals instead of standard guns. These are an improvement from the victim's point of view because they don't cause permanent injury or death.

D The Victim

I had my house burgled last year and after that, I spent a lot of money on a good security system. Crime has increased to the point where we need alarms for everything — not just our houses but other possessions — cars, motorbikes and so on. Things were different when I was young. Sometimes we didn't even use to lock the front door when we went out. That would be unthinkable nowadays! The threat of crime is everywhere. Every time you pay for something by credit card, you don't know if someone might be recording the details to use themselves. Even when you use the cash machine, you have to be careful. I heard a story on the news the other day about a gang of crooks who installed a fake cash machine in a shopping centre! People punched their personal ID numbers into the machine and waited for their money, which, of course the machine didn't give them. While they waited, their cards were copied and the criminals later used the copies to take money out of their accounts!

Work it Out!

E Find words in the text that mean:
1 move from one place to another (A) ....
2 where your money is kept at a bank (A) ....
3 set free (B) ....
4 stops (B) ....
5 smell (C) ....
6 connected to (C) ....
7 position (C) ....
8 lasting forever (C) ....
9 things someone owns (D) ....
10 (criminal) group (D) ....

F Explain what these things are and what they are used for.
1 a cash machine
2 a DNA profile
3 electronic tagging
4 a GPS receiver
5 CS gas spray
6 a stun gun

Quick chat
What computer crimes have you heard about?

Grammar 1

✓ Check infinitives and -ing forms

See pages 141 and 142 for more information about infinitives and -ing forms.

Complete the sentences with the correct form of the verbs in brackets.

1 My parents won't let me .... (buy) a palmtop computer.
2 Pat is really good at .... (solve) mathematical problems.
3 George denied .... (copy) the file, but I didn't believe him.
4 Do you remember .... (see) a strange man outside our house the other night?
5 My mum helped me .... (do) my chemistry homework.
6 We decided .... (follow) the woman to see where she went.

A Complete the text with the -ing form or infinitive form of the verbs in brackets.

Ex-criminals in one US state will soon be able (1) .... (have) free plastic surgery! Authorities hope (2) .... (reduce) crime by giving offenders the chance to alter their appearance. 'Many ex-criminals want (3) .... (change) when they come out of prison,' says the creator of the scheme, Harry Day. 'Giving them a different appearance means that they'll avoid (4) .... (mix) with criminals from their past, and this will hopefully help them (5) .... (make) a fresh start in life!' Several prisoners have already said they're interested in (6) .... (try) the treatment. Bill Cobbley, who is currently serving a ten-year sentence for armed robbery, says he won't mind (7) .... (look) different. 'The treatment will enable me (8) .... (leave) my past behind,' he commented. 'Now nothing can prevent me from (9) .... (begin) a new life. I just hope they make me (10) .... (look) good!'

B Rewrite the sentences. Use the word given followed by the -ing form or the infinitive form.

1 You didn't switch on the answering machine! (forgot)
....

2 Rosie wishes she hadn't stolen the CD. (regrets)
....

3 I tried to interrupt them, but they just continued to talk. (went on)
....

4 I changed the battery, but the camera still didn't work. (tried)
....

5 Don't worry about me! (stop)
....

6 I have no memory of locking the front door. (remember)
....

7 After his talk, the speaker answered questions from the audience. (went on)
....

8 I'll always remember riding a horse for the first time. (forget)
....

9 Jeremy attempted to unlock the door, but he had the wrong key. (tried)
....

10 Please make sure that you feed the dog. (remember)
....

11 I'm sorry, but I have to inform you that all the tickets are sold out. (regret)
....

12 I stopped the car and asked for directions. (to)
....

Vocabulary 1
Technology

A Label the picture with these words.

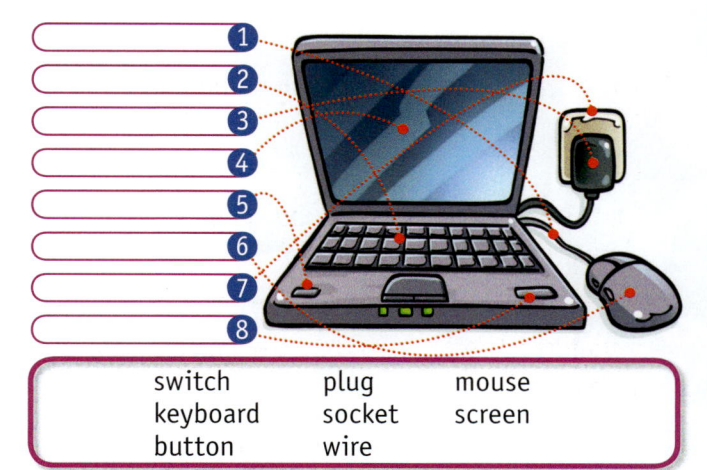

1
2
3
4
5
6
7
8

switch   plug   mouse
keyboard   socket   screen
button   wire

B Circle the correct word or phrase.

A Beginner's Guide to Using the Internet

The first thing you have to do is (1) **switch on / open** your computer. OK, that was easy! Now you have to (2) **log on / log off**. In other words, you have to type your name and password into the correct spaces. Next you have to find where it says 'internet (3) **connection / entrance**' and (4) **press / click** on that. After a few seconds you'll be (5) **online / on top** (connected to the internet). Now enter the (6) **address / number** of the website you want to look at. When it opens, you'll see (7) **paths / links** to different places on the site, where you'll find different kinds of information. You can (8) **unload / download** any of this information and save it on a CD-ROM or on your computer's (9) **hard / flat** disk. If you want to have a copy on paper, you can then (10) **print / scan** it out.

C Say what you can do with these devices using the verbs and structure below.

1 hosepipe   5 torch   9 scales
2 light bulb   6 calculator   10 ruler
3 scissors   7 radiator   11 air conditioner
4 satellite dish 8 thermometer

You use (a) … to …

add up, cool, cut, get, heat, measure, see, wash, water, weigh

D Match the verbs with the nouns.
1 charge ....   a software
2 install ....   b research
3 service ....   c a tap
4 turn on/off .... d a car
5 carry out ....   e a battery

Society and crime

E The highlighted verbs are in the wrong sentences. Write the correct verbs in the spaces.
1 When they **stole** our house, they took everything of value they could find. ....
2 The terrorists **hijacked** the journalist and held him hostage for three days. ....
3 A US plane carrying 200 passengers was **burgled** this morning. ....
4 The man said he **murdered** the bank because he was in desperate need of money. ....
5 The shoplifter only **robbed** small items like CDs and magazines. ....
6 The woman **kidnapped** her husband by poisoning him. ....

Word partners

F Match the words to make compound nouns.
1 prison ....   a limit
2 speed ....   b sentence
3 crime ....   c rate
4 driving ....   d service
5 military ....   e licence

G Match the compound nouns from Exercise F with their definitions.

1 The number of illegal acts that happen in an area.
....

2 You aren't allowed to drive faster than this.
....

3 When you have to be in the army for a certain time.
....

4 One of these might be for several years if you commit a serious crime.
....

5 You need this in order to drive a car.
....

4

Listening

A Which do you think is the most enjoyable way of shopping? Why?

B2 Exam Practice

You will listen to a monologue or dialogue between speakers. You will then have to answer seven multiple choice questions based on what you heard.

Steps to success
- Read the questions first to get an idea of what the recording is about.
- Remember, you hear the recording twice so you have the chance to check your answers.

B Look at the questions below about a conversation you are going to hear, and complete the notes.

Names of speakers: .... and ....
Subject of conversation: .... called ....

1 What did Emma do recently using a website?
A She sold some trainers.
B She advertised some trainers.
C She bought some trainers.

2 What can you buy on the website that Emma mentions?
A clothes only
B clothes and electronic goods
C lots of different things

3 All the items for sale on E-buy are accompanied by
A a photo and written information.
B a photo.
C written information.

4 What does Emma say about the jeans she bought?
A They were brand new.
B They were almost new.
C They had never been worn.

5 The prices of things for sale on E-buy are
A always cheap.
B able to change.
C standard.

6 How do you pay for things that you buy on E-buy?
A You send the money by post.
B You pay the seller in person.
C You pay the money into the bank.

7 What is Liam thinking of buying?
A a digital camera
B a video camera
C a computer

C 🎧 Listen and choose the best answer (A, B or C).

Speaking

B2 Exam Practice
You will have to answer questions related to a theme. You will be asked to give your opinion about different issues.

Steps to success
- Remember to make your answers as full as possible by giving reasons, examples, etc.
- Listen carefully to your partner's answers because you might be asked to comment on them.

A Match the questions with the answers.
1 How do computers help us in our daily lives?
2 Is there any modern gadget that you couldn't live without?
3 How often do you use a mobile phone?
4 What kind of problems does your generation face?
5 Why do teenagers find it difficult to communicate with adults sometimes?

a All sorts of things.
b In several ways.
c Because of their different ages.
d Very often.
e Yes, the TV.

B Expand on the answers in Exercise A by using some of the words and phrases in the groups below.

1 save time / do things efficiently / make communication easier

2 essential to me / useful for / a great way to

3 all the time / several times a day / whenever I …

4 unemployment / pressure to succeed / loneliness

5 generation gap / old fashioned / different points of view

C 🎧 Listen to these candidates answering one of the questions in Exercise A. Which candidate gives a good answer? How could the other candidate have improved their answer?

D 🎧 Listen to Dimitri again and tick any of the Language chunks he uses. Why does he use these expressions?

E Ask and answer with a partner.
Do you think life was easier or more difficult in the past?
What new gadget would you like to buy and why?
Is communication between people easier or more difficult nowadays?
How do you think your life will change in the next ten years?

Language chunks

Conversation fillers
I guess …
I suppose …
you know …
I mean …
you see …
Well, …

4

A
Discuss the ways in which the following might change your life and affect your future:
- Your parents move you to another school.
- You become passionately interested in something such as computing.
- Your father gets a new job and the family has to move abroad.
- You suddenly become very wealthy.

Reading 2

B2 Exam Practice
Some reading comprehension questions require you to find things that are only implied and not stated clearly in the text.
Learn to find implied meanings.

B
Look at the following excerpt from a passage about technology.

His opinions about new technology were quite different from those of most people today. He did not think that high-tech tools are necessarily better than low-tech ones.

Now look at the exam question.

What do most people think about high technology?

C
Read the following extracts and answer the questions that follow.

Jane always carried an umbrella when it was sunny, but preferred a hooded waterproof jacket when it was raining. On her way to work, she received an unexpected phone call. When she heard the news she dropped her umbrella.

What was the weather like when Jane heard the news?

Hydrogen is unlike the sort of fuels that we have been putting in our vehicles up to now. For one thing, it has to be manufactured because we cannot just dig and find reserves of the gas underground.

What does this extract imply about the sort of fuels we have been putting in our vehicles up to now?

D
Read the following passage about Bill Gates and then answer the six multiple choice questions.

Bill Gates: From geek to billionaire

Bill Gates' father was a wealthy lawyer. Because of his son's outstanding record at elementary school, especially in maths and science, he decided to send the boy to the private Lakeside School, where he should have been able to achieve his academic potential. However, when he was 13 the school took the unusual step of buying time on a computer at a company nearby (CCC). Soon Gates and his classmate, Paul

1 What does the passage tell us about Gates' studies at high school?
a He was very good at maths and science.
b His studies suffered.
c He was top of his class.
d He dropped out.

2 What was Bill Gates' and Paul Allen's first job?
a building a home computer
b improving computer security
c writing an article
d selling software

3 What did Gates and Allen get from the first company they worked for?
a a computer of their own
b free access to a computer
c a fixed salary
d $20,000

4 Where did Gates and Allen first see a home computer?
a at Lakeside
b at CCC
c at Harvard
d in a magazine

5 According to the passage, which organization did Gates and Allen lie to?
a Lakeside
b CCC
c Harvard
d MITS

6 The main purpose of the passage is to show
a that computers are extremely important in our lives.
b that we don't have to study to succeed.
c how Bill Gates became a successful businessman.
d that Bill Gates was a bad student.

Allen, were spending most of their time on it. They even hacked into the system to alter the records of the time they were on the computer. When this and other activities were discovered, CCC hired the students to help them prevent this happening, giving them unlimited free computer time as payment. It was not long before they had set up their own company and made $20,000 selling a computer system they had created.

Gates then enrolled at Harvard University, but his studies suffered, just as they had at high school, due to his passion for computers. The turning point came in 1974 when Allen saw a magazine article about the Altair 8080, the world's first home computer, made by MITS. They both realized that this would be the next big thing. They immediately contacted MITS and told them that they had the software that the new computer needed. Actually, the software was only ready eight weeks later, but when the company saw it running they signed a deal with the two young men. This persuaded Gates to drop out of Harvard and start working full-time with Allen. Their company, Microsoft, made Gates a billionaire.

E Complete the sentences with the words in the box.

> access • achieve • alter • deal • hack • hire
> potential • step • unlimited • wealthy

1 The decision to quit her job was a difficult .... to take.
2 Bill Gates is a very .... man.
3 You can't possibly .... anything unless you have dreams and goals.
4 You won't have .... to the website without a password.
5 I don't need one. I can .... my way into the computer system.
6 Broadband gives you .... access to the internet.
7 Anita has a great singing voice. She has the .... to become a huge star.
8 One year later she signed a(n) .... with a major record company.
9 The company is going to .... 16 computer programmers. You should apply.
10 They have different customs abroad so when you go to live there you will have to .... your lifestyle.

Quick chat

What do you like doing on the internet? How much time do you spend on the internet?
Are there any dangers when people focus so much of their energy on things to do with computers?

Grammar 2

✓ Check future forms

See page 142 for information about future tenses.

Match the uses with the sentences.
1 a prediction based on evidence
2 an unplanned decision
3 a request
4 an intention
5 a prediction about something in progress at a future time
6 a fixed arrangement
7 a statement about something that happens regularly
8 a prediction about something completed before a future time
9 an offer

a I think I'll type this essay instead of writing it.
b I'm never going to have plastic surgery!
c Shall I show you how this works?
d We're going on a school trip tomorrow.
e By 2050, they will have found alien life forms.
f The forecast says it's going to snow tomorrow!
g On Tuesday at one pm everyone will be watching the eclipse.
h That mystery series is on at six o'clock.
i Will you explain the results of the experiment?

A Circle the correct word or phrase.
1 The show **shall start** / **starts** at eight o'clock.
2 By 2050, astronauts **will have visited** / **are going to visit** Mars.
3 It will be beautiful in Scotland in October. The trees **are changing** / **will be changing** colour.
4 I hope my parents **will let** / **will have let** me get an iPod.
5 Some scientists predict that a meteorite **is hitting** / **is going to hit** the Earth soon.
6 **Will** / **Shall** you help me carry this heavy box?

✓ Check time clauses in the future

See page 142 for information about time clauses in the future.

Which of these sentences is correct?
1 You should read the instructions before you will use the DVD player.
2 I won't turn it on until he'll tell me to.
3 By the time we've downloaded this film, it will be midnight!

B Complete the sentences with the correct form of the verbs in brackets.
1 When Paul .... (go) out later, he .... (set) the burglar alarm.
2 I .... (bring) a spare battery for my MP3 player in case that one .... (run) out.
3 As soon as we .... (arrive), I .... (send) you a text message.
4 The computer .... (be) OK once we .... (install) the anti-virus software.

B2 Exam Practice
Steps to success
- Read through the whole text quickly before you begin to answer the questions.
- Check that your answers make sense grammatically and in terms of meaning.

C For questions 1-9, read the text below and think of the word which best fits each gap. Use only one word in each gap.

It's difficult to get a multinational company interested (1) .... helping wildlife, but that didn't prevent one British charity (2) .... trying. The British Hedgehog Preservation Society persuaded McDonald's (3) .... change its containers to save hedgehogs' lives. The problem? Hedgehogs, which like (4) .... sweet things, got their heads stuck in McDonald's dessert cartons! The hedgehogs (5) .... to get their heads through the holes in the cartons to eat the tasty leftovers, but their spines prevented them from (6) .... out again. Members wrote to McDonald's asking them to (7) .... something about it. McDonald's agreed to make the opening in the carton smaller. Hedgehogs (8) .... be unable to get their heads through it now and will no longer (9) .... in danger!

Vocabulary 2
Prepositions

A Complete the text with the prepositions below.

> about • against • by • in • on • over
> under (x2) • without

A young man walked into a supermarket, pointed a gun at the cashier and took all the money in the till. Then he asked for some bottles of beer too. The cashier was very calm (1) .... the circumstances. Although she was (2) .... danger of being shot, she refused to give the robber the beer. She told him it was (3) .... the law to give him alcohol since he was obviously (4) .... the age of 18. It annoyed the robber that the woman was in doubt (5) .... his age. Insisting that he was (6) .... 18, he got his driving licence out to prove it. The cashier looked at the licence and gave him the beers. As soon as he had gone, she called the police. It wasn't (7) .... chance that she had asked to see the man's driving licence. She had done it (8) .... purpose in order to find out where he lived. The police went to his house (9) .... delay and arrested him!

Key phrasal verbs

B Match the phrasal verbs with their meanings.

1 break into   a investigate
2 do away with   b escape
3 look into   c betray
4 give someone away   d get rid of
5 go up   e enter illegally
6 get away   f increase

C Complete the sentences with phrasal verbs from Exercise B in the correct form.

1 They should .... experiments on animals.
2 The police are .... the disappearance of a 52-year-old man.
3 The prisoners managed to .... by pretending to be prison guards!
4 The price of petrol has .... again!
5 The hacker managed to .... the bank's computer system.
6 Nick denied breaking the window, but his guilty expression .... him ....

B2 Exam Practice
Steps to success
- Read the text to get an idea of what it's about.
- Consider all the options before choosing the answer!

D For questions 1–10, read the article below and decide which answer (A, B, C or D) best fits each gap.

What's the secret of happiness? Researchers have been (1) .... into this. The research, which was (2) .... recently, suggests that happy people tend to be more successful than unhappy ones.

Happiness is difficult to (3) .... , but happy people are cheerful, sociable and generous. (4) .... , people who aren't happy can do something about it. Happiness levels can go (5) .... by doing things that make you feel good. That doesn't mean (6) .... a bank to get rich! By breaking the (7) .... , you might end up in prison where you would be miserable! (8) .... , activities should be enjoyable without being dangerous.

The study found that it wasn't (9) .... chance that some countries were happier than others. Governments can make their citizens happier by providing good public transport, working conditions and so on. The result will be lower crime (10) .... , which will make people feel safer and more secure – definitely something to smile about!

1	A seeing	B getting	C turning	D looking
2	A given away	B carried out	C broken into	D added up
3	A weigh	B measure	C charge	D scan
4	A Happily	B Sadly	C Steadily	D Fortunately
5	A up	B off	C down	D away
6	A burgling	B robbing	C stealing	D hijacking
7	A rule	B law	C licence	D sentence
8	A Otherwise	B Whereas	C Instead	D But
9	A by	B in	C on	D about
10	A numbers	B rates	C amounts	D limits

Writing: letter (transactional)

B2 Exam Practice

You will be given a situation and some information which you have to use to write a letter. You must write between 120 and 150 words.

Steps to success
- READ all the information carefully.
- Respond to all of the PROMPTS.
- ORGANIZE your answers in a logical order.
- Use clear PARAGRAPHS.
- Use an INFORMAL STYLE.
- Use a VARIETY of language.

A Look at this task. Will the letter you write be formal or informal?

You have received a letter from your cousin. This is an extract from that letter on which you have made some notes. Write a letter to your cousin, using all your notes.

> *big party*
>
> *No, it's the 26th!*
>
> By the way, I know it's your brother Robbie's birthday soon. I think it's the 16th October, isn't it? Is he doing anything to celebrate? Anyway, I want to give him a present, but I've no idea what to get him (I haven't seen him for a couple of years). What kind of things does he like? Has he got any hobbies? I can't spend a lot, but I want to get him something useful. Any ideas?
>
> *Loves music and computers!*
>
> *Yes! Give her some ideas.*

B Look again at the notes marked on the letter. For which one do you have to think of your own ideas?

C Which two presents would be most suitable for Robbie? Why?

D Now read a letter in answer to the task. Complete the four gaps in your own words using the notes marked on the letter in Exercise A.

> Dear Billy,
> Thanks for your letter. It was great to hear from you! I hope your mum is feeling better now.
> You asked me about what to buy Robbie for his birthday. It's really nice of you to suggest buying him something. I know he'll be pleased! His birthday (1) ...., by the way. It will be great because in the evening he (2) ....
> I've thought of a couple of ideas for presents that would be perfect for Robbie. One idea is a radio because he (3) .... Why don't you get him a waterproof radio that he can use in the shower? Then I'll be able to borrow it too!
> Robbie's also really into computers so you could get him anything to do with them. (4) ...., for example? They aren't too expensive.
> I've got to go now because it's my turn to take the dog for a walk! Say hello to your parents from me.
> Bye for now,
> Emma

E Which two paragraphs of Emma's letter do NOT refer to anything in the four notes given? What is their purpose?

F Look at the task below. For which two notes do you have to come up with your own ideas?

You have received a letter from your pen friend. Read an extract from the letter and the notes you have made. Then write a letter to your pen friend, using all your notes. Write your answer in 120–150 words.

How awful! Ask how it happened.

Yes, wallet stolen. Explain.

> You'll never guess what happened to me the other day. Someone stole my mobile phone! I'm really upset about it because it was a present from my parents. Has anything like that ever happened to you?
>
> By the way, I haven't forgotten that it's your birthday next week. Have you got any plans for it? What present would you like? Try to think of something that isn't too heavy so I can send it easily!

Cinema with friends.

Make a suggestion for a present.

G Respond to each of the notes in full sentences that you could include in your letter.

1 How awful! Ask how it happened. ....
....

2 Yes, wallet stolen. Explain. ....
....

3 Cinema with friends. ....
....

4 Make a suggestion for a present. ....
....

3-minute plan!

H Number these things you should do in your letter in the correct order.

Describe birthday plans. ....
Give a reason for finishing letter. ....
Describe how your wallet was stolen. ....
Suggest a birthday present for him/her to send. ....
Ask about your pen friend's family. ....
Say goodbye. ....
Ask how his/her phone was stolen. ....
Thank your pen friend for his/her letter. ....

I Now complete the paragraph plan below.

Beginning: .... , ...
Main Paragraph 1: .... , ...
Main Paragraph 2: .... , ...
Ending: .... , ...

J Now write your letter in 120–150 words using the correct layout, your notes and some of the Language chunks below.

Language chunks

Informal letters

Opening
How's it going?
Thanks for your letter.
It was great to hear from you!

Making suggestions
How about … ?
What about … ?
You could …
Why don't you … ?
One/Another idea is …

Closing
I've got to go now because …
Say hello to … for me.
Give my love to …
Bye for now!
Write soon!
Let me know how/what …

Review 2

A Read the text and choose the best answer, A, B, C or D.

Is university the only route?

The number of students who (1) .... of school each year is increasing. Equally, large numbers of undergraduates are (2) .... to complete a university education. Clearly, not having a school leaving (3) .... is worse than not attaining a degree. But do (4) .... really matter in this day and age?

The school (5) .... doesn't produce plumbers, computer programmers or great actors. Yet these are respectable jobs and their (6) .... potential is much greater than that of teachers or accountants.

Actor Patrick Stewart, better known as Professor Xavier in the *X-Men* films never completed (7) .... At the age of 15 he left to take up full-time acting, and later went on to join the Royal Shakespeare Company. Likewise, Richard Branson didn't need to (8) .... university to become one of the (9) .... people in the world. By age 17, Branson had already gone into business and went on to build an empire.

(10) .... success does help if you want to become a doctor or a lawyer. For these popular professions (11) .... good marks at school or university really will open doors. But not everybody is cut out to follow years of intensive study. The potential of these people lies in different areas. Who cares? These days, with a little ambition and a lot of (12) .... , you can do anything.

1	**A** drop off **B** get out	**C** drop out **D** work out	7	**A** primary school **B** nursery school	**C** university **D** secondary school
2	**A** denying **B** failing	**C** disagreeing **D** stopping	8	**A** get into **B** go into	**C** enter into **D** go
3	**A** degree **B** register	**C** paper **D** certificate	9	**A** wealthy **B** richer	**C** richest **D** rich
4	**A** qualifications **B** skills	**C** assessments **D** scholarships	10	**A** Bachelor's **B** Degree	**C** Academic **D** Master's
5	**A** report **B** exam	**C** timetable **D** curriculum	11	**A** taking **B** winning	**C** getting **D** making
6	**A** money **B** financial	**C** optional **D** cash	12	**A** determination **B** happiness	**C** willingness **D** improvement

B Complete the text with ONE word that best fits each gap. Write your answers in CAPITAL LETTERS.

Crime on TV

Crime makes good entertainment. Producers can't do away (1) .... crime, because TV wouldn't be (2) .... good as it is. From *CSI* to James Bond, viewers switch (3) .... to watch programmes or movies that are based on criminal activity.

BBC producers, however, are taking advantage of this interest to actually fight crime with a programme called *Crimewatch*. So far, *Crimewatch* has shown no less (4) .... 4,000 real crimes, and the cases all come from police files. The programme reconstructs crime scenes using real actors or shows real film footage. Police hope (5) .... make people remember and give evidence. If, just (6) .... chance, a witness comes forward with important information, then the programme has been a success.

Crimewatch will not actually (7) .... crimes happening, but by the end of each episode, viewer calls will (8) .... helped towards solving difficult cases. In some ways, watching *Crimewatch* is (9) .... frightening than watching a thriller. You are in no doubt (10) .... the reality of what you see. Most frightening (11) .... all, however, is the fact that some of these criminals have already got (12) .... with the crime and they are still somewhere out there.

C Complete the text with the correct form of the words in capitals. Write your answers in CAPITAL LETTERS.

School – stressful but survivable

People say that the time you spend at school will constitute the (1) .... years of your life. That may well be true, but it doesn't change the harsh (2) .... that school is actually very (3) .... Throughout secondary school, students are under constant (4) .... They have to keep up with lessons in no less than eight subjects, ranging from chemistry to computer studies. Reading must be done and homework has to be handed in on time. Then, at the end of the school year, totally exhausted, students are expected to show a high level of (5) .... in exams. For many capable students who suffer from 'exam nerves', even endless hours of (6) .... are not sufficient to improve their (7) .... Yet, getting an (8) .... is only one part of life at school. Socializing is just as important, and levels of (9) .... can be the source of unnecessary heartache.
However, (10) .... at school is compulsory. Just remember, most people have experienced it and survived it.

GOOD
REAL
STRESS
PRESS

ACHIEVE
REVISE
PERFORM
EDUCATE
POPULAR

ATTEND

D Rewrite the sentences using the words in capitals. Use between two and five words, including the word given. Write only the missing words in CAPITAL LETTERS.

1 Is it difficult to install this software?
IF
Do you know .... install this software?

2 There wasn't a better person than Jim to give the bride away.
BEST
Jim was .... give the bride away.

3 A GPS is more accurate than a map.
AS
A map .... a GPS.

4 Do you agree that the crime rate will have dropped by the year 2020?
IT
The crime rate will have dropped by the year 2020, ... ?

5 We didn't think the satellite dish would cost so much.
THAN
The satellite dish .... we thought.

6 Joe said I could use his computer.
ME
Joe .... his computer.

7 The police officer wants to investigate the case.
INTERESTED
The police officer .... the case.

8 Would you like us to get you a drink?
SHALL
.... a drink?

5 Movement

A Match the vehicles to the pictures. Have you ever ridden or driven any of them?

1 a mountain bike
2 a car
3 a moped
4 a minibike
5 a scooter
6 a skateboard

Reading 1

B2 Exam Practice

You will be given a text that has had some sentences taken out of it. You have to decide where the missing sentences go.

Steps to success

- Look carefully for time references. Dates or years in the text will help you fill in the gaps. Other references, such as *this/that, now/then, before that, after that, years later,* etc, as well as verb tenses, will also help.
- Linking words help you decide if a sentence continues the previous idea (*and, so, also,* etc), or introduces a different idea (*although, but, however,* etc).

B Circle the correct word or phrase in bold.

1 In the 1970s, roller skates were really popular with children. **But / And** by 1980, the fashion for roller skating had almost disappeared.
2 When I had saved up enough money, I bought a minibike. **After I'd / Now that I've** had it for a week (and crashed it three times) I decided to sell it.
3 Nowadays, we have a lot of choice. **So / However**, back then things were very different.
4 I had a scooter when I was young and I went everywhere on it. **Before that / Then** I think I just grew too big for it.
5 Nowadays, kids can get around on all kinds of powered vehicles. **This is / That was** a big change from the 1950s, when we would have been lucky to have a bicycle!

C Read the article about young people and transport. Seven sentences have been removed from the article. Choose from the sentences (A–H) the one which fits each gap (1–7). There is one extra sentence which you do not need to use.

I get around

What transport options are available for young people? Seventeen-year-old Bruce Dearden tells us that walking is not one of them!

If there's one thing that **characterizes** the younger generation, it's that we want things fast; fast download times on our computers, quick copying facilities for CDs, fast-action games and up-tempo music. We're also in a hurry to get to places and, although walking is very useful, it's not exactly a lot of fun, is it?

Most of us can't wait until we get a car. Having your own car (**as opposed to** borrowing your mum's or dad's) is fantastic. (1) .... Nothing beats that feeling and, even if your car is ten years old and second-hand, it's still *yours*! But you need to pass your test and cars are expensive – both to buy and to run. (2) .... Until then, anything is better than walking, and we should count ourselves lucky that we have such a great choice. For many, their first set of wheels is a skateboard. Now, you're either a skateboard fan or you're not. Some people think that they're just a kids' toy. (3) .... They do jumps and tricks on them, enter competitions and, yes, they consider them to be a means of transport. Whether you like them or not, using a skateboard is a lot quicker than walking everywhere.

Then there's the scooter. The basic model is a simple affair, with two wheels, handlebars and a flat plate to stand

A If you really can't wait until then, you can ride a moped at 16.
B That's the ultimate goal – to be independent, comfortable and safe.
C And it's obvious to any rider that three wheels are safer than two.
D But in all other ways, they're just like the real thing.
E So most people have to wait until they finish studying and start earning before they can get one.
F It has the distinct advantage that pedal power keeps you fit.
G However, they're great fun for going short distances!
H Others, however, take them everywhere they go.

on. They're **compact**, stylish and designed to **appeal** to teenagers. There's no engine – all you do is put one foot on it, push yourself along with the other foot and you're off. You wouldn't want to go for a long journey on one. **(4)** .... If you want even more excitement, you can get electric or petrol-driven models (often called go-peds), which can reach some pretty terrifying speeds.

Motorbikes have, of course, always been popular with teenagers. But you need to be 17 to apply for a **licence**. **(5)** .... A moped engine has to be smaller than 50 cubic centimetres, and they can't go faster than 50 kilometres per hour. To ride any kind of motorbike, including mopeds and motor scooters, you still need to have a licence and pass a test.

A few years ago, they brought out the minibike. This is a smaller version of the modern motorbike. They're so small that some of them only come up to your knees! **(6)** .... And that's just the problem. Minibikes are sold as toys but they have very powerful engines – so powerful, in fact, that they're really dangerous. Some people think they're a lot of fun, but they're not really a **practical** transport option.

Of course, the bicycle, in one form or another, has always been popular. **(7)** .... And they're now much lighter and much more stylish than they used to be. Maybe they're not quite as cool as a sports car, and they certainly aren't as fast! But on the other hand, they're environmentally friendly and very cheap to run.

Work it out!

D Match the words in bold from the text with their meanings.
1 official paper ....
2 taking up little space ....
3 describes ....
4 realistic; useful ....
5 to be liked ....
6 rather than ....

E Match the pictures (a–e) with the sentences (1–5).

1 This car's very cheap to run. ....
2 She's lucky she wasn't badly injured. ....
3 He gets around by pedal power. ....
4 It's just like the real thing. ....
5 All you do is press the button and you're off! ....

Quick chat

How do you normally get around? Do any of the vehicles in the text sound like a good idea?

Grammar 1

✓ Check modal verbs (1)

See pages 142 and 143 for information about modal verbs.

Look at the modal verbs in these sentences. Which express(es)

ability? .... advice? ....
permission? .... obligation? ....

1 I **must** go to school today, but I really don't want to.
2 My little sister **can't** ride a bicycle.
3 My mum says I **can** stay at your house tonight.
4 You **should** be more careful on the road.
5 I **have to** help my mum with the housework.
6 You **needn't** take the bus. I can drive you home.
7 Eric **wasn't able to** fix his car, so he took it to a mechanic.
8 I'**m not allowed to** stay out late.
9 You **ought to** take up a hobby.
10 Will your parents **let** you ride a motorbike?

A Complete the sentences with a word or short phrase. Sometimes there is more than one correct answer. You may have to use negatives.

1 I haven't got a bike so I .... walk to school every day.
2 You .... ride a motorbike unless you're 17.
3 You .... be very careful when you're on the roads.
4 The children .... play on the tractor. It's very dangerous.
5 No, you .... borrow my scooter – you damaged it last time.
6 You don't .... spend a lot of money to buy a second-hand car.
7 I was .... get to school in less than five minutes on my skateboard.
8 I .... go to bed. I'm really tired.

B Complete the text with the words and phrases in the box.

had to • couldn't • could • need • must • be able to
allowed • shouldn't

My driving test

At last, the day had arrived when I was going to take my test. 'After this, I'll (1) .... drive a car – I'll be independent,' I thought.

But in the test, everything went wrong. I felt terrible because I was nervous and I (2) .... control the car. I kept thinking to myself, 'I (3) .... listen to what the examiner says.' But each time he said something, I got confused. When he told me to turn right, I turned left. At one point, I (4) .... stop the car because I was shaking so much. Luckily, I was (5) .... to wait a few minutes until I felt ready to carry on.

Then, I don't know why, but when the examiner told me to slow down I went faster instead. I (6) .... see the bus in front of me, but I was going too fast to stop and I crashed into it. I don't (7) .... to tell you that I failed the test.

My driving test taught me one thing – that I'm not a good driver! I (8) .... take my driving test again because I don't think I'll ever learn. Perhaps I'll get a motorbike. Now *that* sounds like fun!

C Make notes in the spaces below. Then, discuss your answers with a partner.

Write down something that you:
1 shouldn't do ....
2 don't have to do ....
3 had to do yesterday ....
4 must do soon ....
5 ought to do more often ....
6 couldn't do when you were younger ....
7 don't need to do ....
8 aren't allowed to do ....

Vocabulary 1
Means of transport

A Which forms of transport do the following words belong to?

1 .... : platform, ticket, carriage
2 .... : check-in, take off, flight
3 .... : petrol, steering, engine
4 .... : handlebars, pedals, gear
5 .... : cabin, deck, cruise

B Fill in the gaps with words from Exercise A.

1 Just jump on, push the .... and enjoy the best cycling experience available!

2 The train now arriving is the Manchester Express. Would passengers on the .... please stand clear of the tracks. Passengers travelling to Birmingham, please go in the last .... only.

3 Welcome on board the ship. Our .... begins at 12 o'clock, when we set sail for Venice. We would like to ask you to remain in your .... until the staff have checked your tickets.

4 Ladies and gentlemen, as the plane is about to .... , could you please return to your seats and fasten your seat belts. We hope you enjoy your ....

5 With power .... and a very reliable 1500cc .... , this is one car that you'll love to drive!

Easily confused words

C Complete the sentences with the words in the box.

excursion • drive • journey • travel • trip • voyage

1 The .... to Australia took five weeks.
2 Shall we go on a day .... to the seaside?
3 We took Grandma for a(n) .... in the country yesterday.
4 Foreign .... is the best way to learn about other countries and cultures.
5 Our train .... from London to Paris was long and tiring.
6 The students went on a(n) .... to the Transport Museum.

Word partners

D Which verbs do we use with these means of transport? There is more than one answer for each verb.

1 board a ....
2 catch a ....
3 drive a ....
4 ride a ....
5 miss a ....
6 take a ....
7 get in/out of a ....
8 get on/off a ....

Phrases with prepositions

E Circle the correct word or phrase.

1 I've never been **on** / **for** a long journey. I'd love to do that – just to get **in** / **on** a train without caring where it goes!

2 It's only five minutes' walk, so we really should go **with the feet** / **on foot** but we usually go **by** / **with** car.

3 Apparently, Hannah had an argument with her boyfriend and made him get **out of** / **off** the car in the middle of nowhere! She just drove **out** / **off** and left him there!

4 I was reading **in** / **on** the bus and I got off **at** / **to** the wrong stop!

5 We have to arrive **at** / **to** the port by nine o'clock and we can go **in** / **on** board the ship at ten o'clock.

Listening

B2 Exam Practice
Steps to success
- Learn to rephrase things. The correct answer is never written in the same way as it is spoken; it is rephrased.
- If you listen carefully, you can often exclude one or both of the wrong answer options.

A Look at this question and the answer options. What sort of things do you expect the speaker to mention?

You hear a man talking. Why has he sold his car?
A He got a job nearer to his house.
B It took him too long to get to work.
C He wanted to help the environment.

B Listen and choose the right answer from Exercise A. Did he mention any of the things you expected? How did you exclude the wrong answers?

C Look at these phrases from the recording. Which answer option (A, B or C) do they refer to in Exercise A?
1 ... often late ....
2 ... not very far ....
3 ... the pollution problem ....
4 ... the time it took ....
5 ... finding a place to park ....

D You will hear people talking in eight different situations. Before you listen, look at the questions and answer options below. Try to predict some of the phrases you might hear. Then listen and choose the correct answers.

1 You hear a man talking to his daughter. Why is he talking to her?
A to punish her for something she has done
B to explain why he won't let her do something
C to apologize for something he has done

2 You hear an announcement on an aeroplane. Why is the announcement being made?
A because there is an emergency
B because there will be a delay
C because they are preparing to leave

3 You hear a man talking on the radio. What has he done?
A built a new car engine
B bought his first car
C had an accident in his car

4 You hear a travel agent talking about tourists on holiday. What does he say about guided tours?
A They won't answer your questions.
B They are very expensive.
C They help you enjoy your holiday.

5 You hear someone talking on the radio. How did she feel while she was on holiday?
A relaxed
B nervous
C thoughtful

6 You hear part of a lecture about transport. Which problem does the lecturer say is the most serious?
A poor public transport
B lack of parking places
C traffic jams

7 You hear a teenager talking about a problem she has. What is her problem?
A She can't afford to go on holiday this year.
B She doesn't want to go away with her parents.
C She hasn't seen her friends for two weeks.

8 You hear a driver being interviewed on the radio. What has his recent driving course taught him to do?
A teach other drivers to drive better
B be a safer driver
C learn from his mistakes

Speaking

B2 Exam Practice Complete Test

A Follow the instructions below.
   Student A: Look at page 136.
   Student B: Look at page 137.

B Follow the instructions below.

Student A:
Your photographs show different types of holidays. Compare the photographs and say how you think people will spend their time on holiday in these places.

How do you think people will spend their time on holiday in these places?

Student B:
What kind of holiday do you prefer?

Student B:
Your photographs show people travelling in different ways. Compare the photographs and say why you think the people chose to travel in this way.

Why do you think the people chose to travel in this way?

Student A:
Which means of transport do you use the most?

C Look at the situation and the pictures below.

A holiday company wants to provide more activities for young people. Here are some of the things that they are thinking about including in their holidays.

First, talk to each other about how popular these suggestions would be. Then decide which two would attract the most teenagers.

How popular would these suggestions be? Which two would attract the most teenagers?

D Take turns answering these questions, which are based on Exercise C. You should also comment on your partner's answers.

What complaints do young people have about family holidays?

Do you think teenagers should go on holiday with their parents or with other young people?

What problems might there be with holidays just for young people?

How do you think holidays might change in the future?

At what age do you think people should be allowed to go on holiday without an older relative?

If you went on an activity holiday with people your own age, would it matter where you went?

5

A Have you ever been camping or hiking? Did you enjoy it?

What equipment would you need to do these activities? Make a list. After you have read the text, see how many of your words were included.

....
....
....

Reading 2

B Match the words with their explanations.

1 cycling   a tent
2 strenuous   b insect
3 experienced   c not a beginner
4 teepee   d physically demanding
5 itinerary   e important
6 mosquito   f biking
7 major   g programme

B2 Exam Practice
Steps to success
- When scanning for words and phrases remember that the advertisement might use expressions that are different from those used in the question.

C Look at the advertisements for six different vacations. Use the information in the advertisements to answer the questions.

1 Your friend does not want to have to get up early while on vacation or do anything too strenuous. Which holiday is she most likely to prefer?
 a 1   b 3   c 5   d 6

2 You want your group to be able to change the programme during the trip if you all agree. Which vacation might make this possible?
 a 1   b 4   c 5   d 6

3 You and your friend do not want to go camping again this year. Which vacation does not involve sleeping in a tent?
 a 2   b 4   c 5   d 6

4 Your family has two children aged five and six. Which vacation is suitable for your family?
 a 2   b 3   c 4   d 5

5 You have an allergy to mosquitoes. Which vacation should you definitely avoid?
 a 1   b 2   c 4   d 5

6 You have always wanted to see a whale. Which vacation might give you an opportunity to do so?
 a 2   b 3   c 4   d 6

7 You want to have some time to explore on your own while on vacation. Which vacation should you book?
 a 2   b 3   c 4   d 5

8 Your friend wants to go on an activity vacation that is suitable for complete beginners. Which vacation should she definitely NOT go on?
 a 1   b 2   c 4   d 5

9 Your friend wants to be able to spend some time in at least one of the major North American cities. Which two vacations will he have to choose from?
 a 1 and 6   b 2 and 6   c 3 and 6   d 4 and 5

10 Your friend will only come on an adventure vacation with you if she can go cycling at some point. Which two options will she have to choose from?
 a 1 and 3   b 1 and 4   c 3 and 5   d 4 and 6

11 You want to go on a vacation with an organization that helps local communities in some way. Which two vacations are worth considering?
 a 1 and 3   b 2 and 4   c 2 and 6   d 3 and 5

12 You only have nine days' leave this year. Which vacations won't be suitable?
 a 1, 2 and 4   b 1, 2 and 6   c 1, 5 and 6   d 2, 3 and 4

GRAND CANYON RAFTING

8 days

Six nights on the river
Final night: Enjoy the bright lights of the city in Las Vegas.
Price: $2,834
Group size: Maximum 14
Age range: 16+ (Passengers aged 16 & 17 must be accompanied by an adult.)
Difficulty: no rafting experience or swimming ability required

So stunning! A spectacular journey through the Grand Canyon in a motorized raft, camping along the way with short hikes to picturesque spots.

- **Be warned:** We need to be up at 7.00am for breakfast and in the raft by 9.00am.
- We supply all camping equipment (including sleeping bags) and waterproof river bags and these are included in the cost of your trip.
- We donate $500 per trek to the Navajo Nation Youth Programme.

❶

ALASKAN HIKE

A 16-day tour with five days of hiking through some of America's best hiking country.

Join a small group of adventurers to see one of the world's last great wilderness areas with glaciers, forests, lakes and rushing rivers.

Optional activities: Scenic flight around Mount McKinley (N America's highest mountain), whale watching cruise, mountain biking in Denali, ice climbing, rafting, canoeing (paid locally)
Accommodation: ten nights camping (sleeping bags not provided), five nights in comfortable hotels
Minimum age: 16 (Those 16 and 17 years old must be accompanied by an adult.)
Must bring: A good insect repellent, warm and waterproof clothing
Dates: Aug 23 – Sep 7

❹

Turtlewatch Expedition
to Costa Rica

Such an unforgettable experience!
Participate in monitoring and protecting the endangered leatherback turtles on a beautiful beach in Costa Rica, working alongside distinguished scientists. Spend your free time at the beach or the surrounding countryside.

Accommodation: In the Marine Biology Refuge on the beach in comfortable, air-conditioned shared rooms
Hours of work: 8.00am – 4.00pm
Dates: October – February
Duration: 10 Days
Contribution: $1,420

❷

Blazing Badlands

A demanding horseriding trek through wild country in the Bighorn Mountains staying in cowboy teepees (sleep 2).

Enjoy breathtaking views and see eagles, antelope and deer along the trails. Experience memorable evenings with the group around a campfire beneath the stars.

Suitable for experienced adult riders of intermediate or advanced ability.

Duration: 8 Days
Departures: 13th, 20th, 23rd, 30th May
Accommodation: traditional bunkhouses and teepees
Prices: from $2,095 pp
Group size: 12 max

❺

Wisdom Keepers' Tour
July 21 – Aug 2

- Stay on a native American reservation and learn about the wisdom and history of its residents.
- A relaxing vacation (no early morning departures or physically demanding activities!) full of fun for all family members, including the kids.
- Daily group excursions in comfortable vehicles.
- Good quality accommodation on the Cheyenne Ranch plus an opportunity to put up and sleep in your own teepee.
- The income from your vacation will help to support the native Americans living here on the reservation.

Cost: Adults – $3,590, Under 15s – $2,190
Cost includes breakfast and lunch boxes for some days.
You will need: Strong comfortable walking shoes and a warm top (temperatures can drop at night).

❸

Walking tour of the most important cities of America's north east in 7 days
Freedom Trail

- Begin with the historymakers' tour of the White House, Jefferson Monument and Capitol Hill.
- Enjoy the nightlife in the best clubs of New York.
- See the Niagara Falls on board 'Maid of the Mist'.
- Cycle the entire historic city of Boston with its many bike trails.
- Final day trip to the Empire State Building, New York
- Flexible itinerary – you and your fellow trekkers can suggest alterations to the tour.

Departure months: May – Oct
Accommodation: 5 nights camping, 1 night hotel ($45 pp paid locally)
Cost: $820
Group size: Maximum 13
Age range: 18+

❻

5

Grammar 2

✓ Check so and such, too and enough

See pages 143 and 144 for information about *so* and *such*, *too* and *enough*.

Circle the correct phrase.
1 Paris is **so nice place** / **such a nice place** / **so a nice place** that I go there every year.
2 I learnt to drive **so much quickly** / **such quickly** / **so quickly** that everyone was shocked, including me!
3 Debbie's **too young** / **young enough** / **enough young** to get a driving licence.
4 Michael hasn't got **money enough** / **too much money** / **enough money** to buy a bike.

A Complete the sentences with the words and phrases in the box.

> much • so • such • many • too • enough

1 There was .... a lot of rain that we couldn't see the road.
2 Dad's car is .... slow that it's quicker to walk!
3 I think I've finally saved up .... money to go on holiday!
4 Penelope has been to so .... places that she can't remember them all.
5 We stayed in our hotel because it was .... cold for us to walk anywhere.
6 I would like to go to the USA, but it costs too .... money.

B Complete these sentences with ideas of your own.

1 My country is such ....
  ....
2 Last summer, it was so ....
  ....
3 If I save up enough money next year, I'll ....
  ....
4 Some holiday resorts are too ....
  ....

B2 Exam Practice

Steps to success
- When transforming sentences, look carefully at the phrase before the gap — you may need to use the infinitive form.
- Remember that the second sentence might be negative. Make all the necessary changes.

C Complete the second sentence so that it has a similar meaning to the first sentence, using the word given. Do not change the word given. You must use between two and five words including the word given.

1 Would it be alright if I came in your car with you?
  come
  .... in your car with you?
2 Don is such a fast driver that I won't go in the car with him.
  so
  Don .... that I won't go in the car with him.
3 I wish I could play the piano.
  able
  It must be nice .... play the piano.
4 Is it necessary for me to have a licence for this scooter?
  have
  Do .... a licence for this scooter?
5 I think we should leave now, don't you?
  ought
  Don't you think .... now?
6 There was no telephone in the room because the hotel was so old.
  such
  It was .... that there was no telephone in the room.
7 Ronnie's only 15 and you need to be 16 to get a moped.
  old
  Ronnie .... to get a moped.
8 Motorbikes are very fast and I don't like riding on them.
  for
  I don't like riding on motorbikes – they're .... me.

Vocabulary 2
Travel

A Complete the text with the words in the box.

> fares • guide • hire • hitch-hiking • holidaymakers
> package • resorts • service • sites

The basics
This is a very popular destination and most (1) .... go straight to one of the coastal (2) .... , many of which are close to airports. By far the most popular kind of holiday is the (3) .... holiday, and several major tour companies operate in the country.

Archaeology
There are hundreds of archaeological (4) .... in the country and admission to many of them is free. At the larger ones, we recommend that you join one of the many tours, where your (5) .... will be able to give you historical information in your own language.

Getting around
There is an excellent bus and train (6) .... which covers most of the country. Visitors from some countries might find that the (7) .... are quite expensive, however. It may be more economical to (8) .... a car – something which you can do easily in any town. A word of warning: we do not recommend (9) .... because very few drivers are willing to stop, and on many roads it is illegal for them to do so.

Key phrasal verbs

B Match the highlighted words and phrases with the phrasal verbs that can replace them.

> drop off • get back • make for
> pick up • see off • set off
> slow down • speed up • take off

1 Will you come to **say goodbye** at the airport when I leave?
2 You'll have to **go faster** if you want to get there before dark.
3 Please **go slower**. These roads aren't safe at night.
4 I'll phone you as soon as I **return** from Berlin.
5 The only time I get scared is when the plane **leaves the ground**.
6 We'll **start our journey** early to avoid the traffic jams.
7 Shall I **collect** you after work?
8 He said he was going to **go in the direction of** Venice.
9 Is it OK if I **let you out of the car** here?

B2 Exam Practice

C For questions 1–10, read the text below. Use the word given in capitals at the end of the lines to form a word that fits in the gap in the same line. Write your answers in CAPITAL LETTERS.

Let the train take the strain

To some people, for example commuters, the train is a part of their daily life. They might not think that the train is a very (1) .... way to travel – just a way of getting from A to B. But more and more (2) .... are discovering the joys of travelling by train. And when it comes to holidays, many (3) .... are beginning to see the advantages of this means of transport.
To start with, even if your train is (4) .... , regular (5) .... times mean that you will not have long to wait until the next one. Once you are on board, a truly (6) .... experience awaits you, as all you have to do is sit back and enjoy the (7) .... views from your window. On (8) .... at your destination, you are refreshed and ready to go (9) .... – or whatever else you have planned for your holiday. The many (10) .... rail holidays available now mean that there's one to suit everyone. Relax – you're on holiday!

ENJOY
TRAVEL

TOUR

DELAY
DEPART
RELAX

SCENE
ARRIVE
SIGHT
ORGANIZE

Writing: essay

B2 Exam Practice

You might be asked to write an essay giving your opinion about something. You might also be asked to make suggestions. You must write between 120 and 180 words.

Steps to success
- PLAN your answers.
- INTRODUCE and CONCLUDE your essay.
- Use clear PARAGRAPHS.
- Support your points with EXAMPLES and/or EXPLANATIONS.
- Stay on the TOPIC, and make sure it is RELEVANT.
- Use a variety of expressions to LINK or show CONTRAST.

A Do you agree with this statement?

In modern society cars do more harm than good.

B Look at the examples below and put some of your own ideas in the table.

The good that cars do	The harm that cars do
cars help people get from A to B	too many cars mean traffic jams

Did you find more *good* things about cars or more *bad* things? Would you write an essay agreeing or disagreeing with the statement?

C Read the model essay and mark the things below on it.

1. introductory sentence
2. writer's opinion (agree or disagree with the statement)
3. first reason writer thinks cars are bad
4. explanation of the first point
5. second reason writer thinks cars are bad
6. example to support the second point
7. third reason writer thinks cars are bad
8. explanation of the third point
9. conclusion

In modern society cars do more harm than good

Nowadays, most families have at least one car and, as the population grows, so does the number of cars on the road. I believe that these cars are doing a lot of harm.

First of all, cars are dangerous. They are responsible for a large number of accidents every year, mainly because drivers refuse to slow down when they are on the road. Another danger is the threat to our health as a result of the pollution that cars cause.

Secondly, cars actually increase the time it takes us to get to places. For example, we often get stuck in traffic jams due to the number of cars on the road. This problem is made worse by the lack of places to park.

Thirdly, cars create a lot of noise. People in big cities have difficulty sleeping because there is so much traffic noise. The problem is also spreading throughout the countryside. Soon there will be no peaceful places left.

In conclusion, I think that cars are disastrous for our society. We should severely punish dangerous drivers and try to reduce the number of cars on our roads.

D In the last paragraph of the model essay, the writer made some suggestions. What suggestions can you make to reduce the harm that cars do? Use the prompts below and your own ideas.

I think we should …	ban cars from some areas
We need to …	make drivers pay to use certain roads
If …	develop pollution-free cars
It would be a good idea to …	severely punish dangerous drivers
	build quieter cars
One suggestion is to …	improve public transport
	provide more parking places

E Do you agree with the statement? Why/Why not?

Following a class discussion on transport in your town or city, your teacher has asked you to write an essay giving your opinion on the following statement.

We should all use public transport.

Write your essay. You can make suggestions if you want to.

3-minute plan!

F Say whether you agree or disagree with the statement. Then try to think of two or three main points, as well as examples or explanations to support them. Finally, try to think of one or two suggestions of your own.

I **agree / disagree** with the statement.

1st point ....

example/explanation ....

2nd point ....

example/explanation ....

3rd point ....
example/explanation ....

suggestion(s) ....

G Now write your essay in 120–180 words using your plan above. Don't forget to write an introduction and a conclusion. Use the model essay and the Language chunks to help you.

Language chunks

Listing points
Firstly, …
Secondly, …
Thirdly, …
In addition, …
Also, …
Then, …
Another (reason / point / danger / etc) is …

Giving explanations
because …
due to …
as a result of …

Giving examples
for example, …
for instance, …
One example of this is …

Making suggestions
I think we should …
We need to …
If …
It would be a good idea to …
One suggestion is to …

6 Mother nature

A Look at the photos.
Which of these foods contains the most:
vitamins? fat?
calories? sugar?

B Write down everything you ate yesterday and compare your list with your partner's. Whose diet was healthier?

Reading 1

B2 Exam Practice
Steps to success
- Think about the writer's attitude(s) and purpose as you read a text (these might not be stated directly).
- Make sure you understand what words like *this*, *him*, *who*, *it*, etc refer back to.

C Quickly read the text opposite and, in your own words, describe the writer's attitude towards:

school dinners in the 1970s
British children's health
Jamie Oliver's school dinners

D Look at the highlighted words. What exactly do they refer to in the text?

1 whom (line 9)
2 it (line 16)
3 them (line 20)
4 them (line 30)
5 it (line 33)
6 it (line 40)
7 them (line 47)
8 they (line 49)
9 their (line 56)

E For questions 1–6 choose the answer (A, B, C or D) which you think fits best according to the text.

1 What do we learn about school dinners a few decades ago?
A They weren't very tasty.
B They were unhealthy.
C They were varied.
D They were enjoyable.

2 What does 'it' (line 9) refer to?
A The fact that children don't complain.
B The fact that ready-made food can be served.
C The fact that children aren't healthy.
D The fact that school dinners are tasty.

3 What, according to Jamie Oliver, did he want to do through his campaign?
A Improve young people's diets.
B Make eating places in schools more pleasant.
C Do research into children's eating habits.
D Encourage children to keep fit.

4 The kitchen staff at Kidbrooke Comprehensive School had to learn how to
A cook for lots of people.
B prepare ready-made food more quickly.
C work in a restaurant.
D peel and chop food.

5 What does 'boycotted' (line 48) mean?
A damaged
B tried to change
C stayed away from
D criticized

6 What effect did Jamie Oliver's campaign have?
A It made children appreciate the value of healthy food.
B It made the canteen at Kidbrooke School more popular than ever before.
C It stopped children eating junk food.
D It helped to change the rules about food in schools.

70

School dinners

For people who went to school in the UK in the 1970s, the words 'school dinners' bring back unpleasant memories. Day after day, our plates were filled with lumpy mashed potato, overcooked cabbage and meat that was as tough as old boots. Fast forward to the year 2000 when the menu changed. Schools began serving up the kind of food kids love – burgers, chips, pizza and more chips. Most of the food wasn't actually cooked, just taken out of packets and heated up. There were no complaints from the children, for **whom** a diet of junk food had become the norm. It suited the schools too, which didn't even need proper kitchens to prepare it.

It's hardly surprising, then, that top chef Jamie Oliver faced strong opposition when he tried to make changes to the school dinner menu. Horrified by the 'rubbish' children were being fed, Jamie started a campaign in 2005 to improve standards in school canteens across the country. Some called **it** a publicity stunt, but Jamie insists that he was motivated by the state of young people's health in the UK. Indeed, the statistics are worrying. In the last ten years, the number of school children who are overweight has almost doubled, and at least 80% of **them** eat more than the recommended amounts of fat and sugar per day.

The experiment started in Kidbrooke Comprehensive School in Greenwich, London and was the subject of a TV series watched by five million viewers in the UK. The cameras followed Jamie's struggle to convince the authorities, the kitchen staff, but, most of all, the pupils themselves that there was a better alternative to the kind of school dinners they were used to.

Jamie soon discovered the main reason why the quality of school dinners was so poor: not enough money was being spent on **them**. The government allocated only 37 pence – the cost of a packet of crisps – per meal. Jamie's challenge was to come up with a way of feeding school children healthily for the same amount of money. At first, he found **it** impossible, although he eventually managed to come up with a selection of delicious-sounding dishes within the extremely tight budget.

Jamie's next problem was that the 'dinner ladies' responsible for making the school meals didn't actually know how to cook, at least not for such large numbers. As part of their training, the kitchen staff at Kidbrooke were taken to Jamie's own restaurant in London to see how the professionals did **it**. Back at school, the peeling, chopping and cooking of fresh ingredients obviously took much longer than heating up the ready-made food had done. As a result, Jamie needed the staff to work longer hours, which cost more in wages – yet another problem.

The biggest hurdle for Jamie, however, was actually getting the pupils at Kidbrooke to eat the new, healthier dinners on offer. Far from appreciating **them**, many of the pupils protested about the changes to the dinner menu and boycotted the canteen! Addicted to their diet of 'chips with everything', **they** preferred to buy a greasy takeaway at lunchtime rather than sample Jamie's nutritionally well-balanced meals. For the first few days, most of the freshly cooked food was being thrown away because hardly anyone was eating it!

At this point Jamie was feeling very depressed, but luck was on his side. The weather suddenly got really bad and pupils didn't want to go outside in **their** lunch break, so they started coming back to the canteen. The battle still wasn't won, however. The children complained about the lack of chips on the menu and were reluctant to eat things containing vegetables. Slowly, however, the Kidbrooke pupils started to eat the food on offer and today a large number of them use the canteen regularly.

More importantly, the effects of Jamie's campaign have been felt across the whole country. Schools now have to comply with new government guidelines which state that the food they provide must contain certain nutrients, and junk food is no longer allowed. Of course, some children still miss the hamburgers, but then school dinners were never designed to be popular!

Work it out!

F Circle the correct meaning for these words from the text.

1 tough (1) — delicious / hard
2 the norm (1) — unpopular / usual
3 opposition (2) — disagreement / support
4 publicity stunt (2) — dangerous action / something to attract attention
5 convince (3) — excuse / persuade
6 budget (4) — amount of money allowed for something / area where cooking takes place
7 hurdle (6) — difficulty / success
8 reluctant (7) — not willing / enthusiastic

Quick chat
What sort of food is sold in your school canteen? Is it healthy?

Grammar 1

✓ Check passive voice

See page 144 for information about the passive voice.

Complete the sentences with the words and phrases in the box.

has been • had been • is • is being • was
was being • will be

1 Present simple	Oxygen .... produced by plants.
2 Present continuous	Our planet .... destroyed by the human race.
3 Present perfect simple	A new species of flower .... discovered.
4 Past simple	This diet .... created by an American doctor.
5 Past continuous	The dog barked while it .... examined by the vet.
6 Past perfect simple	The rabbit .... fed, so I just gave it some water.
7 Future simple	The beach .... cleaned up by volunteers tomorrow.

✓ Check articles

See pages 144 and 145 for information about articles.

Fill in the gaps with *a* or *the*, or leave blank. Can you explain the rules for using articles in these cases?

1 My mum is .... doctor.
2 .... doctor who examined me was very friendly.
3 I'd love .... slice of that chocolate cake!
4 Abbie never eats .... chocolate.
5 In Ancient Egypt, ... cat was considered to be a very special animal.
6 .... cats are highly intelligent.

A Rewrite the sentences correctly.

1 Cockroaches are hating by most people.
2 Those mushrooms mustn't be ate!
3 Will be animal experiments banned one day?
4 Have the strawberries be washed?

B Complete the paragraph with the correct passive form of the verbs in brackets.

A bear that escaped from a circus in Germany three days ago (1) .... (hunt) by police last night. The dancing bear, which (2) .... (call) Barney, (3) .... (see) by several people in the last 24 hours. The bear managed to escape when its cage (4) .... (leave) open by mistake. Local farmers are worried that their animals (5) .... (attack) by Barney if he gets hungry. People (6) .... (warn) not to approach the bear if they see it, but to contact the police immediately.

C Circle the correct word or phrase.

1 Scientists have discovered that the **dolphin** / **dolphins** might not be as intelligent as we think.
2 My uncle is **farmer** / **a farmer**.
3 Neil Armstrong was the first person to walk on **moon** / **the moon**.
4 The **rich** / **rich people** should do more to help those living in poverty.
5 I went to **hospital** / **the hospital** to visit Frank.
6 **River Nile** / **The River Nile** is in Egypt.
7 How often do you go to **gym** / **the gym**?
8 **A** / **The** sky has gone dark. It's going to rain.
9 Do you come from **Greece** / **the Greece**?
10 Switzerland is one of **the** / **a** most mountainous countries in Europe.

Vocabulary 1

Health and diet

A Write the food items in the box that are or can be ...

> beans • beef • biscuits • cabbage • cake • carrots
> cereal • cheese • chips • fish • ham • honey • ice cream
> lettuce • melon • nuts • olive oil • pasta • rice
> sausages • strawberries • yoghurt

1 eaten raw ....
2 fattening ....
3 nutritious ....
4 juicy ....
5 homemade ....
6 low-fat ....
7 greasy ....
8 delicious ....
9 sweet ....
10 savoury ....

Key phrasal verbs

B Replace the highlighted words with these phrasal verbs in the correct form.

> cut down on • get over • give up • go off
> put on • work out

1 This milk smells funny. It must have **gone bad**. ....
2 I'm trying to **eat less** chocolate. ....
3 All women **gain** weight when they're pregnant. ....
4 If you **stop** eating junk food, you'll feel much better. ....
5 It took Freddie weeks to **recover from** the virus. ....
6 Tina's really fit. She **exercises** at the gym every day. ....

Word partners

C Fill in the gaps with the words in the box. Can you think of any other nouns that can follow them?

> bread • cake • chocolate • crisps • grapes • jam
> tuna • water

1 a bunch of ....
2 a loaf of ....
3 a tin of ....
4 a bar of ....
5 a slice of ....
6 a packet of ....
7 a bottle of ....
8 a jar of ....

Cooking and eating

D Write *e* next to the verbs to do with eating and *c* next to those to do with cooking.

1 taste ...... 5 chew ...... 9 roast ......
2 grill ...... 6 fry ...... 10 bake ......
3 boil ...... 7 swallow ...... 11 lick ......
4 sip ...... 8 suck ...... 12 melt ......

E Complete the sentences with words from Exercise D in the correct form.

1 Don't .... gum in the classroom!
2 .... food isn't healthy because it's very greasy.
3 Try not to .... any bones when you eat fish.
4 Kathy .... her coffee slowly as she read her newspaper.
5 The ice cream started to .... because it was so hot.
6 I want to .... a cake, so I'll need some eggs.

Quick chat

What's the worst dish you've ever eaten? What's the weirdest food you've ever heard of?

Listening

B2 Exam Practice
Steps to success
- When listening, fill in what you can the first time, and check or add to your answers the second time.
- Remember — some answers might require more than one word.

A You are going to hear someone being interviewed about being a vegetarian. What reasons might someone give for becoming a vegetarian? How might being a vegetarian change your life? Write your ideas below.

B Look at the gapped sentences in Exercise C. In which sentence(s) is it clear that more than one word is missing?

C 🎧 Listen to the interview. For questions 1–10, complete the sentences below. You will need to write a word or short phrase in each gap.

1 Suzy became a vegetarian about .... ago.
2 Suzy sometimes .... for herself.
3 A vegan diet doesn't include milk, eggs or ....
4 Suzy says that meat doesn't contain more .... than vegetables.
5 Suzy's .... used to own a farm.
6 Suzy was upset when a(n) .... was killed.
7 Suzy's cousins thought it was .... to kill animals for food.
8 Suzy once saw a(n) .... which showed some negative things about meat production.
9 Lots of people are .... when Suzy tells them she's a vegetarian.
10 Suzy says that people's attitudes can be ....

D 🎧 Now listen again, concentrating on the gaps that you have not yet been able to fill. Listen for these phrases which will help you to locate the answers.

1 '… been a vegetarian for …'
2 '… had to start doing my own …'
3 '… a vegan is someone who doesn't eat …'
4 '… vegetables have just as many …'
5 '… a farm which belonged to …'
6 'I cried for days.'
7 'My cousins couldn't understand my reaction because …'
8 '… a couple of years ago I watched …'
9 'You'd be surprised how many people are …'
10 '… expect me to explain why I'm a vegetarian, which …'

Quick chat
Would you ever consider becoming a vegetarian? Why/Why not?
What other changes do people sometimes make to their diets? Why?

Speaking

B2 Exam Practice
Steps to success
- When you answer a question, offer a reason or an explanation for your answer.

A 🎧 Listen to an examiner and a candidate talking. Did the candidate give a good answer to the question?

B Look at these questions and short answers. Take it in turns with your partner to expand on the answers given.
1 'Do you like cooking?' 'No.'
2 'What's your favourite food?' 'Spaghetti.'
3 'What would you like to change about the place where you live?' 'Nothing.'
4 'Have you got a pet?' 'Yes.'
5 'What kind of animals make the best pets?' 'Dogs.'

B2 Exam Practice
Steps to success
- Look for similarities and differences between the two photographs you will be shown.

C Compare these photographs.
How many differences can you find between them? Find as many as you can in one minute.
eg *The puppy is playful,* **but/while/however** *the cat isn't.*

Are there any similarities between them?
eg **Both** *photos show people with their pets.*

D What effect are the animals having on the people? Use the words and phrases below and the Language chunks to help you.

> relaxed • happy • calm • excited

> cheers them up • is a good friend • keeps them fit stops them being lonely

E Look at the pictures below.
Student A: Compare photos 1 and 2 and say how you think the people are feeling.
Student B: Compare photos 3 and 4 and say how you think the people are feeling.

Language chunks

Describing people's feelings
She/He must be feeling …
She/He might be feeling …
She/He looks as if s/he …
I get the impression she/he …

F Look at the mistakes some candidates made in their speaking test. What did they mean to say? *Howlers!*
1 'I like having baths in the sea.'
2 'My best friend is very sympathetic.'
3 'I'd like to go in Italy.'
4 'I see TV or go out with my friends.'
5 'I have my birthday on January.'
6 'My best friend and I have the same age.'

6

A Which are the most famous areas of natural beauty in your country?

Reading 2

B Match the underlined words with their meanings.

1 a <u>log</u> cabin
2 a park <u>ranger</u>
3 a hot <u>spring</u>
4 a <u>bulletin board</u>
5 <u>peak season</u>
6 <u>surrounding</u> area
7 wolf <u>tracks</u>
8 a <u>remote</u> area
9 <u>therapeutic</u> value
10 extreme <u>caution</u>

a footprints
b a thick piece of wood
c a place to put announcements and notices
d busiest time
e land outside another area
f far away, difficult to access
g a place where water comes out of the ground
h guard
i taking no risks
j healing

B2 Exam Practice
Steps to success
- Underline key words and phrases in the questions and look for their synonyms or similar expressions in the text.
- Pay attention to words that have a negative meaning as they are very important in getting the answer correct.

C You are thinking of visiting Yellowstone National Park. Use the information in the brochure to answer the questions.

1 Your friend insists that you must not go anywhere dangerous. Which place will you not visit?
a Upper Geyser Basin   c Grand Prismatic
b Midway Geyser Basin   d Shoshone

2 How can you find out the title of the next campfire talk?
a by looking at a bulletin board
b by asking at the visitor centre
c by phoning the National Park Headquarters
d by reading the brochure

3 Which is said to be the most well-known geyser in the park?
a Old Faithful   c Steamboat
b Norris   d Madison

4 When did people first come to live in the Yellowstone area?
a 1903   b 1872   c 1918   d 11,000 years ago

5 How much will it cost a family of two adults and three young children to enter the park by car and stay for two nights in their family-sized tent?
a $25   b $40   c $55   d $90

6 You want to hear a talk about how geysers work, but it is raining. Where should you go?
a Mammoth   c Steamboat Geyser
b Norris Geyser Museum d Old Faithful Inn

7 You want to book a place on a campsite. Which will be the best place for this?
a Grant Village   c Norris Meadows
b Spring Creek   d Bay Bridge

8 Your young nephew is about to qualify as a junior ranger. What will he get?
a something to sew on his jacket
b a 12-page booklet
c free hiking
d free accommodation at the Old Faithful Inn

9 Where did the forest fires start in 1988?
a outside the park
b just inside the north entrance
c at a park picnic area
d at the Norris Campsite

10 Which feature of the park is named after an American president?
a a hotel   b a geyser   c an arch   d a museum

Yellowstone National Park

History

The 2.2 million acres occupied by the park have been inhabited for perhaps as long as 11,000 years. The traditional use of the land by native tribes ended in 1872 when the area was turned into the first national park in the world. It was protected by the US Army until 1918 when the National Park Service took over, establishing its headquarters at Mammoth.

One of the first attractions for visitors was the hot springs, particularly for their therapeutic value. In 1903, work began on the Old Faithful Inn, Yellowstone's first hotel. The seven-storey building, which was named after the most well-known geyser, is one of the few remaining log hotels in the USA. In the same year, the park was visited by President Roosevelt and a special arch was built at the park's north entrance in his honour.

Hydrothermal features

The park's 10,000 hydrothermal features include over 300 geysers (almost 70% of the world's total), which spray hot water hundreds of feet into the air. There is easy access to half of these at the Upper Geyser Basin. Further away is the Midway Geyser Basin with the largest hot spring, the Grand Prismatic. The most remote hydrothermal area is Shoshone, which is reached by a 17-mile round-trip hike. There are no boardwalks in this area, so visitors need to be extremely careful.

Picnicking and camping

There are 49 picnic areas in the park. Note that cooking over an open fire is only allowed where there is a park barbecue: Bridge Bay, Snake River, Spring Creek, Cascade Lake Trail, Grant Village, Nez Perce, Norris Meadows, Yellowstone River and East Lot.

Camping is only permitted at the park's 12 campsites. Although all sites have toilets only the one at Fishing Bridge has water and an electrical hookup.

Fee: $15 per tent per night.

Campsites may fill quickly in the peak season (July and August) so arrive before 11.00am. Reservations are possible only at Bridge Bay, Grant Village, Fishing Bridge and Madison.

Junior ranger programme

Open to children aged 5 to 12, the aim of this programme is to get children interested in preserving the natural wonders of Yellowstone. Children need to perform the tasks described in a 12-page activity paper which can be purchased for $3 at any visitor centre. Tasks include hiking on a park trail, writing about geothermal geology, park wildlife and fire ecology. Successful junior rangers will receive a patch featuring the wolf track logo of the National Park Service.

Norris campfire programme
Starting June 8

Get together round the campfire for an old-fashioned night out under the stars. The whole family can participate and hear stories told by a park ranger.

Programme titles and descriptions are posted on local bulletin boards. Meet at the Norris Campsite Campfire Circle.

Geysers made simple
Starting August 3

Come along to the Steamboat Geyser (the world's tallest) to hear how geysers work. To get there, follow the signs from the Norris Geyser parking lot. It's only a 15-minute walk. If the weather is poor, the Norris Geyser Museum hosts the 20-minute talk.

Yellowstone's no-smoking policy

In 1988, 36% of the park (793,880 acres) was damaged by fires that burnt into the park from the surrounding public lands. As a result of the largest fire, the North Fork Fire, more than 410,000 acres were burnt. The fire started when someone carelessly threw down a lighted cigarette, which is why we now operate a no-smoking policy at Yellowstone.

Entrance fees

The cost of a 7-day entrance permit covering both the Yellowstone and Grand Teton National Parks is as follows:

Private, non-commercial vehicle .... – $25
Snowmobile or motorcycle .... – $20
Visitor arriving on foot .... – $12

Entrance is free for people aged 15 or under and for US citizens who are disabled or blind.

---

11 According to the brochure, what is true about Yellowstone?
a It was the first national park.
b It is the only park in the world that has geysers.
c It is the largest park in the world.
d It is owned by the army.

12 What attracted the first visitors to Yellowstone Park?
a the springs with healing powers
b the Mammoth headquarters
c the native tribes
d the breathtaking scenery

Quick chat

Should areas of natural beauty be preserved? Why?/Why not?

Grammar 2

✓ **Check** countable and uncountable nouns

See page 145 for information about countable and uncountable nouns.

Underline the uncountable nouns in three of these sentences. What is the difference between countable and uncountable nouns?

1 Do you want any chips with your hamburger?
2 I need some coffee to help me wake up.
3 The doctor's advice was simple: that I should exercise more often.
4 These apples are delicious!
5 How is this equipment going to fit in my rucksack?

A Complete the sentences with the nouns in the box. Use the plural form where necessary.

> cake • coffee • fruit • glass • hair • information
> jean • room

1 How many .... has your house got?
2 Oh, no. We've run out of .... Would you like tea instead?
3 Mum always wears her old .... when she's gardening.
4 Jenny eats a lot of .... , which is probably why she's so healthy.
5 These .... are delicious. Did you make them yourself?
6 You can find .... about the wildlife park on the internet.
7 Look at this! There are dog .... all over my sofa!
8 I need to get my .... fixed because I can't see without them.

B Complete the second sentence so that it means the same as the first.

1 Can you advise me about training my puppy?
Can you give me .... about training my puppy?
2 Amanda has got very long hair.
Amanda's .... very long.
3 I never watch the news because it's depressing.
The news .... so I never watch it.
4 Nobody has informed me about the gym.
I haven't got .... about the gym.
5 Jack is working hard at the moment.
Jack has got a .... at the moment.
6 There is no food left in the house.
There isn't .... left in the house.

B2 Exam Practice

Steps to success

- After writing an answer, read the sentence again to make sure it fits.
- Don't leave any blanks — you won't lose marks for wrong answers.

C For questions 1–12, read the text below and think of the word which best fits each gap. Use only one word in each gap.

The news (**1**) .... been full of stories recently about vicious dogs attacking babies and children. Some dogs can be aggressive, it's true, but many more deserve to (**2**) .... called 'man's best friend'. Take the recent case of the stray dog that saved (**3**) .... baby in Sheffield. Police believe that (**4**) .... dog found the newborn baby in a wood, where it had (**5**) .... abandoned. The dog then carried the baby to (**6**) .... empty house, where it was sheltering its puppies. A passerby heard cries coming from the house and found the baby girl lying next to the puppies. The baby, who has been (**7**) .... Stella, was taken (**8**) .... hospital, where she is in good health. The mother of the baby is (**9**) .... asked (**10**) .... the police to come forward. In the meantime, a(n) (**11**) .... of people have shown interest in the dog and her puppies, so hopefully a good home (**12**) .... be found for them.

Vocabulary 2
The natural world

A With which seasons do you associate these things? Use some of the words and phrases to complete the sentences.

> blizzard • damp • flood • fog • forest fire • harvest
> heatwave • ice • shower • storm • sunburn

1 There was so much .... on the motorway that we could hardly see where we were going.
2 I don't think the rain will last long – it's just a(n) ....
3 The mountain climbers were stuck in the snow due to the ....
4 High winds made it even more difficult to put out the ....
5 During the .... , people were advised to keep cool and drink lots of water.

B2 Exam Practice
Steps to success
- Look carefully at the words that come before and after the gap to help you find the answer.
- Eliminate answers which you are certain are wrong. You will then have fewer options to choose between.

Prepositions

B Complete the table with the prepositions in the box.

> about • at • between • by • for • from • in • of • to • with

Before nouns	After adjectives	After verbs
.... sale	cruel	pay ....
.... mistake	excited	care .... , ...
.... demand	popular	benefit ....
.... risk	afraid	criticize ....
.... need	similar	choose .... , ...
.... fault	different	refer ....

C Complete the text with phrases from Exercise B.

Most people don't get excited (1) .... beetles, but the Japanese love them! In fact, some people pay thousands of dollars (2) .... them! Beetles are (3) .... with both children and adults. They are for (4) .... in big department stores as well as in specialized beetle shops. However, animal rights groups have criticized authorities (5) .... allowing beetles to be sold in vending machines. They say it's cruel (6) .... the beetles, which are living creatures, not objects.

D For questions 1–8, read the text below and decide which answer (A, B, C or D) best fits each gap.

Restaurants are getting stranger and stranger. I'm (1) .... to restaurants that have turned eating out into a whole new experience.
Why not (2) .... out London restaurant Dans Le Noir (In the Dark). Here you pay (3) .... the pleasure of enjoying your meal in the dark! Choose the surprise menu and you'll have to guess what you're eating just by (4) .... it! Tables are always in (5) ....
Then there's Mim in Barcelona where the waiters don't talk – they communicate through mime! You might order something you don't want by (6) .... , but it will definitely be an unforgettable experience!
In Berlin there's a restaurant where all the dishes are made from potatoes! (7) .... potatoes, known as chips, are everyone's favourite junk food, but potatoes can be cooked in a number of different ways – even made into pancakes.
Finally, there's a trendy restaurant in Taiwan called Toilet Bowl. The seats are in the shape of toilets and so are the food bowls! No one seems to (8) .... about that, though – it's full every night! Bon appetit!

1	**A** talking	**B** referring	**C** mentioning	**D** saying
2	**A** go	**B** get	**C** try	**D** work
3	**A** about	**B** for	**C** to	**D** from
4	**A** tasting	**B** sipping	**C** sucking	**D** licking
5	**A** question	**B** demand	**C** need	**D** desire
6	**A** fault	**B** regret	**C** failure	**D** mistake
7	**A** Baked	**B** Melted	**C** Boiled	**D** Fried
8	**A** criticize	**B** disagree	**C** care	**D** fear

6

Writing: report

B2 Exam Practice
You might be asked to write a report. You must write between 120 and 180 words.

Steps to success
- Write **To:** .... , **From:** .... and **Subject:** .... at the top of your report.
- MAKE UP names if necessary.
- Divide your report into short PARAGRAPHS.
- Give each paragraph a HEADING.
- Use FORMAL language.

A Look at this task and tick what you have to do in your report.

A group of British students have just arrived in your town and their leader has asked for information about a suitable restaurant to go to during their stay. Write a report for the group leader giving useful information about the restaurant you recommend and giving reasons for your recommendation.

1 Suggest several restaurants for the students to choose from.
2 Choose one restaurant in your town and describe it.
3 Address your report to the students.
4 Say why you think your choice is suitable.

B Read the report. Which of the pictures below shows Thursday's Restaurant?

To: Jenny Myers
From: Alex Kingston
Subject: Thursday's Restaurant

....
This report is about Thursday's Restaurant, which I would like to recommend to you and your group.

....
Thursday's has a varied menu including both vegetarian and meat dishes. The portions are large and the quality is excellent. I particularly recommend the apple pie and ice cream for dessert!

....
The staff at Thursday's are both friendly and efficient. Generally speaking, you are served quickly unless the restaurant is very busy.

....
Prices are reasonable and students are given a discount of 10% on weekdays. A meal for one person including a starter, main course and dessert costs about 15 euros.

....
Thursday's is open every evening from 7pm till midnight and at lunchtime on Sundays from 12.30 to 3pm. Tables should be booked in advance, especially at weekends.

....
To sum up, I strongly recommend Thursday's Restaurant. It's a great place to eat cheaply and the friendly atmosphere makes it ideal for young people.

C Match the headings below with the paragraphs of the report.

Cost   Service
Food   Introduction
Conclusion   Opening Times

D What style is the report written in?

H Choose four headings from Exercise E for the main part of your report and complete the plan below.

3-minute plan!

To: .... (name of manager of tourist office)
From: .... (your name)
Subject: .... (name of café)

Introduction
state purpose of report: ....

Heading 1: ....
notes: ....

Heading 2: ....
notes: ....

Heading 3: ....
notes: ....

Heading 4: ....
notes: ....

Conclusion
sum up reasons for recommendation:
....

E Which of the things below are important to young people when they go to a café? Can you think of anything else that is important?

- prices
- music
- service
- decoration
- menu

F Complete the sentences with the words in the box, then match them with the categories in Exercise E.

both • especially • including • till • unless

1 There is a live band from 10pm .... midnight every Saturday.
2 Everything is black, ... the walls!
3 The café serves .... drinks and snacks.
4 Everything is very good value, ... the coffee.
5 The waiters are very fast, ... you go on Saturday night when it's very busy.

G Look at this task. Underline the key words.

Your local tourist office has asked you to write a report about a café that is popular with young people. Write a report describing your favourite café and saying why it is suitable for young people.

I Now write your report in 120–180 words using the model, your plan and some of the Language chunks to help you.

Language chunks

Explaining purpose
The purpose/aim of this report is to …
This report is about …

Making recommendations
I would recommend … because …
I would particularly recommend …
… is suitable for … because …

Speaking in general
On the whole, …
Generally speaking, …

Concluding
To sum up, …
In conclusion, …

Review 3

A Read the text and choose the best answer, A, B, C or D.

Travel – I think I'll stay at home!

(1) .... is not nearly as romantic as it used to be. In the 19th and early 20th century, only the very rich could (2) .... for it. In those days, going abroad might well have involved a(n) (3) .... by ship or a long journey by train. This would inevitably require expensive clothes and a comfortable (4) .... Passengers might have to dress for dinner with the captain of the ship or enter the dining car of the train. In the 21st century, everybody travels, and (5) .... on holiday is a completely different experience.

Online booking might have made organizing a holiday cheap and easy, air (6) .... may well be more economical than ever before, and yes, you can (7) .... a car or a private plane in any country worldwide at the touch of a button. But this means that whatever destination you make (8) .... , you are at (9) .... of finding swarms of tourists.

On a recent trip to Granada in Spain, a visit to the Alhambra was recommended. I arrived at 9.00am to find a queue of eager (10) .... waiting patiently outside. A big digital screen showed the approximate waiting time before being able to (11) .... — three hours. Apparently, I should have booked online. There was a (12) .... and after the first hour I had run out of water. By the time I got into the Alhambra, my mood was so bad that I couldn't enjoy the experience. I started wishing I had stayed at home.

1	A Vacation	B Trip	C Holidaying	D Travel
2	A go	B look	C pay	D try
3	A trip	B voyage	C excursion	D drive
4	A space	B cabin	C room	D hotel
5	A seeing off	B setting off	C going on	D making off
6	A fares	B prices	C lines	D packages
7	A close	B buy	C hire	D borrow
8	A for	B up	C out	D to
9	A danger	B risk	C fault	D need
10	A holidaymakers	B hitchhikers	C commuters	D guides
11	A enter	B get	C be	D walk
12	A harvest	B flood	C heatwave	D shower

B Complete the text with ONE word that best fits each gap. Write your answers in CAPITAL LETTERS.

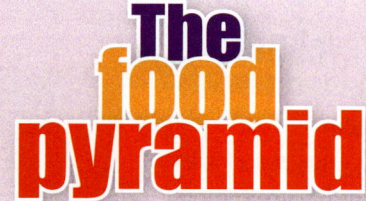

The food pyramid

Food and feeling good go together. Our mental and physical well-being (1) .... directly affected (2) .... what we eat. (3) .... healthy and nutritious diet is the key. But what makes a 'good' diet? Firstly, it is important to eat (4) .... of each different food group.

There are four different food groups, which fit into a food pyramid. (5) .... pyramid indicates which foods we are most (6) .... need of. Complex carbohydrates, such as bread, rice, pasta and cereals, are the (7) .... important food group. They can (8) .... found at the base of the pyramid. Then come fruit and vegetables, followed by proteins, which include meat, fish, milk, cheese, eggs and beans. Lastly, at the tip of the pyramid, are oils, fats and sweets. We (9) .... only eat small quantities of the last group.

The food guide pyramid helps promote three basic rules – variety, balance and moderation. Eat as (10) .... different foods as possible from each different level of the pyramid. Eat the correct amount of food from each level of the pyramid. Don't eat (11) .... much of any one food group.

Amounts of food vary depending on your age or sex, but the balance of foods in the pyramid stays the same. Logically, by following the pyramid guidelines you will be (12) .... healthy that there will be no stopping you!

C Complete the text with the correct form of the words in capitals. Write your answers in CAPITAL LETTERS.

Forget the Tube, use the Thames!

London Transport is a nightmare for most (1) .... **COMMUTE**
Trains are overcrowded and frequently (2) .... **DELAY**
Underground tube lines are consistently problematic and
punctual (3) .... at work can never be guaranteed. **ARRIVE**
The majority of peak-time (4) .... in London are heading **TRAVEL**
towards the City, which is London's (5) .... centre. **FINANCE**
It is also the oldest part of London, and is visited by both
(6) .... and Londoners alike. **TOUR**
The City is just a short trip along the river, and in 1999,
Thames Clippers came up with a (7) .... alternative to the **RELAX**
busy tube – the (8) .... of boat travel along the Thames. **ORGANIZE**
Using just one catamaran, *Thames Clippers* started ferrying
people to their destinations quickly and efficiently. Now there is
a fleet of 12 catamarans, and passengers can get on or off at
16 piers along the Thames including the Tower of London
and Greenwich. There are ferry (9) .... every 20 minutes **DEPART**
and the route is far more (10) .... than the Northern line. **SCENE**
Thames Clippers now transport 7,000 passengers a day. The
route includes some of London's most important landmarks,
so the catamarans are also popular with (11) .... **SEE**
It's the most (12) .... way of getting around London! **ENJOY**

D Rewrite the sentences using the words in capitals. Use between two and five words, including the word given. Write only the missing words in CAPITAL LETTERS.

1 The forest fire was so big that the firefighters could not control it.
TOO
The forest fire was .... to control.

2 Since you're feeling ill, you needn't come to work.
TO
You .... to work if you're feeling ill.

3 Drivers are obliged to carry a licence at all times.
BE
A licence .... at all times.

4 The fog was so thick that we couldn't see further than a metre.
SUCH
There .... we couldn't see further than a metre.

5 Our gym is equipped very well.
SOME
There .... in our gym.

6 My mum thinks I'm too young to get a skateboard.
OLD
In my mum's opinion, ... to get a skateboard.

7 The hotel was fully booked.
ANY
There .... the hotel.

8 A blizzard caused a three-hour delay until take-off.
WAS
Take-off .... because of a blizzard.

7 Beauty

Dive in!

A What do these statements mean? Which ones do you agree with? Which do you disagree with?
- Beauty is in the eye of the beholder
- Appearance is everything
- Beauty is only skin deep

Reading 1

B Look at the statements about cosmetic surgery. Which are advantages and which are disadvantages?

- It is expensive.
- It can help you feel more confident.
- It goes against nature.
- It makes you more beautiful.

C Which sentence (a or b) follows on most naturally from the first sentence?

1 Fashion affects many things in our lives.
a These include the clothes we wear, the way we style our hair – even the mobile or car we choose.
b Fashion affects other things too, but the most important things are the clothes we wear.

2 I asked my friend which shirt I should buy.
a It was the wrong answer because he doesn't know anything about clothes.
b He said it was a difficult question, but in the end he chose the blue one.

B2 Exam Practice
Steps to success
- The missing sentence must fit logically with those that come before and after it. Read the three sentences together to make sure there is a logical flow.

D Now read this article about young people and cosmetic surgery. Seven sentences have been removed from the article. Choose from the sentences A–H the one which best fits each gap (1-7). There is one extra sentence which you do not need to use. The underlined words and phrases are clues to help you.

Madeleine Dumont talked to a group of young people about what they were prepared to do to improve their appearance … and found a few surprises!

We all know that, for the average teenager, the way they look is very important. They are under increasing pressure to fit in so

All in the name of

there is a huge **range** of clothes, accessories and hair products to help them do just that. You only have to walk down any high street, and you'll see countless shops selling the latest designer **gear**.

Things have changed since I was a teenager. It's very easy for young people today to buy trendy clothes for reasonable prices, and there's no shortage of hairdressers, their chairs are filled with youngsters keen to have the latest hairstyle. (1) …………… Yes, <u>those two things</u> are as important today as they were in my youth, probably even more so.

<u>But other things have changed</u> quite dramatically in the 20 years since I became an adult. (2) …………… It seems that more

A Kelly then went on to describe in great detail how she's saving up to have an operation that will change the shape of her nose.

B I must admit that I didn't agree with Martin, 17, when he said that girls always spend too long getting ready to go out.

C The first to answer was Maria, a shy 18-year-old who had said very little up until this point.

D And Kelly wasn't alone.

E One in particular was 18-year-old John.

F One of those changes is the availability of cosmetic surgery.

G But there are many more ways to change your appearance than simply buying the latest clothes or having a modern haircut.

H Many ordinary people, some as young as 13, have had cosmetic surgery.

beauty

...and more people are prepared to go under the knife in order to look just the way they want.

And it's no longer just the super-rich (with money to burn) or top models (whose careers depend on it). (3) .... And even more of them are planning to change their appearance with this method. As the mother of a ten-year-old daughter, this **bothers** me, so I asked a group of teenagers about it. Surely they wouldn't use such **drastic** measures to change the way they look? What they said shocked me.

According to Kelly, who's 15, 'It's every person's right to look the way they want and, if cosmetic surgery is available, and you can afford it, why not?' (4) .... After that she told me, to my complete amazement, that she would also like to have work done on her eyes, her cheeks and finally her chin. I asked her if she would stop there and she laughed, 'I'll probably stop when the money runs out!'

I was shocked to discover that someone so young was prepared to do this. (5) .... Over half of the group (including two or three boys) said that they are thinking about having some form of cosmetic surgery in the near future. Alison, 16, made a very interesting point, 'By the time you're in your 20s — and have money to spend on these things — it's too late. Now is the time to do it, while you're young and can get the **benefit** from it.'

Since they had only mentioned the advantages of having surgery done, I felt that I had to ask whether they were worried about the pain or the risks involved. Most of them just **shrugged** and said it was worth it, but one or two members of the group expressed their concern. (6) .... His argument was 'What if it all goes wrong and you come out looking worse than when you went in?' I felt I had to agree with John. After all, I reminded them, there are no guarantees when you put your life in the hands of a surgeon.

Again, most of the group seemed to think that our fears weren't important. 'You're just being **pessimistic**,' they told me. 'The doctors know what they're doing,' one girl snapped at John. Desperate to make them think again, I asked the group one last question: 'Don't you think we all have our own beauty — just the way nature **intended**?' (7) .... She said that, yes, everyone is beautiful in their own way. She went on to talk about the emphasis on appearance in today's world, and about the ways in which you can look good without turning to cosmetic surgery. I liked what she had to say and felt that my final question had really made them think. Until she added, 'But if we have to put on make-up to look our best, nature's not that good, is it? Nature's fine, but you can always improve on it.'

Work it out!

E Match the words in bold from the text with their meanings.

1 meant
2 raised his or her shoulders
3 variety
4 extreme
5 advantage
6 disturbs or worries
7 clothes and accessories
8 only seeing the negative side of things

F Match the pictures (a–d) with the sentences (1–4).

1 His money has run out. ....
2 There's no shortage of shops. ....
3 He's got money to burn. ....
4 He's trying hard to fit in. ....

Quick chat

How do *you* feel about cosmetic surgery?

Grammar 1

✓ Check zero, first and second conditionals

See page 146 for information about conditionals.

Look at the conditional sentences below. Which expresses:

something that you probably won't do? ....

something you do regularly? ....

something that you probably will do? ....

a If I wear make-up, it makes me look older.
b If I wear a suit, I will look very smart.
c If I dyed my hair red, I would look funny!

A Circle the correct word or phrase.

1 Joanna would be very happy if she **could / would** make all her own clothes.
2 If you **buy / bought** cheap clothes, they don't usually last very long.
3 You will never be a good painter if you **didn't / don't** try.
4 If you **will see / see** Tom tomorrow, tell him to phone me.
5 What **would / will** you do if you won the art competition?
6 If I **had / would have** some money, I would be able to have a haircut.
7 If I **was / were** you, I wouldn't buy those trousers.
8 Whenever I **will get / get** a tan, I look healthier.

B Use the prompts to make conditional sentences. Sometimes more than one answer is possible.

1 Fiona wants to get a tattoo, but her mum will be really angry.
If Fiona ....

2 The jeans are so expensive. Otherwise I would buy them.
I would ....

3 Each time I wear make-up, I look like my sister.
Whenever I ....

4 You should buy this T-shirt. You can wear it to the party tonight.
If you ....

5 You might need help with your art project. You can phone me.
Phone ....

6 I'm studying. That's why I can't come to your house.
If I ....

7 I'm not good at painting. I won't join the art class.
If I ....

C Look at the pictures and write your own conditional sentences.

Vocabulary 1
Appearance and fashion

A Label the picture with these phrases.

1 ....
2 ....
3 ....
4 ....
5 ....
6 ....
7 ....
8 ....

bleached hair • high heels • pierced lip
dark glasses • nose ring • skate shoes
goatee beard • painted nails

Quick chat
Which of the things in the picture are fashionable at the moment? Which of the things do you like and would wear? Are there any things in the picture that you wouldn't wear?

Word partners

B Complete the text with the words in the box.

casual look • fashion designer • hair gel • lip gloss
make-up artist • ponytail

Charles is a top (1) .... who works in Paris. He's a very distinctive man – tall and slim with a long brown (2) .... His latest collection features mainly formal wear, but you would never imagine that to look at him – he prefers the (3) .... and was wearing scruffy jeans when I met him.

Tina has been a (4) .... for as long as I've known her, but people are surprised to see that she wears very little herself. In fact, she almost never bothers with make-up or lipstick; she just uses a little (5) .... , and a small amount of (6) .... to stop her hair from going in her eyes when she's working.

Key phrasal verbs

C Match the highlighted phrasal verbs in the sentences with their meanings.

INTERESTING, BUT I DON'T THINK IT WILL EVER CATCH ON!

1 That's a really interesting hairstyle, but I don't think it will ever **catch on**.
2 I'm going to have the hem **taken up** on this skirt because it's too long.
3 I know a woman who **puts** her make-up **on** just to take the rubbish out!
4 You need a lot of money if you want to **keep up with** the latest fashions.
5 John **rolled up** his sleeves and started work.

a become popular   d stay up-to-date with
b make shorter   e apply; wear
c turn back

Word patterns: *match, suit, fit, go with*

D Correct the words in bold.
1 That jacket really **goes with** you – you should wear it more often.
2 Marina loved the skirt so much that she bought a blouse to **fit**.
3 People say that green doesn't **match** blue, so don't wear your green shirt with that blue pullover.
4 I tried on a size nine but it didn't **suit**, so I must be a size ten.

E Complete the text with the correct form of *match, suit, fit* or *go with*.

One of the problems with being a redhead is finding clothes that (1) .... your hair colour. I mean, everyone knows that red doesn't (2) .... green, so green jumpers or blouses are out. And if I wear red I just look ill! So red doesn't (3) .... me either. Most people have difficulty finding clothes in a size that (4) .... them, but my problem is finding the right colour – I tend to wear a lot of brown things, but I'm so bored with brown!

Listening

B2 Exam Practice

Steps to success
- Look at the list of answer choices and try to guess what each of the speakers might talk about.
- Listen very carefully to what each person says — where they are, if they are talking about themselves or someone else, etc.

A 🎧 Listen to two people talking about art and tick the things each speaker mentions. Then decide who the speaker is.

Speaker 1
- The type of art ☐
- How much it is worth ☐
- The subject ☐
- The artist's technique ☐
- How it makes the speaker feel ☐
- Biographical information about the artist ☐

The speaker is **an expert on art / someone who knows very little about art**.

Speaker 2
- Different ways to paint a picture ☐
- Studying the work of artists ☐
- Studying books about art ☐
- Learning from your mistakes ☐
- Getting qualifications in art ☐
- Learning about painting techniques ☐

The speaker is **an art student / an artist**.

B 🎧 Listen again and make a list of words and phrases that helped you decide who the speaker is.

Speaker 1: ....
....
....

Speaker 2: ....
....
....

C What would you expect the following people to talk about? Choose from the list of topics (a–f) and add your own suggestions.

1 someone talking about a favourite painting
.... , ...
....

2 someone who makes statues
.... , ...
....

3 someone who sells or displays art
.... , ...
....

a what kind of art he/she likes (landscapes, portraits, etc)
b the cost of works of art
c what he/she likes about a particular artist/piece of work
d the materials he/she uses
e the kind of artists he/she deals with
f the way he/she works

D 🎧 You will hear five people talking about different aspects of art. For questions 1–5, choose from the list A–F who is speaking. There is one extra letter which you do not need to use.

A an art collector
B an art critic
C a painter
D a visitor to an exhibition
E a sculptor
F a gallery owner

Speaker 1 ☐ 1
Speaker 2 ☐ 2
Speaker 3 ☐ 3
Speaker 4 ☐ 4
Speaker 5 ☐ 5

Speaking

B2 Exam Practice
Steps to success
- Keep the conversation flowing — when your partner stops talking, you should say something.
- Listen very carefully to what your partner says because you will need to comment on it.
- If you have spoken for some time, ask your partner his or her opinion.

A 🎧 Listen to four short extracts from a speaking test. What is wrong with the second candidate's answer in each extract?

Extract 1 ....
Extract 2 ....
Extract 3 ....
Extract 4 ....

B 🎧 Now listen to another candidate. Why is his response better?

C Take turns responding to what your partner says using the Language chunks below to help you.

Student A: Look at page 136.
Student B: Look at page 137.

Language chunks

Keeping the conversation going
And also …
I think you're right, and …
I see what you mean about …
Wouldn't it be better to/if … ?
I (don't) think I would … but …
That's a good point, but/and …
Yes, but …

D Do the following task with your partner.

A new magazine called *In Fashion* is going to be published. The pictures show different things that could appear in the magazine. Talk about whether the items would appeal to boys, girls or both. Then choose the two items which you would most like to see in the first issue of the magazine.

Would these items appeal to boys, girls, or both?

Which two would you most like to see in the magazine?

B2 Exam Practice

E In pairs, answer questions 1–4. Use the star diagrams to help you. When your partner answers first, listen to his or her answer and add your own opinion.

1. What kind of magazines do you usually read?
2. What do you like about them?
3. Would you like to work in the fashion industry?
4. Some people say that the fashion business is just a way to make money out of young people. Do you agree?

magazines: interesting, free time, music, monthly, articles, fashion, weekly

the fashion industry: (super)models, peer pressure, designers, expensive, fashion shows, new styles, exciting

7

A Look at the pictures. Are there any differences between the two types of personal decoration?

Reading 2

B Complete the sentences with the words in the box.

> ancient • fierce • heal • hut • mark • primitive
> slave • unique

1 The tattoos might look similar, but each one is ....
2 The cut on his face took many days to ....
3 The earliest humans lived in .... societies that did not know about agriculture.
4 Plato's philosophy is written in a(n) .... language.
5 A tattoo is a(n) .... on the skin made with a needle and ink.
6 A(n) .... was someone who could be bought and sold.
7 There is a simple wooden .... on the mountain where climbers can stay if the weather is bad.
8 The dog sounds .... when he barks, but really he is gentle.

B2 Exam Practice
Steps to success
- Learn to work quickly by timing yourself. Try to read the text about tattoos and answer the questions in five minutes.

C Read the following passage about tattoos and then answer the questions.

Throughout history tattoos have been used in different ways and have had different meanings. In ancient Rome, for instance, tattoos were used to identify criminals. In parts of northern India it is still common for tattoos to be used to prevent disease and protect against the evil eye. In the native peoples of North America, tattoos were statements about which family or tribe a person belonged to. And in northern Japan, a tattoo around the lips was used to exaggerate their size and make women more attractive.

Among the Maoris of New Zealand, men had to have their faces covered with black spirals in

The functions of

order to be respected as the fierce warriors that Maori men were supposed to be. Although it was a painful process, as a sign of bravery Maori men didn't react when being tattooed. With the exception of slaves, all men had facial tattoos, while women had markings on other parts of their bodies.

Unlike other primitive cultures, the Maoris did not decorate their faces by hitting the back of a

1 According to the passage, in which part of the world did tattoos have a magical purpose?
a New Zealand
b northern India
c North America
d Japan

2 What was the purpose of moko?
a to protect against the evil eye
b to make the enemy afraid
c to make someone look more beautiful
d to show a person's family identity

3 According to the passage, who wouldn't have had tattoos on their faces?
a Maori women
b Japanese women
c Roman slaves
d native Americans

tattoos

sharp comb. To do what they called moko, they cut lines right through the skin and put ink in the cuts. The decoration, which was always unique, started in adolescence and, until the cuts of the first pattern had healed, the young man had to remain hidden in a special moko hut. In following years, the design was added to and, to look its best, each hair of the beard had to be plucked.

4 What do we know about moko designs?
a They were all different.
b They were red and black.
c They only had straight lines.
d They showed animal figures.

5 What was needed to improve the appearance of the Maori moko?
a to change the colour of the hair
b to practise facial expressions
c to stay in a hut
d remove hair from the face

6 The main purpose of the passage is
a to show why different people had tattoos.
b to warn us about which Maoris to respect.
c to inform us about how moko is carried out.
d to show that slaves and criminals were treated differently.

D Complete the sentences with the correct form of the word in brackets.

1 Tattoos are not just a ……………………… ; they have a symbolic purpose too. (decorate)
2 A laser can be used to remove ……………………… hair. (face)
3 ……………………… is often a difficult period in a person's life. (adolescent)
4 Everyone must take part. There will be no ……………………… . (except)
5 Warriors from the same tribe could ……………………… each other from their tattoos. (identity)
6 Maori tribesmen were known for their ……………………… . (brave)
7 A Maori man was expected to be a good ……………………… . (war)
8 Does this design have a symbolic ……………………… ? (mean)

E Complete each sentence with a word from the text.

1 'How did the police ……………………… the robber?' 'They found his fingerprints at the scene of the crime.'
2 Making furniture by hand is a very lengthy ……………………… .
3 'Honestly, the fish I caught was huge!' 'Oh, don't ……………………… !'
4 That's a very interesting ……………………… on your wallpaper, but doesn't it give you headaches?

Doesn't it give you a headache?

Quick chat

How would your family, friends and teachers react if you did the following things?
- had a tattoo done
- had all your hair shaved
- had your hair dyed blue
- had your lip/nose/ear pierced

Grammar 2

✓ Check causative form

See page 146 for information about the causative form.

Look at these examples of the causative.
Laura **has had her nails painted** blue.
I **am having a new dress made**.
Did you **get your clothes cleaned**?

Now put the words in the correct order to make causative sentences.

1 cut / Jane / her / has / hair / month / every
....

2 jacket / I / cleaned / had / have / my
....

3 boots / I / having / am / my / repaired
....

A Complete the text with the correct causative form of the verbs in brackets.

As a model, my appearance is very important to me, so there are some things that I do regularly – just to keep myself looking good. For example, once a month, I visit the hairdresser's to (**1**) .... (my hair / cut). I have a manicure and (**2**) .... (my nails / paint) once a month too.

But that's just to maintain my looks in case I have to go for a job. In between times, when I'm working, my hair and nails can change colour up to five times a week. Last week, I (**3**) .... (my hair / style) four times – and each time it looked totally different!

Usually I put on my make-up myself, but if I'm on a photo shoot, I (**4**) .... (my make-up / do) by a professional make-up artist. That's quite nice, actually, because you just have to sit there while someone else does the work.

The worst thing about my job? Well, I should say that I don't always like (**5**) .... (my photograph / take) – the flash can give me a terrible headache.

But next month, I (**6**) .... (my picture / published) on the front cover of a magazine. That will be the first time for me – and I'm sure that when I see myself in the newsagent's, I'll think all the effort was worth it!

B Find the mistakes in these sentences and correct them.

1 We have our letters sending to my aunt's house because the postman doesn't come here.
2 My neighbours are going to have built a garage under their house.
3 My dad had his car break into when it was in the car park at work.
4 I have been having my photograph taken thousands of times.

B2 Exam Practice
Steps to success
- Remember that you may need to change nouns into adjectives, verbs into nouns, etc.
- Pay attention to your spelling. You will lose marks if you spell a word incorrectly.

C Complete the second sentence so that it has a similar meaning to the first sentence, using the word given. Do not change the word given. You must use between two and five words including the word given.

1 I'm really busy today, so I can't come shopping with you. **able**
If I wasn't so busy today, I .... shopping with you.

2 You can borrow my hairdryer tomorrow, but you'll have to come and get it. **if**
You can borrow my hairdryer tomorrow .... and get it.

3 I want to go to the show, I'm waiting for John to invite me. **me**
If .... to the show, I will go.

4 I look thinner in black clothes. **I**
If I .... thinner.

5 Someone stole Margaret's bag while she was trying on clothes. **her**
Margaret .... while she was trying on clothes.

6 You have to sit very still when an artist is painting your portrait. **portrait**
When you are .... by an artist, you have to sit very still.

7 Take Tim's book with you in case you see him. **give**
If you .... his book.

8 I am going to get a professional photographer to take the photographs. **taken**
I am going to .... a professional photographer.

Vocabulary 2
Art

A In which of the pictures below can you see:
1. a still life painting? ....
2. a landscape painting? ....
3. a sculpture? ....
4. abstract art? ....
5. a portrait? ....

B Circle the correct word or phrase.
1. This picture **shows** / **paints** a scene from nature.
2. The artist has chosen to use **canvas** / **water colours** as his medium.
3. The best **studios** / **exhibitions** have paintings from all over the world.
4. This painter has an unusual **method** / **ability** – he paints with his fingers, not brushes.
5. She needed a lot of **fantasy** / **imagination** to create such an amazing piece of work.

Word formation

C Complete the table with the correct forms.

Noun (thing)	Noun (person)	Adjective	Verb
paint, painting			
art			–
		–	sculpt
	exhibitor	–	
	–		attract
	–		appreciate
	critic		
value	–		
amazement	–		
	–		beautify

B2 Exam Practice

D For questions 1–10, read the text below. Use the word given in capitals at the end of the lines to form a word that fits in the gap in the same line. Write your answers in CAPITAL LETTERS.

Art – or just child's play?

When Sean Rourke agreed to meet me for an interview, all I really knew about him was that he is a (**1**) .... and that his work is starting to receive very good reviews. But I don't think I have ever met a more (**2**) .... person than Sean.
As well as painting the most (**3**) .... pictures, Sean is a (**4**) .... and a writer. He has written four children's books, for which he provided some of the most (**5**) .... drawings I have ever seen in a book. 'Children are very (**6**) .... ,' he tells me. 'They know what they like and they understand that (**7**) .... is all around us. Children know how to look at pictures – and their (**8**) .... of art is often highly developed.'
'I don't care if my work becomes (**9**) .... or not – I'm not in it to make money', he told me. 'What's important is the art.' With his first major (**10**) .... at the Walker Gallery this month, we now have the chance to judge for ourselves.

PAINT
ART
AMAZE
SCULPT
ATTRACT
CRITIC
BEAUTIFUL
APPRECIATE
VALUE
EXHIBIT

7

Writing: article

B2 Exam Practice
Steps to success
- Read the task carefully to see how many POINTS or QUESTIONS you need to write about.
- Write a PARAGRAPH for each MAIN POINT.
- Give EXAMPLES or EXPLANATIONS to support the points you make.

A Read the writing task below and then answer the questions.

You have seen this announcement in an international magazine.

> **Keeping up with fashion**
> How far are you and your friends prepared to go in order to stay in fashion? Why is it important for young people to be fashionable? Send us an article telling us your opinion on the subject. We will print the best articles in next month's magazine.

1. What do you have to write?
2. Who is going to read it?
3. What style of writing will you use?
4. How many points should you write about?

B Complete the model article with the words and phrases in the box.

> addition • also • because of • believe • conclude
> however • just because

Keeping up with fashion

Fashion plays a big role in our lives and, **(1)** .... this, we spend quite a lot of time and money on our appearance.

Like most teenagers, my friends and I enjoy getting new things and, if we have enough money, we usually buy new designs when they come out in the shops. We **(2)** .... try to keep up with things like hairstyles. For example, most girls my age have had their hair cut short because that's what is in fashion here at the moment. **(3)** .... , there are limits to what we would do. I don't think any of my friends would get a tattoo done **(4)** .... it was fashionable, for instance.

I **(5)** .... that it's important to stay in fashion because if you don't, it means that you don't fit in with the others. In **(6)** .... , modern clothes give you self-confidence – when you look good, you usually feel good too.

To **(7)** .... , being fashionable is very important to most people of my age, but we need to make sure that we don't take it too seriously.

C Find examples or explanations for the following points in the model. The first one has been done for you.

1. My friends and I enjoy getting new things.
   Example: ... we usually buy new designs when they come out ...
2. We also try to keep up with things like hairstyles.
   Example: ....
3. There are limits to what we would do.
   Example: ....
4. It's important to stay in fashion.
   Explanation: ....
5. Modern clothes give you self-confidence.
   Explanation: ....

D Number the points below in the order in which they appear in the model.

- Answers question, 'Why is it important for young people to be fashionable?' ☐
- Summarizes main points in the article. ☐
- Gives general comments about the importance of fashion. ☐
- Answers question, 'How far are you and your friends prepared to go in order to stay in fashion?' ☐

E Read the writing task below. Discuss the question with your partner and complete the table.

You have seen this announcement in a magazine for school students.

What should we wear to school?
Write an article giving examples of some of the things you can and can't wear at your school. Give us your views on what you think students should wear. The best articles will be published in the magazine.

	Allowed	Not allowed	Would like
clothes			
hair			
jewellery			
shoes			
make-up			
other (eg, tattoos)			

F Make sentences about your own school. Use the Language chunks to help you. Give an example or an explanation for each point you make.

We're not allowed to wear jewellery because our teachers say that school is not a place for dressing up.

3-minute plan!

G Complete the paragraph plan for your article.

First paragraph: introduce the subject
Is your school strict or relaxed about what you wear?
....

Middle paragraph(s): give the information asked for in the task
What clothes are allowed at your school? Give examples or explanations.
....
....

Are there any school rules about:
make-up? ....
hair? ....
jewellery? ....
Give examples/explanations for any of these.
....

How would you rather dress for school? Why?
....

Final paragraph: make a final comment
How do you feel about the way you dress for school?
....

H Now write your article in 120–180 words using your notes, paragraph plan and some of the Language chunks to help you.

Language chunks

Writing about what people do
I/We (don't) usually …
Most of the time I/we …
I/We (don't) tend to …
We're (not) allowed to …

Expressing preferences
I (don't) like (to) …
I'd (much) rather (not) …
I prefer …
We should (not) …
It would be nice/good if …
I would like to be able to …

Linking words and phrases
However, …
In addition, …
… just because …
… also …
… because of …
for example
for instance
to conclude, …

8 For pleasure

snowboarding

go-karting

modern dance

Dive in!

A Which of these activities would you like to try?

B Which would be:

exciting?   creative?
dangerous? expensive?
relaxing?   physically demanding?

Reading 1

B2 Exam Practice

Steps to success

- Practise finding information quickly in a text without reading every word.
- Remember, if there are two answers to a question, you can write them in any order.

C Look at the article and see how quickly you can find:

1 the names of two past winners of Highland dancing competitions ...., ...
2 the price of something Highland dancers wear ....
3 the title of an international competition ....
4 a possible danger of Highland dancing ....
5 when women started taking part in Highland dancing ....

D For questions 1–15, choose from the paragraphs (A–F). Underline in the text where you found your answers.

Highland dancing

A Highland dancing is, perhaps, among the most competitive and disciplined sports available to young people in Scotland. Those who get involved tend to make it central to their lives, often entering competitions twice-weekly in the season. Though the number of those practising has apparently **declined** in recent years, this has not yet been reflected in the professional field. The World Highland Dancing Championships, which take place next weekend, will attract over 500 competitors from around the globe.

B For many of those involved, Highland dancing is far more sport than art form. Partly it is the extreme competitiveness, partly the nature of the dance. It's not a form of self-expression, but of precision and coordination, of strength and athleticism. Though it used to be **predominantly** a male **pursuit**, it now attracts more women than men. Yet it was only in the late 19th century that the first woman, Jenny Douglas, competed.

C Highland dance, of course, is not just a physical activity, it is a social scene: one that involves parents, relatives, sitting out in the rain under **damp** tents at Highland Games, early mornings, late nights and international travel. The current juvenile world champion, Robyn Hart-Winks, was the first dancer in her family. She was just six years old when her mother, Ann, signed her up for the local Highland dancing class. Ann was concerned that her daughter was a little shy and wanted to get her involved in something social. She explains how of her four children, Robyn

Which section or sections mention(s):

the history of Highland dancing? **1**
the need for Highland dancers to have physical power? **2** **3**
Highland dancers' ability in other areas? **4**
an international competition? **5**
the prizes won by a Highland dancer? **6**
special clothes worn by Highland dancers? **7**
the characteristics needed to be a Highland dancing champion? **8**
the involvement of dancers' families? **9**
the popularity of Highland dancing? **10**
the physical damage that Highland dancing can do? **11**
the advantage that male Highland dancers seem to have? **12**
competing against people you know? **13**
the amount of time and effort involved in Highland dancing? **14** **15**

is the most expensive child: even more costly than their daughter who rides horses. Her husband jokes that they kept secret from her the cost of the Highland dance socks, which are £90 a pair.

D There are three living rooms in the Hart-Winks' home; another seems to be devoted to the storage of Robyn's treasure trove of cups and trophies. A quick count suggests at least 70, not including the small trophies piled in the corner. 'When I do well,' Robin says, 'I feel so amazing. But what's so great is everybody's pleased for you.' She admits she is intensely competitive, but at the same time enjoys and **participates** in an atmosphere of mutual support. The dancing community for her is really like an extended family. 'Everyone wants to win, but in the end, the dancers just dance. And some of your closest friends are your biggest competitors.'

E It's a sign of the **toughness** of the pursuit that Highland dancers have a relatively short career life. Delma Wilson, ex-Highland dancing champion and teacher, was 17 when she ripped the tendons and ligaments along the top of her foot and found herself unable to dance. She wishes she hadn't had to stop dancing so early. '**Injuries**,' she says, 'are really quite prevalent in Highland dancing. I think the body gives out before the will does.' Men, she believes, often last longer than women. It's as if developing that kind of strength more naturally suits their body type.

F So what is the formula that makes for a championship winner? Wilson believes there is an element of biology, but mostly it is character that counts. 'Sometimes you find the ones who have the most natural talent aren't going to be your top dancers because it's all down to how hard a worker you are,' she says. Highland dancers are almost always highly **disciplined** in all aspects of their life. They often excel at school. 'They are high achievers, full stop,' says Wilson. Often it seems that the dancing is just the pursuit they have happened to direct their energies into.

E Match the words in bold from the text with their meanings.
1 wet
2 takes part
3 difficulty
4 become less
5 mostly
6 physical damage
7 behaving in a controlled way
8 activity

F Match the adjectives and nouns from the text to make common pairs.
1 natural .... a century
2 close .... b talent
3 physical .... c activity
4 nineteenth .... d sport
5 competitive .... e friend

G Complete the sentences with pairs of words from Exercise F.
1 Sarah used to be a .... of mine, but we've grown apart now.
2 Kyle is so lazy – he hates any kind of .... !
3 This theatre was built in the ....
4 Nick has got a .... for gymnastics.
5 Football is probably the most popular .... in the world.

Quick chat

Give an example of
• a pursuit that you enjoy
• a world champion in a popular sport
• an injury that you've had
• an event that you have participated in recently

Grammar 1

✓ **Check** relative clauses

See pages 146 and 147 for information about relative clauses.

Complete these sentences with relative pronouns. Why are there commas in sentence 1?
1 That film, ... stars Keanu Reeves, is fantastic.
2 The DVD .... we rented last night was a bit boring.

A Complete the sentences with the relative pronouns in the box. In which sentence(s) can the relative pronoun be replaced by *that*? In which sentence(s) can the relative pronoun be omitted completely?

when • where • which • who • whose • why

1 Harry, ... is an experienced skier, has offered to give me lessons.
2 This is a book .... will change your life!
3 Sunday is the only day .... I get up late.
4 Sarah, ... cousin has got a yacht, has invited us to go sailing this weekend.
5 Is this the place .... you dropped your purse?
6 He didn't explain .... he was angry.

C Join the two sentences. Use relative pronouns and make any other necessary changes.

1 Claire's dad works in a circus. He's very funny.
....

2 I've just been to the gym. That's why I'm hot and sweaty!
....

3 Ricky got us free tickets for the show. His friend works at the theatre.
....

4 The Oscars are awards. They're given to people in the film industry.
....

5 That's the new stadium. The Olympic Games were held there.
....

6 At the weekends I have more free time. I go out with my friends then.
....

B Complete the text with the correct relative pronouns. Insert commas where necessary.

Snowkiting (1) .... is like skiing and flying a kite at the same time is an exciting new winter sport. Snowkiters use kites (2) .... have been specially designed for the sport to pull them up mountains, along the ground and through the air. Some Arctic explorers (3) .... have to travel huge distances across the snow are fans of the sport too. Another reason (4) .... snowkiting is becoming popular is that it's very easy to learn. Skiers and snowboarders for (5) .... winter sports are a way of life only have to learn how to control the kite and they're off! Snowkiting also enables you to go to places (6) .... skiers and snowboarders can't go.

Vocabulary 1
Sports, hobbies and pastimes

A Write *go*, *do* or *play*.

1 .... skiing
2 .... aerobics
3 .... swimming
4 .... karate
5 .... chess
6 .... horseback riding
7 .... tennis
8 .... climbing
9 .... a musical instrument
10 .... basketball
11 .... jogging
12 .... ballet
13 .... diving
14 .... table tennis
15 .... cycling
16 .... sailing
17 .... hiking
18 .... weight training

Quick chat

Which of the above
- have you done?
- would you like to do?
- would you never do?

Sports equipment

B Label the pictures with these words. Which activities in Exercise A are these items used for?

bat • compass • goggles • helmet • lifejacket • racket
rope • rucksack • saddle • wetsuit

1 ....
2 ....
3 ....
4 ....
5 ....
6 ....
7 ....
8 ....
9 ....
10 ....

Key phrasal verbs

C Match the phrasal verbs with their meanings.

1 take up ....
2 put off ....
3 turn up (for/at) ....
4 be into ....
5 put on ....
6 turn down/up ....

a arrange to do something at a later time
b make the sound quieter/louder
c perform
d like
e arrive at a place
f to start doing a new activity/sport regularly

D Complete the sentences with phrasal verbs from Exercise C in the correct form.

1 The organizers of the festival didn't expect so many people to ....
2 My sister .... heavy metal music, but I hate it!
3 They decided to .... the party because Steve was ill.
4 Sammy has just .... windsurfing and she's crazy about it!
5 Can you .... the TV? I can't hear myself think!
6 Our local amateur dramatic society .... a play once a year.

Listening

B2 Exam Practice

Steps to success
- Listen for expressions which show the speakers' point of view or feelings.
- Remember, the order of the questions is the same as the order in which you will hear the answers on the recording.

A 🎧 Listen to five short dialogues and tick the phrases you hear in the recording.
1 Never mind. ☐
2 You can say that again! ☐
3 Go on! ☐
4 Speak for yourself! ☐
5 No worries. ☐
6 You're joking! ☐
7 It goes without saying. ☐
8 To tell you the truth … ☐

B Now match the phrases you ticked in Exercise A with their meanings below.
a I don't believe it. ....
b In my honest opinion. ....
c It doesn't matter. ....
d Do it! ....
e I don't agree with you. ....

C Look at questions 1–7 in Exercise D and number the points below in the order you expect to hear about them.
meals ....
transport ....
accommodation ....
problems they had ....

D 🎧 You will hear a conversation which takes place between three friends, James, Vicky and Lucy. For questions 1–7, choose the best answer (A, B or C).

1 Why didn't James go to the festival?
A He doesn't like music festivals in general.
B He didn't have enough money.
C He wasn't impressed by the same one last year.

2 Vicky and Lucy
A stayed in a cheap hotel.
B stayed in a luxurious hotel.
C camped.

3 What spoilt one performance for Vicky?
A She couldn't hear very well.
B She hurt her head.
C She didn't have a good view.

4 What was wrong with the food at the festival?
A It was mainly vegetarian.
B There wasn't enough variety.
C It was too expensive.

5 How did Vicky and Lucy get to the festival?
A by train
B by car
C by coach

6 The Blue Goldfish's performance
A didn't go very well.
B was cancelled because of rain.
C was a great success.

7 Pete Dove is
A a famous singer.
B related to James.
C giving a concert soon.

Speaking

B2 Exam Practice
Steps to success
- When answering questions about your interests, explain why you like doing certain things.
- If you don't know the specific word for something in a picture, try to describe it in your own words.

A Complete the sentences with the correct prepositions.
1. What do you like doing .... your spare time?
2. What's your favourite programme .... TV?
3. What kind of music do you listen .... ?
4. Do you prefer spending time .... friends or family?
5. What did you do .... your last birthday?
6. Do you like being .... your own?

B Now choose four of the questions in Exercise A to ask your partner.

C Describe these things to your partner without using the specific words for them. Use the Language chunks to help you.

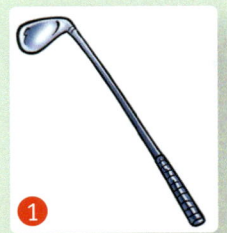

D Compare the two photos and say why the different people are making music. If there are objects in the pictures whose names you don't know, describe them in your own words. Use the Language chunks to help you.

Why are the different people making music?

E Now ask and answer these questions with a partner.

Is there any musical instrument that you would like to play?

What kind of music don't you like?

Say it right!

F 🎧 One word in each pair contains a letter that is not pronounced. Underline the 'silent' letters, then listen to see if you were right.
1. balle**t**, hit
2. s**c**reen, s**c**ience
3. **a**lbum, **a**erobics
4. clim**b**, glo**b**e
5. instrument, party
6. walk, golf

Language chunks

Describing objects and places
It's something that you use to …
It's for …
It's a bit like a …
It's a kind of …
It's a place where …

8 Science

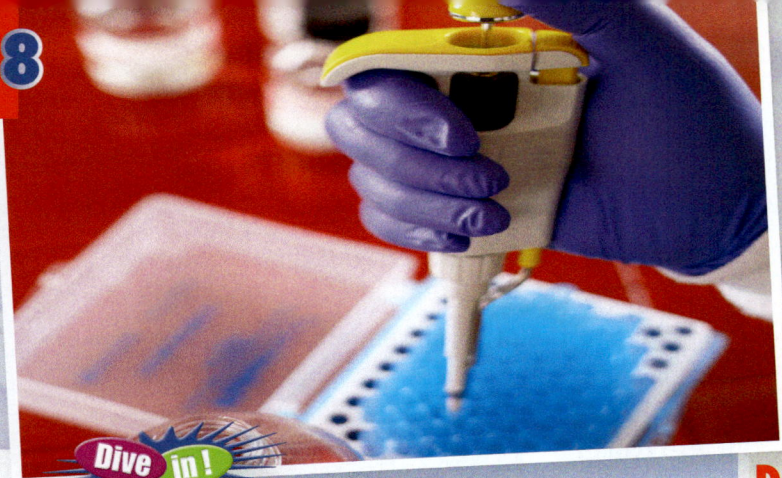

A What would you expect to see and be able to do at a science museum?

B How well do you know our solar system? Write the names of the planets in the correct order.

1 ....
2 ....
3 ....
4 ....
5 ....
6 ....
7 ....
8 ....

Earth • Jupiter • Mars • Mercury • Neptune
Saturn • Uranus • Venus

Reading 2

B2 Exam Practice

Steps to success
- It's important to locate relevant information quickly by scanning the texts. Use section headings to help you.

C Find the following information in the museum brochures as quickly as you can.

1 The cheapest museum for children to visit is ....
2 The museum in San Francisco is the ....
3 You can see fish at the ....

D Read the extracts from six museum brochures. Use the information in the brochures to answer the questions.

1 You are staying at Fisherman's Wharf in San Francisco and are travelling around by bicycle. Which is the easiest museum to get to?
  a 2   b 3   c 5   d 6

2 You are interested in the study of Earth's earliest creatures. Which museum should you visit?
  a 1   b 2   c 4   d 5

3 Which museum is situated next to a hotel that will give you free admission to museum exhibitions?
  a 3   b 4   c 5   d 6

4 Which museum will let you stay overnight?
  a 3   b 4   c 5   d 6

5 Which museum would be able to bring part of its exhibition to your school?
  a 1   b 2   c 5   d 6

6 A new teacher needs help developing her teaching skills. Which museum should be able to help her?
  a 1   b 2   c 3   d 4

7 Your niece is doing a project called 'Fashions of the future'. Which museum might give her useful information for her project?
  a 2   b 3   c 5   d 6

8 Your teenage friend wants to get involved in a programme that will help his community. Which museum might give him this opportunity?
  a 1   b 3   c 5   d 6

9 An American family have a visitor from abroad. Which museum will almost certainly refuse him admission?
  a 1   b 2   c 3   d 4

10 Which two museums sell tickets that also give you admission to other local attractions?
  a 2 and 3   b 3 and 4   c 4 and 5   d 5 and 6

11 Which two museums would be good places for a child to celebrate a birthday?
  a 1 and 5   b 2 and 6   c 3 and 5   d 5 and 6

12 Which three museums enable you to do something creative and make something artistic?
  a 2, 3 and 5   b 2, 5 and 6   c 3, 4 and 5   d 4, 5 and 6

SPACE VISITOR CENTRE ①

A wide range of interactive exhibits: Try out the module used to train shuttle crews; experience the thrill of a countdown to a launch; and do experiments in gravity. Visit the Solar System Hall and find out if there really is life on Mars and find out how much you weigh on each of the planets in our solar system.

Travelling Exhibitions: If you can't come to us, we can bring one of our mobile exhibitions to you. (Note that arrangements must be made at least eight weeks in advance.)

Important security notice: All visitors must be US citizens holding government-issued photo ID.

City Museum ②

Super Aquarium: *Home to over 10,000 sea creatures, including octopus, stingrays and seahorses. You can even slide through a 50,000 gallon shark tank!*

Art House: *See painters, potters, sculptors and glassblowers at work. Try your hand at pottery and decorate your own ceramic objects.*

Professional Development Programmes for Educators: *Popular courses to improve the classroom success of newly-qualified teachers.*

Prices
- General admission (ages 3 years and up): $12.00
- After 5pm Friday & Saturday: $10.00
- Let us organize your party for $20 per person.

Scientorium ③

Founded in 1960, the Scientorium is located near the Golden Gate Bridge.

Touch Dome: Lose your sense of sight and see only with your hands on this tour of total darkness.

Second Skin: See futuristic clothing designs that use the very latest technology.

Getting here:
The museum is easily accessible on all forms of public transport and is an easy two-mile bicycle ride from Fisherman's Wharf, San Francisco.

Admission
Adults – $14
Children – $9
First Wednesday of every month: admission free
City Pass: Save 50% on five famous city attractions.

Museum of Science and Industry ④

As hundreds of teachers know, we provide inspiring activities that really get youngsters interested in science.

Dinosaurs Alive: Accompany the world's most famous palaeontologists as they discover the most amazing dinosaurs.

Discovery DNA: Discover the secrets of genetics as you watch baby chickens develop and see the DNA in your own cheek cells.

Admission
Adult: $23 • Child: $14 • City Pass: Visit 5 attractions for $59

Museum of Science ⑤

Exhibition: Mythical Creatures
Trace the natural and cultural roots of dragons, unicorn, mermaids and other mythic creatures. Amazing exhibits bring to life myths from around the world.

Event: Global Teen Summit
Teenagers from around the world can come together to use their technology skills, teamwork and imaginations to solve some of the problems of their communities. Learn how to make digital art, radio and video documentaries.

Accommodation: *Stay in the hotel next door to the museum and get free access to the museum the following day.*

National Centre for Science (NCS) ⑥

The mission of the NCS is to motivate young people to seek careers in technology and engineering.

Become a graphic designer: Make original pictures with media software, make your own website, direct and edit your own videos.

The Night of the Robots: Explore the world of robotics as you programme your own robot and then watch it in action.

Admission • Adults – $8 • Children – $6

It's party time! It's the coolest place for a party. Only $150 (including a live science demonstration) for up to 10 children and 15 adults.
Only $30 for members, including dinner, evening snack, accommodation and breakfast.

Quick chat
Which museum would you most like to go to?
What sort of activities do you enjoy doing in your free time that enable you to learn new things?

Grammar 2

✓ Check unreal past

See page 147 for information about the unreal past.

Which sentence in each pair is correct?

a If only I was a good dancer.
b If only I am a good dancer.

a I wish I went to the party.
b I wish I had gone to the party.

a I'd rather you don't shout.
b I'd rather you didn't shout.

a It's about time you took a rest.
b It's about time you take a rest.

✓ Check third conditional

See page 147 for information about the third conditional.

Look at this sentence. What happened? What was the result?

If it **hadn't rained**, they **wouldn't have cancelled** the match.

Complete these third conditional sentences in your own words. For each one say:
a) what happened/what didn't happen
b) what the result was

1 If Joe had won the chess championship, he …
2 If Zara hadn't gone to the party, she …

A Complete the sentences about Rosie's regrets and wishes.

not go shopping   not have to write an essay
not go to bed late   not make so much noise

1 I wish I ……………… .
2 If only I ……………… .
3 I wish he ……………… .
4 I'd rather we ……………… .

B Read the facts and complete the sentences using the third conditional.

1 I had a headache so I didn't go to the concert.
If ……………………………………… to the concert.
2 We had a picnic because the weather was hot.
If ……………………………………… a picnic.
3 Tim hadn't finished the book so he didn't lend it to me.
If ……………………………………… to me.
4 My grandfather was very fit because he walked everywhere.
If ……………………………………… very fit.
5 They didn't go to the match because the tickets were too expensive.
If ……………………………………… to the match.

B2 Exam Practice

C For questions 1–12, read the text below and think of the word which best fits each gap. Use only one word in each gap.

'Isn't it (**1**) ……………… you left?' I said impatiently to my parents, (**2**) ……………… were supposed to be going away for the weekend. 'There might be lots of traffic on the motorway.' As they finally got into the car, my mum said to me, 'I don't mind if you invite a few friends round while we're away, but I'd (**3**) ……………… you didn't have a party.' As soon as the car was out of sight, I sent a text message to my friend, Craig. 'Party at my house on Saturday night,' it said. 'Invite everyone (**4**) ……………… know.' I hadn't realized that he knew so many people! My friend Jo, (**5**) ……………… brother was a DJ, provided the music and I provided the drinks and the food (**6**) ……………… my mum had thoughtfully left for me. By ten o'clock the house was full of people dancing, talking and having a good time. At midnight (**7**) ……………… the phone rang, my friend Gobbo answered it. It was my mum. 'Can you tell me (**8**) ……………… someone called Gobbo answered the phone?' she asked. 'Well, you did say I could invite some friends round,' I replied. Gobbo was apologetic. 'If I'd known it was your mum, I wouldn't (**9**) ……………… answered it,' he said. I decided then that it was time everyone (**10**) ……………… home. Then I started tidying up and I noticed the stain on the sofa. Just my luck – someone had spilt orange juice all over it! (**11**) ……………… if it wouldn't come off? Now I was going to be in big trouble. If (**12**) ……………… I hadn't had a party!

Vocabulary 2
Entertainment

A What do we associate these words with? Music, cinema/TV or books/newspapers?

> audience • author • band • best-seller • chapter
> character • composer • concert • fiction • forecast
> hit • novel • opera • orchestra • page • plot • screen
> series • singer • stage

B Complete the sentences with words from Exercise A.

1 That song was a(n) .... last summer.
2 I got a headache in the cinema from sitting too near the ....
3 That band gives a great performance on ....
4 That book you lent me was really boring! I couldn't even finish the first ....
5 Have you seen The Kaiser Chiefs in .... ?
6 The .... was so complicated that I couldn't understand what was going on!

Word partners

C Use words from Exercise A to make compound nouns and then match them with their meanings.

1 main ....
2 lead ....
3 science ....
4 soap ....
5 front ....
6 live ....

a a fictional TV series about everyday lives
b the most important person in a story
c the first page of a newspaper
d films or books about imaginary future events
e people who watch a performance as it takes place
f usually the most famous person in a band

Easily confused words

D What's the difference between:

1 a **professional** and an **amateur**?
2 a **play** and a **game**?
3 a **supporter** and a **fan**?
4 a **viewer** and a **spectator**?
5 a **stage** and a **studio**?
6 a **microphone** and a **speaker**?
7 a **DVD player** and a **DVD recorder**?
8 an **opponent** and a **teammate**?

B2 Exam Practice

E For questions 1–10, read the text below and decide which answer (A, B, C or D) best fits each gap.

Rock School

Calling all girls! Have you ever dreamt of being the (1) .... singer in a rock band? The Rock School was set up by Chrissie Pane, guitarist and songwriter, to help girls become rock musicians. 'Many girls are (2) .... music when they're young, but very few actually make it in the music industry,' says Chrissie. 'At Rock School we show girls that they don't have to just (3) .... ballet in their spare time. They can (4) .... the drums, the electric guitar or another musical instrument. We show them that it's OK to (5) .... up the volume and make lots of noise!' The girls who attend Rock School are divided into groups and work with the other members to think of a name for their group and write a song together. They then take part in a(n) (6) .... at the end of the course when they perform their song on (7) .... The (8) .... audience is made up of friends and family, but as ex-Rock School student Amy Watts says, 'It's still quite a scary experience.' However, she believes that without Rock School, she wouldn't have become a(n) (9) .... musician or written an album which is already a big (10) ....
'Although I was talented, I didn't have the confidence needed to succeed,' she says. 'Rock School taught me to believe in myself.'

	A	B	C	D
1	main	lead	big	great
2	in	into	up	down
3	do	play	go	make
4	take up	put off	put on	take down
5	put	turn	make	go
6	play	opera	game	concert
7	screen	studio	stage	floor
8	real	present	living	live
9	front	amateur	main	professional
10	plot	hit	winner	best-seller

8

Writing: essay

B2 Exam Practice
You might be asked to write an essay giving your opinion about something. You can present both sides of an argument, illustrated with examples and suggestions.

Steps to success
- Present arguments FOR and AGAINST in separate paragraphs.
- Use a NEUTRAL style (neither very formal nor informal).
- Use LINKING WORDS to join your ideas together.

A Do you agree with this statement?

It's much better to take part in a sport than to be a spectator.

B Read these comments and write A (if they agree with the statement) or D (if they disagree).

Sabina, 16, Argentina 
'Some people just aren't into doing physical exercise and there's nothing wrong with that.'

Jean Paul, 15, France 
'Playing in a team teaches you how to get on with other people.'

Anna, 15, Ireland 
'Physical activity is a great way to get rid of tension.'

Julie, 14, USA 
'I love watching tennis, but I hate playing it!'

C Read an essay in response to the statement in Exercise A and fill in the gaps with the words and phrases in the box.

also • because • however • on the other hand
so • what's more

Sport is something which most people enjoy. Some like to participate in sports themselves while others prefer just to watch. In my opinion, both activities can be fun for different reasons.

On the one hand, actually taking part in a sport helps keep you fit and healthy. It gives you the opportunity to socialize with other people, especially if you play in a team. It's (1) .... a great way to relax after work or school. (2) ...., competing with other people is both exciting and challenging.

(3) ...., sport can be enjoyable even when you don't take part in it. Watching your favourite team play, either live or on TV, is great entertainment. The only drawback is that being a spectator doesn't involve physical activity (4) .... it doesn't keep you fit!

To sum up, watching sport can be a very enjoyable pursuit, especially when you support one of the teams or players. Taking part in a sport is, (5) ...., more beneficial (6) .... it is both good fun and good for the health!

D Which of the words and phrases from Exercise C are used to:

1 add further points?

....

....

2 introduce an opposite point of view/idea?

....

....

3 explain the effect/result of something?

....

4 explain the reason for something?

....

E Look at this example of how the *-ing* form can be used as a noun:

Watching sport can be a very enjoyable pursuit.

Rewrite these sentences using the *-ing* form of the underlined verbs and making any other changes necessary.

1 It's great entertainment <u>to watch</u> your favourite team play.

....

2 It helps keep you fit and healthy <u>to do</u> a sport.

....

....

3 It's both exciting and challenging <u>to compete</u> with other people.

....

....

4 It's more beneficial <u>to take part</u> in a sport.

....

....

F Now look at this question. Do you agree with the statement? Why/Why not?

Your class has had a discussion about sport. Your English teacher has now asked you to write an essay giving your opinion on the following statement:

Students should be allowed to choose whether to take part in sports at school or not.

3-minute plan!

G Complete the table below with two or three ideas of your own in note form. Then try to think of some ideas for the opposing point of view.

Agree	Disagree
1	1 ....
2	2 ....
3	3 ....

H Now write your essay using your plan for the two main paragraphs of your essay. Don't forget to write an introduction and a conclusion. Use the model and some of the Language chunks to help you. Write between 120 and 180 words.

Language chunks

Introducing arguments
On the one hand, …
On the other hand, …

Giving reasons
… because …
… due to (+ noun) …
… because of (+ noun) …
The reason why … is that …

Describing results/effects
… so …
Consequently, …
As a result, …

Review 4

A Read the text and choose the best answer, A, B, C or D.

A dedicated follower of fashion

Fashion is an industry that generates billions, and has an enormous (1) .... base. Most people want to (2) .... with the times, and stay fashionable. This applies to all clothes, from everyday clothing to sports (3) .... Being trendy or fashionable plays a big role in being able to (4) .... in. People rarely want to appear too different. As a consequence, there is a general tendency to wear outfits that don't actually (5) .... us, just because they are similar to what everybody else is wearing. Yet, a quick look around the shops is (6) .... to realize that the (7) .... of styles on offer is enormous. There are clothes for every shape and (8) .... , so individuality should not be frightening.

Many people (9) .... want to look good believe that you need to have money to (10) .... in order to be fashionable. However, a good 'look' can always be achieved by simply recycling old clothes. Fashion never really changes, it goes round in circles. So if your parents were into fashion in their (11) .... , they might have some cool clothes that would be trendy today. Alternatively, if those clothes were thrown out years ago, when you do shop try to (12) .... clothes that will last.

1	A supporter	B fan	C follower	D opponent	7	A group	B range	C stage	D variation
2	A go on	B get in	C keep on	D keep up	8	A quantity	B size	C number	D amount
3	A gear	B range	C identity	D clothes	9	A which	B whose	C who	D whom
4	A sit	B be	C put	D fit	10	A throw	B burn	C use	D give
5	A match	B suit	C fit	D go with	11	A phase	B adolescence	C times	D teen
6	A too much	B enough	C very much	D so much	12	A identify	B intend	C benefit	D match

B Complete the text with ONE word that best fits each gap. Write your answers in CAPITAL LETTERS.

Exercise with a difference

Capoeira doesn't (1) .... everybody, because it isn't your average sport. But, if you want to take (2) .... a hobby (3) .... keeps you fit, and you are (4) .... world music and dancing, then it (5) .... be just the thing for you.

Capoeira is a combination of Brazilian and African martial arts, but it is performed like a dance to music. Rather (6) .... injure your opponent, you aim to demonstrate skill. Capoeiristas form a circle around two opponents playing a 'game'. The people (7) .... form the circle clap or play the 'berimbau', a Brazilian string instrument. Anyone can clap, but if you are new to Capoeira, entering a 'game' (8) .... only recommended once you have learnt a few moves.

As in karate, (9) .... you have progressed to a different level, you are awarded a different coloured belt. The belt is presented (10) .... a Capoeira master at a 'batizado' or 'baptism', (11) .... many different Capoeira troupes meet. These ceremonies are a fantastic opportunity to see many different Capoeira styles.

It may take a lifetime to become a Capoeira master. If you are in your teens and thinking of starting Capoeira, you (12) .... take time to progress, but it doesn't matter. Enjoy what you can teach your body to do.

C Complete the text with the correct form of the words in capitals. Write your answers in CAPITAL LETTERS.

Is *beauty* really in the eye of the beholder?

Without (1) .... , in past and present cultures and civilisations, a human ideal has existed which is considered more (2) .... than others. The common Greek adjective for (3) .... was 'oreos'. It is derived from the word 'hour', (4) .... that beauty is looking the way you should at the right moment in time – neither older nor younger.
Natural beauty is generally (5) .... in both men and women, but truly beautiful people should (6) .... a balance of both inner and outer beauty.
If one were to compare supposedly perfect (7) .... characteristics in different cultures, it would reveal an interesting fact – that beauty is universal. This is because a strong indicator of (8) .... beauty is 'averageness'. If many images of faces are superimposed one on top of the other, the average face created by combining all the other faces, is better-looking!
Art is a (9) .... guide for beauty. For centuries, both artists and (10) .... have been creating wonderful portraits and beautiful bodies to capture the (11) .... Although the shapes of the bodies change, the faces stay the same.
In the highly (12) .... world of the supermodel, unusual faces will not get a job, but an exquisite face with totally average features will.

EXCEPT
ATTRACT
BEAUTY
MEAN
APPRECIATE
EXHIBITION
FACE
PHYSICS
VALUE
SCULPT
IMAGINE
COMPETE

D Rewrite the sentences using the words in capitals. Use between two and five words, including the word given. Write only the missing words in CAPITAL LETTERS.

1 Wearing make-up makes me look older.
 IF
 I look .... make-up.

2 My advice is to bleach your hair and wear dark sunglasses.
 WERE
 If .... bleach my hair and wear dark sunglasses.

3 A big production company is making a film based on Sarah Dean's best-seller.
 MADE
 Sarah Dean is .... into a film by a big production company.

4 Someone painted my portrait while I was in Paris.
 GOT
 I .... while I was in Paris.

5 A live audience watched the show and it was a great success.
 WHICH
 The show, ... live audience, was a great success.

6 I ought to get a new rucksack – this one is falling apart.
 BOUGHT
 It's .... rucksack – this one is falling apart.

7 I don't like you bothering me with unimportant issues when I'm working.
 BOTHER
 I wish .... with unimportant issues when I'm working.

8 Because of the bad weather, the game was cancelled.
 BEEN
 If the weather .... wouldn't have been cancelled.

9 Words

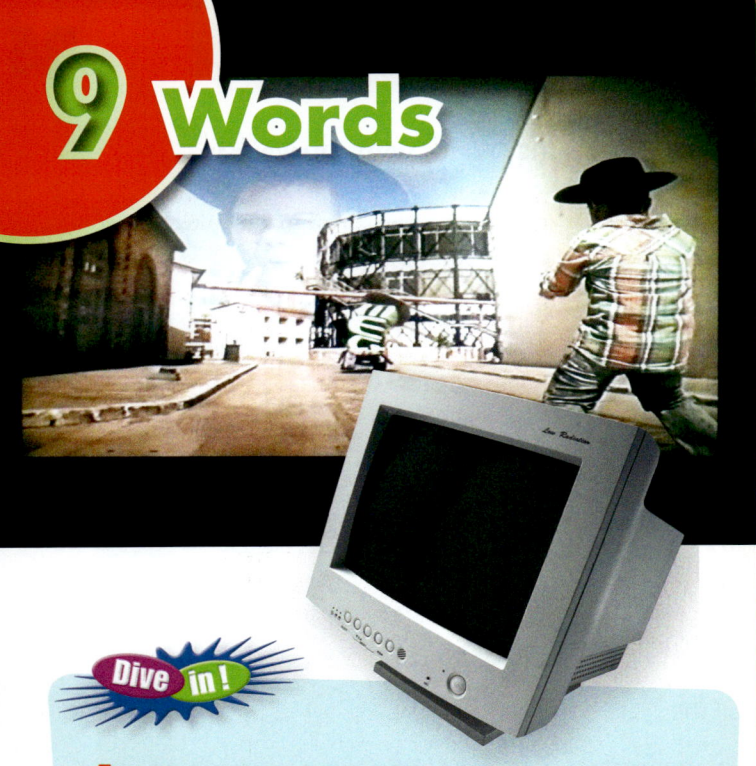

A Discuss these questions with a partner.

Which commercials on television do you think are the most effective?

Have you ever bought anything after seeing it advertised? What was it? Were you happy with it?

Have you ever recommended a product (eg a mobile phone, an MP3 player, a CD) or a service (eg an email provider, a website) to a friend?

Have any of your friends ever bought anything because you recommended it?

Do you forward things that you receive by email (eg photographs, jokes, videos)? What sort of things do you forward?

Reading 1

B2 Exam Practice

Steps to success
- Read through the text quickly and decide what the main point of it is.
- Remember to use key words in the question stem to help you find where the answer is in the text.

B Quickly read the text and choose which of the following best describes what it is about.

1 Different types of TV commercials
2 The spreading of information about products and services
3 The use of computers and the internet in advertising

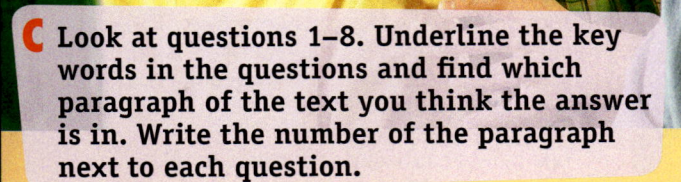

C Look at questions 1–8. Underline the key words in the questions and find which paragraph of the text you think the answer is in. Write the number of the paragraph next to each question.

D For questions 1–8 choose the answer (A, B, C or D) which you think fits best according to the text.

1 The writer says that celebrity endorsements of products and services
A make us admire the celebrity.
B are only used by advertisers when something is very good.
C suggest that satisfied customers include famous people.
D fail to convince anyone that something is worth buying.

2 Who are we most likely to believe about a product or service?
A a friend   B an expert   C a company   D the media

3 The writer uses the phrase 'weigh up what you've heard' (paragraph 3) to show that we
A often act foolishly.
B decide according to the information we have gathered.
C don't believe people who have mistakenly bought something.
D have difficulty remembering what people have told us.

4 What do we sometimes do if we really want to buy something?
A persuade critics to buy it
B believe the opinions of a critic
C ignore the criticisms of another person
D doubt our own beliefs

5 The writer describes word-of-mouth advertising as 'limited' (paragraph 5) because we
A are never satisfied with what we buy.
B don't often recommend things to people we meet.
C tell the wrong people about things we have bought.
D cannot persuade people to buy something.

110

Word-of-mouth advertising

Manufacturers have always told us that their products are good. But they soon realized that we doubted them, so adverts and TV commercials began to feature well-known faces, like David Beckham, telling us that they have bought the product or used the service and are happy with it. These celebrity endorsements work because we trust what we're being told. Because we believe that something is so good that successful people – people we admire – use it. But there's something more convincing than the best advertising campaigns. Something that doesn't cost a penny.

Word-of-mouth advertising is probably the oldest form of advertising. No matter how much a company advertises something, whether it's through sponsorship, on TV or in the press, if a friend tells you they're happy with it, you'll trust their judgement. No matter what the so-called experts tell us, we tend to believe people we know.

Equally, though, if someone told you that they were dissatisfied with what they'd bought, you would be influenced on some level. What usually happens is that you balance the information you've gathered with the credibility of the person who told you. You store this information in your memory, and then, if you really want to buy something, you weigh up what you've heard. If you've heard five people telling you they made a mistake buying something, and you haven't spoken to a single satisfied customer, you'd only buy the product if you were brave, desperate or foolish.

But if the only negative comment you've heard was from one person, and all the other factors (such as advertising, good things you've heard, and your own needs and desires) make you want to buy it, you might start to doubt that one person. If you really want the item, you'll blank out the opinion of the person who criticized it. You may even ridicule them or dismiss them as a crank.

When it works well, word-of-mouth advertising can be very effective, but limited. How many people do you meet? And how many of those people do you discuss the merits of a product or service with? Look at it another way: when was the last time you were satisfied with something you paid money for? How many people did you tell, and how many of those people went out and bought it? For word-of-mouth advertising to work, at least one person must buy it based on what you said. If one person does buy it because of you, and they persuade another person, it starts a chain. If the chain stays unbroken, everyone in the world will eventually own that one thing. But the key word is eventually. It will take a very long time!

At least, that was true until the internet. Through emails and messaging services, weblogs and file-sharing, we now 'meet' more people than we used to, and we hear a lot more opinions, which we often pass on. By forwarding an email to everyone in our address book, we can reach many more people. If that email contains a reference to a product or service, and if the receivers forward it to everyone in their address book, it's easy to see how quickly the word can spread.

Companies are now using this method to advertise. It's called viral marketing (because it spreads like a virus, each person infecting many more). One of the first examples was Hotmail. By adding the message 'Get your private, free email at http://www.hotmail.com', to every email its subscribers sent, the company gained 12 million members in one and a half years at a cost of just four cents per member. So when the next amazing product comes out, and you forward a funny video about it to everyone in your address book, it might not be long before the whole world has bought it – on your recommendation!

Work it out!

6 Why is product information spread more quickly because of the internet?
A because we always forward emails
B because we are in contact with more people
C because we can't control the spread
D because we tell people to pass it on

7 How did Hotmail increase its membership?
A by advertising on emails
B by sending emails
C by reducing its prices
D by changing its web address

8 Overall, the writer feels that word-of-mouth advertising
A makes us buy things we don't need.
B doesn't work as well as it used to.
C is an unfair method.
D has always been effective.

E Choose the correct meaning for these words from the text.

1 manufacturers (1)
a they make items   b they buy items

2 convincing (1)
a successful   b believable

3 judgement (2)
a opinions   b choices

4 influenced (3)
a satisfied   b made to think or act differently

5 blank out (4)
a refuse to listen   b take into consideration

6 crank (4)
a expert   b eccentric

Quick chat

Do you find TV commercials annoying? What would make you decide to buy (or not to buy) something?

Grammar 1

✓ Check reported speech

See pages 147 and 148 for information about reported speech.

Circle a or b to show what the person said.

1 She said she was really tired.
   a 'I was really tired.'   b 'I'm really tired.'
2 She said she hadn't slept the night before.
   a 'I didn't sleep last night.'   b 'I haven't slept the night before.'
3 She said she didn't like it there.
   a 'I didn't like it here.'   b 'I don't like it here.'
4 She said she was going to bed.
   a 'I was going to bed.'   b 'I'm going to bed.'
5 She said she couldn't understand.
   a 'I can't understand.'   b 'I couldn't understand.'

A Rewrite the sentences in reported speech.

1 'We'll meet you at the café.'
   They said ....

2 'I'm not doing anything at the moment.'
   Tony said ....

3 'I've been working all day!'
   Bill said ....

4 'I saw a really stupid ad on TV.'
   Barbara said ....

5 'We aren't going to see the new Bond film.'
   Ernst said ....

6 'I've already read that book.'
   Angela said ....

B Read the email which your friend sent you and then do the task.

Sorry, but I'm not going to come to the media class tonight. I've been working all day and I'm not in the mood for any more lessons! I was studying French all morning and I had to write two compositions this afternoon! I'm tired and I want to go to bed early because I have a test tomorrow. Have fun!

Nigel

A few days later, another friend asked you about Nigel. What did you say?

Nigel sent me an email. He said he wasn't going to go to the media class that night.
He said ....

C Rewrite the sentences in reported speech using the reporting verbs in the box.

agreed • claimed • denied • refused • suggested

1 'Why don't we all subscribe to Bebo?'
   Harry ....
2 'Yes, I'll help you write your essay on advertising.'
   Joanna ....
3 'I've read every single newspaper this week!'
   Gordy ....
4 'I didn't say she was stupid!'
   Adam ....
5 'I'm not answering that question.'
   The politician ....

The rat said it wasn't a race.

I'VE ALREADY READ THAT BOOK!

TEACH YOUR BABY TO READ

IT'S NOT A RACE

Vocabulary 1
Radio and television

A Circle the correct word.
1 The DJ interrupted the programme for an important news **bulletin** / **forecast**.
2 This **description** / **commentary** is coming to you live from the stadium, where the match has just started.
3 This was on last week! Why do they show so many **repeats** / **reviews**?
4 Don't miss tonight's exciting **episode** / **version** of this popular programme.
5 The picture's clearer on my new high definition TV **channel** / **set**.
6 My favourite programme is a great murder **mystery** / **sitcom** – it's really scary!

B Explain the difference between:
1 a **talk show** and a **reality show**
2 an **episode** and a **series**
3 a **TV channel** and a **satellite channel**
4 the **news** and a **newsflash**
5 a **repeat** and a **remake**
6 a **newsreader** and a **DJ**

Key phrasal verbs

C Match the phrasal verbs with their meanings.
1 tune in   a turn pages very quickly
2 turn over   b change channels on the television
3 flick through   c find a radio station or TV channel
4 come out   d stop watching television
5 turn off   e receive a radio signal
6 pick up   f be published

D Complete the sentences with phrasal verbs from Exercise C in the correct form.
1 Why don't you .... the TV and do something different for a change?
2 This radio's great. I can .... all the stations really clearly.
3 I was just .... the newspaper when I saw your picture!
4 Can I .... it .... ? There's a documentary on Channel Four which I'd rather watch.
5 Make sure you .... at nine tonight for all the latest news.
6 It's a weekly news magazine and it .... on a Friday.

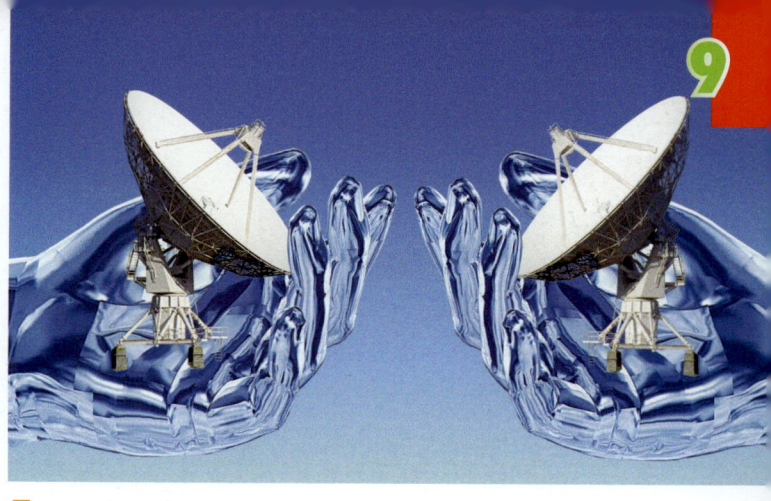

E Complete the text with the words and phrases in the box.

> aerial • broadcast • pick up • signal
> stations • studio • turn on

What is pirate radio?

The government controls which radio (1) .... are allowed to (2) .... programmes. At the moment, most radio stations operate on the FM band and sometimes, when you (3) .... your radio, you might be able to (4) .... a pirate station.

Pirates operate without a license. Sometimes, they block out other stations and they could interfere with emergency services. In order to avoid getting caught, pirates don't usually have a(n) (5) .... They often transmit from open places using recorded material, with car batteries to power their equipment. The antenna or (6) .... for sending the (7) .... can be as simple as a long piece of wire tied between two trees.

Quick chat
What do you watch on TV?
What do you listen to on the radio?

Listening

B2 Exam Practice
Steps to success
- Look for key words in the notes and listen for them on the recording — the missing information is usually just before or just after the key words.
- If the recording is an interview, pay attention to what the interviewer says, as this might also contain key words.

A Look at the gapped sentences below and pay attention to the key words in bold. What kind of words can go in the gaps?
1 The **iPod Shuffle** can **hold** .... **songs**.
2 For **watching videos**, the size of the .... is important.
3 The **life of a battery** can range between six and .... hours.

B 🎧 Now listen to a short extract from an interview. Listen carefully for the key words to sentence 1 in Exercise A. When your teacher stops the recording, fill in the gap. Do the other gaps in the same way.

C Look at the gapped sentences in Exercise D. Look at the key words and try to guess what kind of word or phrase is missing from each gap.

D 🎧 Now listen to an interview about a kind of broadcasting called podcasting. For questions 1–10, complete the sentences. You will need to write a word or short phrase in each gap.
1 The word 'podcast' comes from the words 'iPod' and ....
2 You can listen to podcasts on an iPod, an MP3 player or a(n) ....
3 The first podcasts appeared in ....
4 Bill says that podcasts were first made by people who .... the radio.
5 Early podcasters made shows at home and chose their own ....
6 One of the limitations of radio is that it's easy to ....
7 The computer saves the podcast so you can .... when it's convenient for you.
8 An individual podcast is sometimes called a(n) ....
9 Bill gets excited about the way podcasts can be used in ....
10 Students who use podcasts can study subjects that are not available ....

Speaking

B2 Exam Practice
Steps to success
- Remember that you often have to talk hypothetically — say *would* rather than *will*.
- You can agree or disagree with the other candidate but make sure you explain your reasons clearly.

B2 Exam Practice
Steps to success
- It is often better to talk about your own experiences (rather than what you think the examiner wants to know). If it's appropriate, mention examples from your own life or about people you know.
- Questions that ask you about your own country often come up. Be prepared to talk about what happens where you live.

A 🎧 Work in small groups. Listen to some short comments on the subject of the media. Take turns responding to the comments with one of the sentences below.

That would be great!
I don't think that would be such a good idea.
That would be OK, I suppose.
That sounds good/bad/interesting, etc.
I (don't) like the sound of that.

B What do you think about the following types of TV programme? Discuss them in pairs. Use some of the words and phrases to help you.

soap operas • mysteries • chat shows • comedy shows • sports coverage • quiz shows • romances • documentaries • music programmes • horror films

too much talking • not enough action • too violent • boring • gripping • unwatchable • only for fans • educational • informative • thrilling • exciting • addictive • fun

D Take turns answering the questions below. When your partner answers first, listen to the answer and add your own opinion.
1. What do you watch most on TV?
2. Would you like to work in the media?
3. What is the biggest complaint people have about TV in your country?
4. Some people say that television is very harmful. Do you agree?

Say it right!

E Read these words aloud and underline the stressed syllable in each. In which three pairs are the same syllables stressed?
1. advertise, advertisement
2. recommend, recommendation
3. effect, effective
4. refer, reference
5. satisfied, satisfaction
6. difficult, difficulty
7. apology, apologize
8. comedy, comedian

F 🎧 Now listen to see if you were right.

C Now do this task with your partner.

A popular TV station is planning to change some of its programmes so that they appeal more to people your age. The pictures show different types of programmes that they have. Talk about how popular these programmes would be with young people. Then decide which two would attract the most young viewers.

How popular would these programmes be with young people?
Which two would attract the most young viewers?

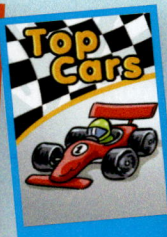

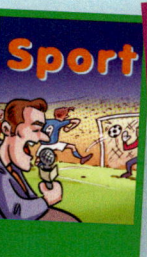

Homes & Gardens • Romance • Murder Mystery • Top Cars • Quiz Show • Music • Sport • Documentary

9

Dive in!

A What do you know about the production of books?
Who invented paper?
Who invented the printing press?

Reading 2

B Match the underlined words with their meanings.

1 an <u>annual</u> event
2 a <u>rare</u> species
3 to be <u>issued</u> with a badge
4 to <u>maintain</u> an old car
5 to <u>house</u> an exhibition
6 an ancient <u>artefact</u>
7 a <u>reproduction</u> of an old painting
8 the artist's <u>studio</u>

a provide a place for
b keep in good condition
c not common
d place of work
e given
f a copy
g yearly
h object made by people

B2 Exam Practice

Steps to success

- Before the exam, time yourself to see how long you need to spend on the reading exercises. Then, in the exam, keep an eye on your watch and make sure you leave yourself enough time to do the reading exercises. Remember you won't be given extra time at the end to transfer your answers.

C You are thinking about visiting a museum. Use the information in the brochure opposite to answer the questions that follow.

1 According to the brochure, who was the first person to print written material in English?
a Juan Pablos
b William Caxton
c AK Forte
d JR Ewling

2 Which of the following benefits will members of the museum enjoy?
a price reductions at the Gift Shop
b free access to the museum for one guest
c free participation in one workshop per year
d a newsletter once a year

3 Who can receive a certificate from the museum?
a patrons   b sponsors   c pupils   d teachers

4 The brochure says that guided tours are particularly appropriate for
a scholars.
b artists.
c tourists.
d students.

5 Your friend wants to see the stone lithopress. What will she have to do?
a phone a day earlier
b join a group
c enrol on a course
d pay an extra fee

6 The only printed material your sister enjoys is comics. Which of the following might she like?
a the JR Ewling Studio
b the Book Fair
c the Summer Studio
d the Living Plants exhibition

7 A brother and a sister want to take part in a Summer Studio course. What will the cost be for both of them?
a $240   b $200   c $180   d $120

8 Where can visitors see how the pages of a book are stitched together?
a on a guided tour of the collection
b at the COVER exhibition
c at the Book Fair
d at the JR Ewling Studio

9 You know a couple who have enrolled their daughter on a Summer Studio course. What must the parents do?
a become members of the museum
b pay the fee seven days in advance
c pick their daughter up each day
d visit the museum 72 hours earlier

10 According to the brochure, what is the earliest known example of printing?
a a Japanese text
b a Spanish dictionary
c a Mesopotamian artefact
d a book by William Caxton

The Museum of the Printed Word

About the museum

The Museum of the Printed Word displays a collection of artefacts from the earliest writing to the 21st century. The first evidence of printing is the Mesopotamian clay tablets from around 3000 BC. Visitors can also see an eighth century Japanese text which may be the earliest example of printing words on paper, and a page by William Caxton, the first printer in English, as well as a Spanish dictionary printed by Juan Pablos.

Guided Tours

Scholars and artists demonstrate the printing technique on an accurate reproduction of an old-fashioned press. Other presses from different periods will also be demonstrated. Our tours are relevant to students doing a range of subjects, from science and technology to English and history.

Working Studios

These are operated and maintained by artists using studios at the museum for their creative work.

The AK Forte Studio is one of the few in the country using a stone lithopress. Next door is the JR Ewling Studio where visitors can see the various stages of bookbinding from cutting paper, stitching, applying leather and gold leaf lettering.

Note: To visit the studios and meet the artists, appointments must be made at least one day in advance.

Summer Studio

Students can experience every stage of the process of bookmaking, beginning with the manufacture of the paper itself. Courses last four mornings, from Monday to Thursday.

We also offer classes in the afternoons appropriate for teachers (both primary and secondary) and parents who want to learn activities they can do with children. Certificates of Completion will be issued to any teacher who needs proof of professional development.

Summer Studio Fees

- $120 for adults, $100 for children
- Parents enrolling more than one child will receive a discount of 10%.
- Supplies fee (for afternoon classes only) — $20
- Enrolments can be cancelled only if there is 72 hours' notice.
- Please note that children must be accompanied to and from the museum each day by an adult. A safety form must also be signed for each child enrolled on a course.

Current Exhibitions

COVER — See the 50 most impressive book cover designs in a range of categories.

Joe Davies — Wonderful photographs of old street signs

Living Plants — Original prints of local plant species by Mark Bulb

Book Fair

The sixth annual Book Fair is your chance to buy rare and out-of-print books and comics from over 20 dealers. At 2.00pm on the opening day visitors will be treated to a special guest lecture by Bill Mathers, who will discuss his recent book on some of the unusual stories behind historic city street names.

Upcoming Events

From September 25 the museum will be housing an exhibition of works by artist Ornella Tutti whose pictures combine printing and painting techniques to create unique works of art. The exhibition is partly sponsored by Helen Martin.

Membership

Members benefit from our free monthly newsletter, invitations to all events, half-price admission to the museum for guests, reduced enrolment fees for workshops and a discount on purchases at the Museum Gift Shop.

Membership costs $500 for patrons, $250 for sponsors, $100 for friends, $35 for individuals and $20 for senior citizens and students.

---

11 Who will give a talk at the museum about unusual stories connected with the city?
- **a** Bill Mathers
- **b** Ornella Tutti
- **c** Mark Bulb
- **d** Helen Martin

12 How long has the museum been holding the Book Fair?
- **a** two years
- **b** six years
- **c** 14 years
- **d** 20 years

Quick chat

Do you think reading books is becoming more or less popular? Why?
Could there be a time in the future when people will stop publishing traditional paper books?
Will this be a good thing or a bad thing?

Grammar 2

✓ Check reported questions

See page 148 for information about reported questions.

Which of the following are correct?
1 He asked me **why haven't you done** / **why hadn't I done** / **why I hadn't done** my homework.
2 She asked me **was I going to** / **if I was going to** / **am I going to** watch the documentary.
3 Benny wanted to know **what time it was** / **what is the time** / **what time is it**.

A Look at the picture and what Pete and Alison said. Report the conversation.

1 'What's wrong?'
  Pete asked Alison ....
2 'Why are you always watching television?'
  Alison asked him ....
3 'This is great! Have you seen it?'
  Pete said ....
4 'Didn't we see it at the cinema?'
  Alison asked if ....
5 'Well, what do *you* want to watch?'
  Pete asked her ....
6 'There's a love story on Channel Four!'
  Alison told Pete ....

B Correct the mistakes in the reported questions (there is more than one mistake in some of them).

1 'Why didn't you go to school yesterday?'
  He asked me why hadn't I been to school yesterday.
2 'How did you become so famous?'
  The reporter asked the celebrity how did she become so famous.
3 'Is there anything I can do to help you?'
  Fiona asked me was there anything she can do to help me.
4 'Don't be so silly.'
  Peter said to her to not be so silly.

B2 Exam Practice
Steps to success
- Don't forget that in reported speech you usually have to make more than one change to the first sentence.
- Remember that pronouns may need to change as well, eg *I, my, mine, his, your(s), him, he*.

C Complete the second sentence so that it has a similar meaning to the first sentence, using the word given. Do not change the word given. You must use between two and five words including the word given.

1 'I am not looking forward to this test,' John said. **was**
  John said that .... to the test.
2 'Will you help me with the dishes?' Mum said. **would**
  Mum asked .... her with the dishes.
3 'I haven't been working hard enough,' Maggie admitted. **been**
  Maggie admitted that she .... enough.
4 Donna said she wouldn't help me. **refused**
  Donna .... me.
5 'I saw her yesterday, but I haven't seen her since then,' Molly said. **the**
  Molly said that she .... before, but not since then.
6 'I'll call you tomorrow,' Ann promised. **me**
  Ann promised that she .... day.
7 'What have you been doing all day?' he asked. **I**
  He asked .... doing all day.
8 'Can you get satellite channels on your television?' Ellen asked. **whether**
  Ellen wanted to know .... satellite channels on my television.

Vocabulary 2

Newspapers

A Match the words with their meanings.

1 reporter/journalist
2 editor
3 headline
4 captions
5 gossip column
6 horoscope

a part of a newspaper where you read about your sign of the Zodiac
b short pieces of writing that go with pictures
c part of a newspaper where you read about celebrities
d person who gathers and writes the news
e the first part of a news article we see
f person who decides what goes in a newspaper

B Fill in the gaps using words from Exercise A.

1 I read my .... every day, but I don't really believe what they say.
2 If the .... says no, then the article won't appear in the paper.
3 To be a good .... , you have to be able to ask the right questions.
4 Sometimes I look at the photographs and read the .... to decide whether I want to read the article.
5 I often read the .... to find out what my favourite pop stars have been doing!
6 I haven't read the paper today – I just looked at the ....

Word formation

C Complete the table with the correct forms.

Noun (thing)	Noun (person)	Adjective	Verb
edition editorial		editorial	
presentation		–	
	–	(un)exciting excited	
photograph photography			
view		–	
product production			
report			
broadcast broadcasting		–	

Advertising

D Where might you find these?

1 slogan – in an email or in an advertisement?
2 logo – on the product itself or on a wall?
3 jingle – in a newspaper or on the radio?
4 poster – on the product itself or on a wall?
5 commercial – on television or in a newspaper?
6 classified ads – in a newspaper or on the radio?

Quick chat
Give examples of each of the items in Exercise D and discuss the more memorable ones you have seen or heard. What makes an advertisement successful?

Jobs in the media

B2 Exam Practice

E For questions 1–10, read the text below. Use the word given in capitals at the end of the lines to form a word that fits in the gap in the same line. Write your answers in CAPITAL LETTERS.

There are a great many jobs in the media, especially if you include positions in advertising. A lot of people start their careers with newspapers, often as a junior (1) .... , which is a good way to get started. I found it (2) .... though, and couldn't wait to move on. Being a (3) .... is more interesting because you get out of the office and meet lots of people. And the job of press (4) .... is a good one, especially if you manage to be in the right place at the right time.
The majority of people want to work in (5) .... though, particularly in television, because they think it's a glamorous job. They hope they will be able to get a position as a (6) .... , where they will be able to meet interesting (7) .... Or else they want to be a (8) .... , watched and loved by millions of (9) .... every night. But most people in television work behind the scenes as members of (10) .... teams and, although these jobs can be very interesting, very few of them will ever make you famous!

EDIT
EXCITE
REPORT

PHOTOGRAPH

BROADCAST

PRESENT
CELEBRATE
NEWS
VIEW
PRODUCE

Writing: review

> **B2 Exam Practice**
>
> You might be asked to write a review of a book, play, film, restaurant, exhibition, etc.
>
> **Steps to success**
> - Mention the TITLE or NAME of the book, play, film, programme or restaurant.
> - DON'T waste too many words describing.
> - You must give your own PERSONAL OPINION.
> - Break your review up into different PARAGRAPHS.
> - End with a RECOMMENDATION.
> - Use a VARIETY of good vocabulary and structures.

A Look at this task and read the model.

You recently saw this notice in an English-language magazine called *TV Now*!

> **Write a review**
>
> We are looking for reviews of documentaries that have been shown on television. If you have seen a documentary recently, send us your review, saying what the documentary was about and what you liked about it. Tell us whether you would recommend the documentary to others.
>
> The best reviews will be published in the magazine.

Write your **review**.

B Now label the paragraphs with the following descriptions.

1 what the reviewer liked about it
2 recommendation
3 the subject of the review
4 what the documentary was about

C Think about TV programmes, films or books that you liked and complete the sentences below with your own ideas. Use some of the following adjectives.

> amazing • strange • impressive • lively • fascinating
> thrilling • mysterious • incredible • shocking

1 I'm not usually a fan of .... However, I recently saw/read ....
2 The programme/film/book began/begins with ....
3 We learn/learnt that ....
4 The programme/film/book went on to ....
5 What I really liked about the programme/film/book was ....
6 In addition, ...
7 I would definitely recommend this programme/film/book to others because ....

Documentary about Kenyan elephants

I'm not usually a fan of nature programmes. However, I recently saw an amazing wildlife documentary.

The programme began with a mystery. Inside a cave in Kenya, they found some strange marks on the walls. One theory was that they had been made by prehistoric man. We learnt, however, that the marks had been made by elephants. The programme went on to explain that they needed salt in their diet, but couldn't find enough of it in plants, so they cut the salt out of the cave walls.

What I really liked about the programme was the filming, which was very impressive. They used special cameras to film the elephants at night. We could clearly see whole families, including baby elephants, walking into the cave. In addition, the narration was very lively and made the programme more interesting.

I would definitely recommend this documentary to others because it was very well made. I think a lot of people would find it as fascinating as I did.

D Read the task and put a tick or a cross next to the statements below.

You have seen this announcement in a magazine called *TVGuide*.

> **Tell us what you think!**
> Send us a review of any programme you have enjoyed over the last week. It could be a comedy, a documentary, a current affairs programme or a soap opera – anything, in fact. Just tell us what you thought of the programme and whether you would recommend that it should be repeated.

Write your **review**.

1 You can write about more than one programme. ☐
2 You can choose which programme to write about. ☐
3 You need to know what *TVGuide* magazine thought of the programme. ☐
4 You have to write about a recent programme. ☐
5 You should include your opinion about *TVGuide* magazine. ☐
6 You need to say whether you thought it was good or bad. ☐

E Think of a programme that you have seen and would like to review.

What was it about?
What did you think of it?

What could you say about some or all of the following in the programme?

story/plot • acting • costumes • narration
filming/animation • soundtrack • presentation
commentary • characters/people • interviews
script • dialogue

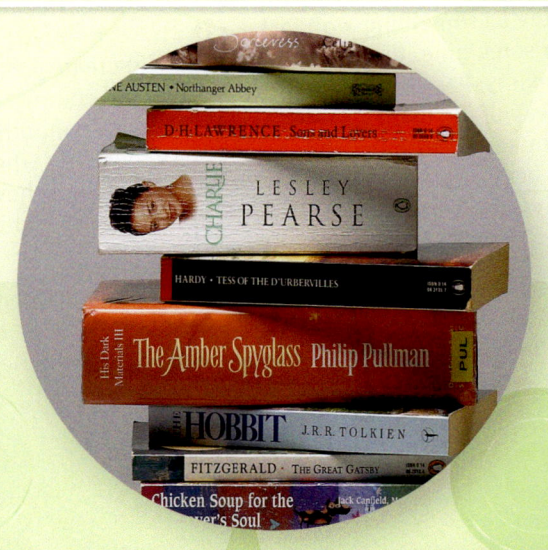

3-minute plan!

F Complete the paragraph plan for your review.

First paragraph: Introduce the subject
What are you going to review?
....

Paragraph 2:
What was it about?
....

Paragraph(s) 3, 4:
Which aspects of the programme are you going to write about?
What will you say about each one?
....
....
....

Final paragraph: Recommendation
Would you recommend that the programme be repeated? Why/Why not?
....

Language chunks

Introducing the subject
I recently saw/read/watched …

What it is about
The programme/film/book is about …
The film is set …
It begins …
In the beginning, …

What you liked about it
What I particularly liked about the … was …
I really liked …
The best thing about … was …

Making recommendations
I would definitely recommend … because …
I don't think I would recommend it …
I would strongly advise …

G Now write your review in 120–180 words. Use the model, your notes, your paragraph plan and the Language chunks to help you.

10 Different places

Dive in!

A What would be most difficult to get used to in a foreign country?
- the food
- the weather
- the language
- the television programmes
- being away from your family
- something else

B How could you prepare for a stay in a foreign country?

Reading 1

B2 Exam Practice

Steps to success
- Make sure the missing sentences fit logically into the gaps you choose to put them in.
- Remember, they might be **examples** of, **explanations** for or **responses** to what has come before.

C Match each sentence with one that follows it logically. There is one extra sentence that you don't need to use.

1 Don't expect to make friends immediately.
2 I didn't want to try the snails, but it would have been rude to refuse.
3 'Why don't we go out and explore?' I suggested.
4 I thought I had ordered a cup of tea, but the waiter brought me a coffee.
5 I decided to forget about being polite.

a To my surprise, they were delicious.
b I didn't want to complain, so I drank it anyway.
c The locals might feel suspicious of strangers.
d I didn't agree.
e I pushed my way to the front of the queue and nobody seemed to mind.
f Helen didn't seem to have heard me.

D Read this article about culture shock. Seven sentences have been removed from the article. Choose from the sentences A–H the one which fits each gap (1–7). There is one extra sentence which you do not need to use.

Culture shock

The worry and feelings people experience when they have to live and **survive** within a new culture, such as a foreign country, are known as culture shock. **(1)** .... They develop from the difficulties faced when people have to **adjust** to a new culture and don't know how to function within it.

Gemma Atkinson, who is British, lived in Italy for three years. 'Everything was exciting at first,' explains Gemma. 'I was thrilled by the **charm** of Italy, but as I settled into my new life, I began to feel overwhelmed and frustrated. Trying to find accommodation, get a new phone line in a **remote** area and get my work permit seemed impossible. **(2)** .... I couldn't understand the Italian way of doing things. There were times when I wanted to pack up everything and return to Britain. Eventually though, I got a handle on my new environment and felt at home.'

Psychologist Rowan Bates explains what Gemma describes as the distinct phases of culture shock. 'The **majority** of people who relocate to a new country, whether to study there or as a permanent move, go through the following phases. The first, known as the honeymoon phase, lasts for a few weeks and is characterized by seeing the new culture as something wonderful. **(3)** .... However, after some time, the new culture begins to create feelings of anxiety. People may start to miss their old country and the way of life there. **(4)** .... After about six months, most people enter the adjustment phase, which is when they become used to their new culture. They know how to behave appropriately and have accepted the new culture.'

But not all people react in the same way, as Rowan explains. 'There are three different forms of adjustment. Many people actually find it impossible to accept the new culture. **(5)** .... Other people integrate so completely

A This is known as the negotiation phase and it is when people start to feel annoyed with their new culture.

B Of course, once he returned to his homeland, everything was different.

C What was wrong? All I could say was 'English? Do you speak English?'

D Once there, develop new friendships both with locals and other foreigners.

E These feelings may include surprise, uncertainty and confusion.

F The food, lifestyle and architecture, for example, are admired and seem far more interesting than what one has left behind back home.

G They are miserable and only wish to return to their own culture, where they feel safe and secure.

H Doing the normal things the average person did seemed so incredibly difficult.

---

into their new environment that they lose their original identity. Finally, there are those people who successfully manage to combine the best parts of their new culture with their old culture. These people experience few problems and are the happiest of all.'

Canadian Simon Hart, who went to Greece for a year-long working holiday, says a sense of humour helped him enormously. 'I couldn't speak a word of Greek when I arrived, which led to some pretty funny misunderstandings. On my second day there, I bought what I thought was a bus ticket from an old man who had dozens of them stuck to a wooden pole. After **queuing** for a few minutes I got on the bus. At the next stop an inspector asked the passengers to show him their tickets. He **glanced** at mine and gave me a very hostile look. He was looking hot under the collar and I was getting anxious. **(6)** .... Another passenger offered to help by translating. She looked at my ticket and burst out laughing. So there I was with a **silent**, angry inspector and a woman in fits of laughter. When she finally brought herself under control, she explained to me that I'd bought a lottery ticket, not a bus ticket! I felt really foolish, but couldn't help laughing anyway!'

Rowan has this advice for people thinking of relocating to a new country. 'Before you travel, learn as much as you can about the new culture so that you are better prepared for what you will face. Obviously, learning the new language will help. **(7)** .... You can share your feelings with fellow expatriates who will provide a support network for you and are a very valuable resource because they've already been in your shoes. Keep an open mind about the new culture and enjoy the differences rather than see them as obstacles. And try to see the funny side in your experiences.'

Work it out!

E Use the words highlighted in the text to complete the sentences below.
1 My aunt lives in a small village in a(n) .... part of Norway.
2 I .... at my watch and realized that the boat was leaving in two minutes.
3 Joe has got so much .... that you can't help liking him.
4 No matter what time I go to the bank, I always end up .... for ages!
5 Everyone went .... when the managing director walked in.
6 Would you be able to .... alone in a foreign country?
7 Tina was able to .... to living on an island quicker than she expected.
8 The .... of my relatives live in Canada.

F What do you think these expressions mean?
1 got a handle on (paragraph 2)
2 hot under the collar (paragraph 5)
3 brought herself under control (paragraph 5)
4 been in your shoes (paragraph 6)
5 keep an open mind (paragraph 6)

G Write the adjectives for these countries, then check your answers in the text.
1 Britain ....   3 Greece ....
2 Italy ....   4 Canada ....

H Write the nationalities of people from these countries.
1 China ....   4 France ....
2 Sweden ....   5 Japan ....
3 the USA ....   6 Australia ....

Quick chat

Would you like to live abroad? Why/Why not? Where would you like to live?

Grammar 1

✓ Check modal verbs (2)

See pages 148 and 149 for information about modal verbs of probability.

Label the sentences 1–3 in order of probability (1 = most probable, 3 = least probable).

a This temple **might** be 4,000 years old. ....
b It **must** be cold in Norway at this time of year. ....
c The letter **should** take about a week to arrive. ....

Complete the sentences with the correct form of the verbs in brackets.

Jason **will** .... (move) into his new house by now.
The ancient Greeks **must** .... (be) very clever.
I **could** .... (study) Spanish, but I chose French instead.

A Circle the correct modal verb.

1 The doorbell rings and you know who it is at the door.
 'That **can / will** be Anna!'
2 You are worried about your friends who haven't returned from a trip to the mountains.
 'They **may / ought to** have had an accident.'
3 Your friend has said there's a possibility she'll meet you at the airport.
 'Jane **might / will** meet us at the airport.'
4 You are annoyed that no one told you the shops are closed today.
 'Someone **must / could** have told us that the shops were closed today!'
5 You see a hotel that is being built at the moment.
 'This **mustn't / can't** be the hotel where we're staying!'
6 You sent a parcel to your cousin in Australia six months ago.
 'He **could / should** have got the parcel by now.'

B Complete the second sentence so that it has a similar meaning to the first sentence, using the word given. Do not change the word given. You must use between two and five words including the word given.

1 It was probably hard to build the pyramids!
 been
 It .... hard to build the pyramids!
2 I bet moving to another country at the age of 13 wasn't easy.
 can't
 Moving to another country at the age of 13 .... easy.
3 I'm sure you've heard of Winston Churchill.
 will
 You .... Winston Churchill.
4 They aren't definitely getting married next year.
 may
 They .... married next year.
5 I'm sure he'll know the answer; he's brilliant at maths.
 bound
 He .... the answer; he's brilliant at maths.

Vocabulary 1

Buildings

A Label the pictures with these words.

block of flats • bridge • bungalow • cathedral • cave
cottage • hut • lighthouse • temple • tunnel

1 ....
2 ....
3 ....
4 ....
5 ....
6 ....
7 ....
8 ....
9 ....
10 ....

Quick chat

Where would you find the following structures?
Notre Dame Cathedral
The Channel Tunnel
The Golden Gate Bridge

B Circle the correct word.

1 Our flat has got a great view because it's on the fifth **level** / **floor**.
2 The **ceiling** / **wall** of the cottage was so low that I almost banged my head on it!
3 Dad keeps his wine downstairs in the **attic** / **cellar**.
4 The dog escaped because someone left the garden **gate** / **door** open!
5 My **landlord** / **owner** is very understanding when I don't pay the rent on tine.
6 No wonder it's freezing in here! The **inside** / **central** heating isn't working
7 We have breakfast on the **corridor** / **balcony** when the weather's nice.
8 There was a huge fireplace in one **corner** / **edge** of the room.

Adjectives

C Match the adjectives with their opposites.

1 old-fashioned ....   a luxurious
2 huge ....   b quiet
3 busy ....   c modern
4 simple ....   d tiny
5 cramped ....   e dry
6 damp ....   f spacious

D Complete the text with words from Exercise C.

The flat wasn't exactly what Greg was looking for. The estate agent had described it as 'compact', which really meant that it was (1) .... Most of the furniture was really (2) ...., like the stuff in his grandmother's house. There was a(n) (3) .... ugly wardrobe in the bedroom that almost filled the whole room and a sofa that looked as if it would collapse if you sat on it. Even though the central heating was on, the air felt slightly (4) .... The only good thing about it was that it was in a(n) (5) .... neighbourhood, away from the noise and traffic of the city centre. Greg knew that he couldn't afford anything more (6) .... 'I'll take it,' he said.

125

10 Listening

B2 Exam Practice
Steps to success
- Conversations you hear might include references to things that are part of British culture.
- Use the context to work out what these things might be.

A 🎧 Listen and circle the correct definition of each word or phrase.
1 custard = **food** / **weather**
2 tube = **a kind of car** / **a kind of train**
3 50p = **50 pence** / **50 pounds**
4 BBC 1 = **website** / **TV channel**
5 Grimsby Town = **a station** / **a football team**

B Do you agree with these stereotypes about Europeans? Can you think of any others?

The French are excellent cooks.
The Germans are very punctual.
The British have a good sense of humour.

C What stereotypes exist about people from your country? Is there any truth in them?

D 🎧 You will hear someone being interviewed about European people and culture. For questions 1–7, choose the best answer (A, B or C).

1 What does David think about European stereotypes?
A They are no longer true.
B They have never been true.
C They are truer now than they used to be.

2 According to the interviewer, what opinion do people often have of Italians?
A They're good cooks.
B They're organized.
C They're friendly.

3 What is affecting people's attitudes towards other nationalities according to David?
A Increased opportunities for travel.
B Changes in climate.
C New theories based on recent research.

4 According to David, British people are considered to be
A very complex.
B too polite.
C less European than other Europeans.

5 Humour is something that
A most Europeans can share.
B can help when doing business with someone from another country.
C can cause misunderstandings between different nationalities.

6 What might make someone from another country feel uncomfortable according to David?
A not speaking their language
B too much physical contact
C turning your back on them while speaking

7 David believes that
A people forgive foreigners for their mistakes.
B Europeans will always be very different from each other.
C English will become the only language spoken in Europe.

Speaking

B2 Exam Practice Complete Test

A Follow the instructions below.
  Student A: Look at page 136.
  Student B: Look at page 137.

B Follow the instructions below.

Student A:

Look at the two photographs below. You are going to talk about the photographs on your own for about a minute. These are your instructions.

Your photographs show different kinds of homes. Compare and say what would be good about living in these places.
What would be good about living in these places?

Student B:
Which of the two homes would you prefer to live in?

Student A:

Look at the two photographs below. You are going to talk about the photographs on your own for about a minute. These are your instructions.

Your photographs show people celebrating different things. Compare and say how you think the people are feeling.
How are the people feeling?

Student B:
What do you like doing on your birthday?

C Do the following task with your partner.

You are planning a 3-month trip to an English speaking country. These are some of the things you want to take with you, but you have only got room in your luggage for three of them.

First, talk to each other about how useful these different things would be. Then decide which **three** would be the most useful to you on your trip.

How useful would these things be? Which three would be the most useful?

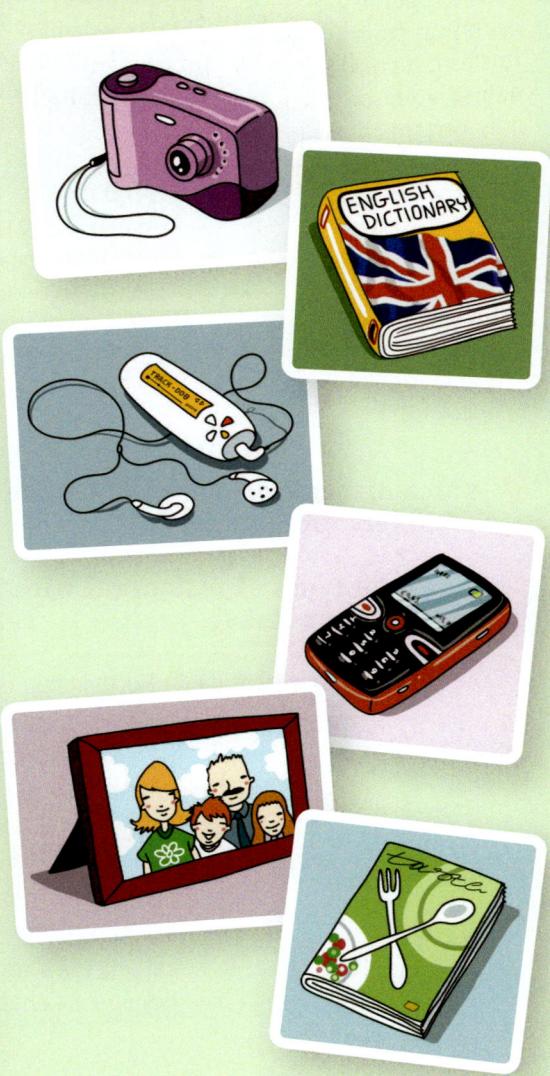

D Follow the instructions below.
  Student A: Look at page 136.
  Student B: Look at page 137.

10

Dive in!

A Read the descriptions of unusual dishes. Which countries do you think these foods are from? Match them from the list.

Iceland • Japan • Scotland • South Korea

Fugu
Tens of people die each year from eating this fish. It contains a deadly poison and only certain chefs are allowed to prepare it.

Haggis
The heart, lungs and liver of lamb or beef are chopped up and mixed with onions, herbs and spices, then stuffed into a sheep's stomach and cooked.

Sannakji
The octopus is cut and eaten while it's still alive. This raw octopus is usually served with a special pepper paste.

Hakarl
This is shark meat that has been buried in the ground for 3-4 months. It is then dried for a few more months before it's ready to eat.

B Which dishes from your country might foreigners find unusual?

C Match the types of restaurant with the correct list of dishes.

Mexican • North African • North Indian • Thai

1 .... fajitas, tortillas, enchiladas, guacamole
2 .... spicy fish cakes, noodles, fried rice
3 .... lassi, rogan josh, naan bread, chicken tandoori
4 .... tajeen stew, falafel, hummus, kebab

Reading 2

B2 Exam Practice

Steps to success
- Pay attention to information in numerical form, for example, times, dates and prices. Questions are often asked about such information.

D Read the five advertisements for restaurants. Use the information in the advertisements to answer the questions.

1 At which restaurant is the owner assisted by members of his family?
a 2   b 3   c 4   d 5

2 Which restaurant is located in a historical building?
a 1   b 2   c 4   d 5

3 Which restaurant has been recommended by locals?
a 1   b 2   c 3   d 4

4 Which advert makes it clear that you will get in wearing your jeans?
a 2   b 3   c 4   d 5

5 You want to eat meat tonight. Which restaurant says it prepares a meat dish particularly well?
a 1   b 2   c 3   d 5

6 You will celebrate your graduation soon. Which restaurant with catering can provide a suitable room for a group of about 60 people?
a 2   b 3   c 4   d 5

7 Your sister wants to find a quiet restaurant to have lunch in. Which restaurant should she avoid?
a 1   b 2   c 3   d 4

8 You would like to sit and eat outside. Which two restaurants will let you do this?
a 1 and 3   b 2 and 4   c 3 and 5   d 4 and 5

9 At which two restaurants might you be able to listen to live music?
a 1 and 4   b 1 and 5   c 2 and 3   d 2 and 5

10 It's 4.15pm and you're hungry. Which restaurants can you NOT eat in?
a 1, 3 and 5   b 2, 3 and 4   c 2, 3 and 5   d 3, 4 and 5

Fajita Restaurant ❶

Hours: 11.00am – midnight daily

The best place in town for flaming fajitas: marinated steak grilled to perfection served on warm flour tortillas.

Finish with our special dessert: fried ice cream.

* **Generous portions**
* **Free Mexican guacamole** with each Family Takeout Special
* **Catering with free delivery** for groups of over 30

Don't miss our Friday night shows featuring famous entertainers and top bands.

Pa Thong ❷

Pa Thong has been serving delicious Thai meals for over a decade.

Located in the old Post Office dating from 1888, now beautifully restored.

At the back, meals can be served in our Thai garden (weather permitting).

Our specialities: Thai doughnuts, sushi and spicy fish cakes.

Beverages: homemade lemonade, fresh fruit juice, freshly brewed iced tea

Catering provided for graduations, retirements and anniversaries.

Hours: Daily 11.00am – 3.00pm, 5.00pm – 10.30pm

Srinagar ❸

Specialists in North Indian cuisine.

A huge range of tasty dishes on offer for both meat lovers and vegetarians.

Beverages: iced tea, soft drinks and lassi (traditional Indian yoghurt shake)

- Many years of experience catering for parties from 50 to 500 people.
- Services for parties include live tandoori cooking at a location of your choice or at our function room (up to 65 people).

Lunch served: Daily 11.30am – 3.00pm
Dinner served: Sunday – Thursday 5.00pm – 10.00pm
Friday – Saturday 5.00pm – 11.00pm

Jim's Oyster Bar ❹

Voted by readers of *The City Gourmet Magazine* as the most fun restaurant to visit in town

Serves only the freshest seafood
Choose your own live lobster

We are extremely busy at lunchtimes so make a reservation to avoid disappointment.

Amenities include: free parking, outdoor seating, private rooms, late-night opening, all credit cards accepted.

Dress code: casual

Hours: Mon - Fri 11.00 am – 12 midnight, Sat and Sun 12 noon – 1.00 am

The African Queen ❺

- A cosy family-run restaurant serving North African cuisine
- Famous for its generous portions of tajeen stews, falafel, kebab and hummus – all at very reasonable prices.
- While dining, enjoy Moroccan melodies live from the African Quartet.
- Situated close to University Village, the African Queen offers discounts to students.
- Open for breakfast Monday to Saturday Closed 3.30 pm – 5.30 pm

Quick chat

Have you tried any unusual or foreign dishes? Describe the occasion and the experience.

If you met some foreigners visiting your country, which dishes would you say they really must try?

Grammar 2

✓ Check inversion

See page 149 for information about inversion.

Match the two halves of the sentences.

1 Never before had I ....
2 Little did Eva know ....
3 No sooner had we set off ....
4 Under no circumstances ....

a than it started to rain.
b felt so lonely in my whole life.
c should you drink the tap water.
d that she would never return to Poland.

A Complete the sentences with the words in the box.

> hardly • nor • not • little • rarely • no

1 .... do you see people walking around in Los Angeles.
2 .... only has he painted his bedroom, but he has also changed the furniture around.
3 .... sooner did our new neighbours move in than the problems started!
4 .... did I know how long the journey would take.
5 Nadia's parents don't speak English and .... does her brother.
6 .... had we sat down when the phone rang.

B Complete the second sentence so that it means the same as the first.

1 I have never spoken to that man.
   At no time ....
2 When he had searched every room, he felt safe.
   Only when ....
3 I won't forgive him until he apologizes.
   Not until ....
4 I have never been so shocked in my whole life.
   Never ....
5 You mustn't try to contact Jim under any circumstances.
   Under ....
6 The meeting began as soon as I arrived.
   No sooner ....

B2 Exam Practice

Steps to success
- Check that you've used the correct part of speech (verb, noun, etc) in each gap.
- Don't leave any blanks — you don't lose marks for wrong answers!

C For questions 1–12, read the text below and think of the word which best fits each gap. Use only one word in each gap.

Going to study abroad for the first time is an adventure, but don't expect it to be easy! You may have (1) .... years studying the language of your host country, but that won't have prepared you for the realities of everyday life. (2) .... sooner have you got off the plane than the problems start. 'Where are you from?' asks the 'friendly' local taxi driver, immediately spotting your foreign accent and hoping he (3) .... be able to overcharge you. When he tells you the fare, you realize you should have (4) .... the bus instead! The student accommodation is the next problem. You knew you (5) .... be sharing a bathroom, but not with eight people! As for your bedroom, the word 'shoebox' comes to mind. Then there's the food. Your mum might (6) .... filled your suitcase with delicious homemade pies, but you will have (7) .... them by the end of the week. Then what are you going to do? You (8) .... have learnt to cook while you had the chance, but now it's too late. The truth is that nothing will (9) .... what you expected when you go and live in a foreign country. You're bound (10) .... feel homesick for the first few weeks as you get used to your new life. The good news is that it (11) .... not last and you'll gradually start to enjoy yourself. (12) .... again will you have so much freedom, so enjoy it!

Vocabulary 2

Places

Prepositions

A Fill in the gaps with *on*, *by* or *in*, then talk about where you live.

Do you live ...
1 .... the coast?
2 .... the sea?
3 .... the city centre?
4 .... a main road?
5 .... the suburbs?
6 .... the outskirts of ... ?
7 .... a village?
8 .... a busy area?

Easily confused words

B Explain the difference between:
1 a **habit** and a **custom**
2 a **stranger** and a **foreigner**
3 a **guest** and a **host**
4 **weather** and **climate**
5 a **country** and the **countryside**
6 a **rural** area and an **urban** area
7 the **cost of living** and the **standard of living**
8 a **local** area and a **regional** area

Key phrasal verbs

C Match the highlighted phrasal verbs in the sentences with their meanings.
1 I didn't **take to** life in a big city at first, but now I love it.
2 Could you **put** me **up** at your house for a couple of days?
3 Adam found it hard to **fit in with** the other children at his school.
4 They've bought an old cottage and they're going to **do** it **up**.
5 You mustn't **look down on** another person because of their race.
6 I don't know how you **put up with** your noisy neighbours!

a accept somebody's behaviour
b be accepted by
c like
d feel that you're better than
e repair and decorate
f let somebody stay at your house

B2 Exam Practice

D For questions 1–12, read the article below and decide which answer (A, B, C or D) best fits each gap.

More and more people are getting fed up with (1) .... life and moving to (2) .... countryside. The internet has made it easier to work from home and home can be anywhere! Take Emily Potter, an IT consultant, who has just bought an old lighthouse on the (3) .... of Cornwall. 'I fell in love with the building as soon as I saw it,' she says. 'The view from the top (4) .... is amazing! People wonder how I (5) .... living in such a remote place. I tell them it's definitely better than living in a block of (6) .... in the city centre.' Peter Moore bought an old farmhouse in Wales, which he's doing (7) .... at the moment. 'The (8) .... of living in London had become so high that I had to work from morning to night to make ends meet,' he says. 'I know farmers have long working (9) .... too, but at least I'll be out in the fresh air doing something I enjoy.' What about being a (10) .... in a small village? Isn't it hard to fit in? 'No, as a matter of fact, the (11) .... people here have been very welcoming,' says Moore. 'They have their old, (12) .... ways of doing things and I obviously have to respect them.'

#	A	B	C	D
1	central	urban	inside	main
2	an	another	the	a
3	coast	sea	suburbs	area
4	level	corridor	floor	corner
5	bring up	look down on	pick up	put up with
6	huts	flats	houses	cottages
7	up	on	in	with
8	price	amount	rate	cost
9	times	hours	periods	spaces
10	stranger	foreigner	guest	host
11	nearby	local	close	regional
12	rural	national	political	traditional

10 Writing: email

B2 Exam Practice
You will be given a situation and some information which you have to use to write an email (or letter).

Steps to success
- ORGANIZE your information in a logical order.
- Lay out your email in PARAGRAPHS.
- Cover all four points in the NOTES.
- Use an appropriate STYLE.
- CHECK for spelling, grammar and punctuation mistakes.

A What do you think a foreign visitor would enjoy most about your country?

the scenery   the traditions   the weather
the architecture   the shops   the nightlife

B Look at this task and complete the four sentences in the notes with your own ideas.

Your English pen friend, Sam, is coming to visit you in your country. Read his email and the notes you have made. Then write an email to Sam using all your notes.

C Read an email that was written in answer to the task. What's wrong with the layout?

Hi Sam. Thanks for your email. I'm really looking forward to see you! Don't forget to tell me what time you arrive so we can meet you at the airport. You asked me for the weather. It might be quite cold in October, so bring some warm clothes with you! It could raining too, but don't worry about that. i can lend you an umbrella! Milan is a very historical city and it's full of interesting buildings. My favourite is the Duomo in the city centre, which is one of the biggest churches in the world! Milan have lots of examples of beautiful architecture, so you'll enjoy walking around the city. As for food, being a vegetarian isn't a problem at all. We have lots of delicious kinds of pizzas and pasta without the meat and my dad's a really good cook! By the way, I want to ask you a favour. Could you bring me a Manchester United football shirt. I'll give to you the money back when I will see you. Thanks! See you soon! Paolo

D Find twelve mistakes in the email and label them as follows:

sp = spelling   ar = article
ve = verb form   pu = punctuation
pr = preposition

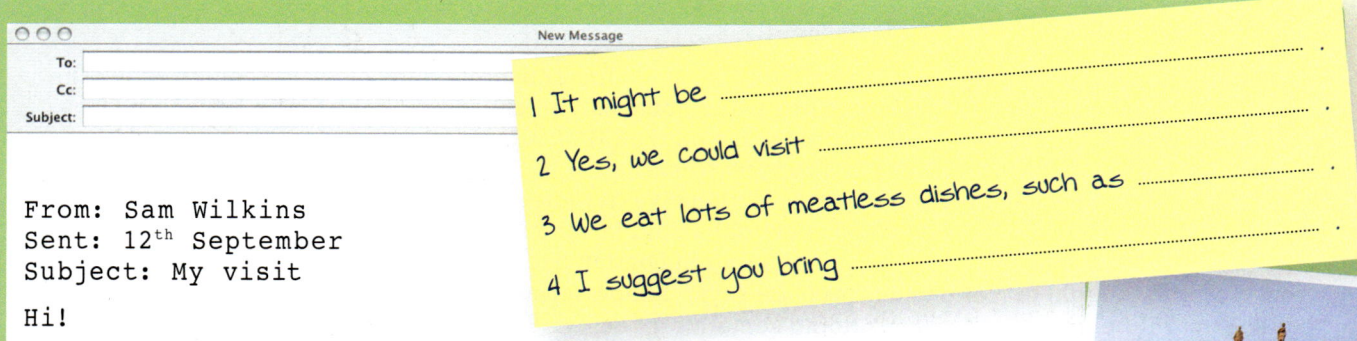

From: Sam Wilkins
Sent: 12th September
Subject: My visit

Hi!

How are you? I can't believe I'll be there in three weeks! I just want to ask you a few questions about my trip.

First of all, what's the weather like at that time of year? I don't want to bring the wrong kind of clothes with me.

Also, you know I'm really interested in architecture, so I'd love to see some of the famous buildings in your city while I'm there. Do you think we'll have time?

By the way, I must have told you that I'm a vegetarian. I don't eat meat at all. I hope that won't be a problem.

Let me know if there's anything else I need to bring with me!

See you soon!
Sam

---

1 It might be ....
2 Yes, we could visit ....
3 We eat lots of meatless dishes, such as ....
4 I suggest you bring ....

E Look at this task and expand on each of the four notes on the email.

A friend from Ireland, Jenny, is coming to stay with you in your country. Read her email and the notes you have made. Then write an email to Jenny using all your notes.

```
New Message
To:
Cc:
Subject:
```

Hello!
How are you? I can't wait to see you next week!
Although I'm excited, I'm a bit worried about travelling on my own. Will you be able to meet me at the airport? ◄ — *Yes*

Another thing is I'm not sure how much money to bring with me. Will we have the chance to go shopping while I'm there? What kind of shops are there? ◄ — *Tell her*

I'd also love to sample some culture in your country. It would be great if we could go to the theatre or to a live concert while I'm there. Is anything good on that week? ◄ — *Yes. Give details.*

Finally, I want to buy a gift for your parents. Have you got any idea what they might like? ◄ — *Suggest something*

Email me soon!
Jenny

3-minute plan!

F Complete the paragraph plan in three minutes using your notes from Exercise E.

1 Respond to Jenny's opening comment:
....
....

2 Note 1: give details about meeting her at the airport:
....
....

3 Note 2: describe the shops in your town, what you can buy, etc:
....
....

4 Note 3: give details about a cultural event you could attend:
....
....

5 Note 4: suggest a possible present she could bring for your parents:
....
....

6 Make a final comment:
....
....

G Now write your email to Jenny in 120–180 words using your notes and some of the Language chunks to help you. Remember to check carefully for mistakes when you've finished.

Language chunks

Answering questions
You asked me about …
As for … ,
In answer to your question about …

Reminding and reassuring (informal letters/emails)
Don't forget to …
Don't bother to …
Don't worry about …
Bring … with you
Let me know when/how/if …
Write soon!
By the way, …

Review 5

A Read the text and choose the best answer A, B, C or D.

Living through teenage eyes

It is inevitably parents who choose where their family will live. Their choices are frequently governed by the (1) .... of living. City life is expensive, and getting costlier by the day. Additionally, living in a polluted, (2) .... area can be stressful and tiring. Adults find themselves drawn by the (3) .... and the promise of fresh air, clean living and a more (4) .... property for less money. They (5) .... also feel that their children will benefit from the lifestyle change that such a move entails. But many teenagers, if asked to express an opinion, would probably (6) .... to give up city life, believing that they would never (7) .... such a different environment. Living in a cramped block of (8) .... is still preferable to limited access to where the action is.

The fact is that teenagers need the freedom that a city offers. That means cinemas, cafés, public transport and all the added conveniences that a (9) .... urban area boasts. Even living on the (10) .... of a city provides access (11) .... to entertainment (12) .... also to good schools and universities. Given the option what would you choose?

1	**A** price	**B** cost	**C** money	**D** standard	7	**A** put up	**B** fit with	**C** take to	**D** look on
2	**A** suburb	**B** outskirt	**C** central	**D** urban	8	**A** cottages	**B** flats	**C** bungalows	**D** huts
3	**A** countryside	**B** village	**C** rural	**D** country	9	**A** busy	**B** local	**C** huge	**D** coastal
4	**A** big	**B** spacey	**C** spacious	**D** bigger	10	**A** edges	**B** outskirts	**C** sides	**D** surrounds
5	**A** ought	**B** may	**C** should	**D** have	11	**A** not only	**B** neither	**C** not until	**D** hardly
6	**A** deny	**B** claim	**C** refuse	**D** agree	12	**A** when	**B** nor	**C** but	**D** and

B Complete the text with ONE word that best fits each gap. Write your answers in CAPITAL LETTERS.

Being the odd one out!

Never (1) .... I felt more like a foreigner than on my trip to Japan. Don't misunderstand me, rarely (2) .... you find people as polite and friendly as the Japanese, but with Japanese women averaging a height of 1.55 m and me being 20 cm taller and a little wider, I was (3) .... to feel a little uncomfortable.

This became painfully apparent when my luggage got lost in transit. At the airport the officials apologized profusely (4) .... the delay and claimed (5) .... my clothes would be sent within 48 hours, but the day after arrival we were going to a posh central Tokyo restaurant, and I had flown in my tracksuit bottoms. I knew I (6) .... to have taken a change of clothes in my hand luggage.

Suwako said she (7) .... take me shopping the (8) .... day. The department store was full of beautiful things, but I am a generous size 14 and take size 8 shoes. When I saw the sizes, I asked Suwako (9) .... we had bothered to come. There was nothing over a dress size 12 or size 6 shoe! 'I'm not sure, but you (10) .... find something in the outsize section', she said.

Two hours later, as I was leaving the store, I (11) .... whether I looked as awkward as I felt in my new outfit. But no (12) .... had I arrived at the New York Grill high up at the Hyatt Regency than all thoughts of my appearance were gone. The buffet was magnificent. I'd never be a size 12 in Japan or any other country!

134

C Complete the text with the correct form of the words in capitals. Write your answers in CAPITAL LETTERS.

Reality TV keeps us watching

Reality TV is not a new phenomenon. In fact, TV (**1**) .... have been (**2**) .... programmes which are unscripted or live, and therefore real, since the 1940s. But it was not until the beginning of the decade that this form of entertainment really started pulling in the (**3**) .... with very little effort from the TV companies making the programmes. (**4**) .... channels were coming up with very (**5**) .... and appealing television by throwing together a group of (**6**) .... and seeing how they would behave with each other. In *Big Brother* this required little more than a house with carefully placed TV cameras and some volunteers wanting to become (**7**) .... The recorded footage didn't even need any serious (**8**) .... because audiences wanted to see what was happening in real time. There are many different categories of Reality TV now, ranging from 'fly on the wall' (**9**) .... about finding jobs or swapping wives to shows like *Survivor* which has achieved (**10**) .... success globally.
Clearly, the one important (**11**) .... that maintains the popularity of this kind of TV is that we as a society need to observe and compare ourselves to others and through this make a (**12**) .... regarding our own behaviour. It is never less than fascinating to see how people really react to difficult or embarrassing situations.

PRODUCT
BROADCAST

VIEW
SUDDEN
EFFECT
STRANGE

CELEBRATE
EDIT

DOCUMENT

COMMERCE
FACT

JUDGE

D Rewrite the sentences using the words in capitals. Use between two and five words, including the word given. Write only the missing words in CAPITAL LETTERS.

1 I feel certain that Bob didn't recommend this documentary because he isn't interested in animals.
HAVE
Bob .... because he isn't interested in animals.

2 Why didn't you tell us that you weren't satisfied with the production?
MIGHT
You .... that you weren't satisfied with the production.

3 'Can I watch the horror film tonight?' asked George.
WHETHER
George .... the horror film that night.

4 Maggie said that she would not take part in the reality show.
REFUSED
Maggie .... the reality show.

5 I'm sure the exhibition was a great success.
BEEN
The exhibition .... a great success.

6 It is rare to see such sensational headlines in this newspaper.
RARELY
.... sensational headlines in this newspaper.

7 The acrobats never have any difficulties during the performance.
TIME
At no .... the acrobats have any difficulties.

8 His photographs are unexciting and of poor quality.
BUT
Not only .... they are also of poor quality.

Pairwork

Unit 5, page 63, Exercise A

Student A:

Ask Student B these questions.
Where are you from?
What do you like about living there?
What time of year do you like the most?
What kind of people do you make friends with?

Unit 7, page 89, Exercise C

Student A:

Complete each sentence below in your own words. Wait for your partner to respond.
1 I think girls are more interested in …
2 Fashions in pop change rapidly, so …
3 Both boys and girls like …

Now swap roles. Listen to what your partner says and respond using the Language chunks.

Unit 10, page 127, Exercise A

Student A:

Ask Student B these questions.
Which school do you go to?
What's your best friend like?
What do you hope to do when you finish school?
What do you like doing on holiday?

Student A:

Answer Student B's questions. Use the Language chunks to help you.

Language chunks

I usually … to school, but sometimes I …
What I enjoy most is/are …
When I have some free time, I usually …
I'd really like to visit … because …

Unit 10, page 127, Exercise D

Student A:

Ask Student B these questions.
Would you like to spend some time living abroad?
What do you think you would miss the most if you lived in a foreign country?
Why do some people choose to live in a foreign country permanently?

Student A:

Answer Student B's questions. Use the Language chunks to help you.

Language chunks

A few months ago I went to …
I really liked …
I haven't yet, but I'd like to …
I'd have to say that the worst thing is …
The worst thing would have to be …
Most foreign visitors come here for the … and …
My country is famous for …

Unit 5, page 63, Exercise A

Student B:

Ask Student A these questions.

How much television do you watch? What kind of programmes?

Do you have a computer at home? What do you do on it?

What did you do on your last holiday?

What are you going to do after this speaking test?

Unit 7, page 89, Exercise C

Student B:

Listen to what your partner says and respond using the Language chunks.

Now swap roles. Complete each sentence below in your own words. Wait for your partner to respond.

1 I think most people our age are interested in …
2 It's only girls who care about …
3 I think cars and bikes …

Unit 10, page 127, Exercise A

Student B:

Ask Student A these questions.

How do you get to school?

What do you enjoy at school?

What do you do in your free time?

Which country would you most like to visit?

Student B:

Answer Student A's questions. Use the Language chunks to help you.

Language chunks

I go to … / I attend …
He's/She's really … and …
What I really like about him/her is …
I'd like to go to university and study …
When I'm on holiday, I really like …

Unit 10, page 127, Exercise D

Student B:

Ask Student A these questions.

Have you ever been on a long journey alone? Did you enjoy it?

What's the worst thing about travelling?

What makes people want to visit your country?

Student B:

Answer Student A's questions. Use the Language chunks to help you.

Language chunks

Yes, I'd like to study abroad …
I'd like to work in …
I'm sure I'd miss … and …
I'd probably miss …
What I would miss the most is/are …
For a number of reasons. Firstly, …

Grammar reference

Unit 1

Present simple

We use the present simple:

- for habits
  I **send** emails every day.
- for permanent situations
  We **live** in the city centre.
- for future events that happen regularly at the same time, such as timetables, transport schedules and programmes
  The train **arrives** at 5.30 in the afternoon.
- for general facts/truths
  Children **learn** foreign languages more easily than adults.
- with *always, never, occasionally, often, rarely, sometimes, usually
  Jane **never** watches television.
  *used with the present continuous for complaints (see below)

← more frequent		less frequent →
always usually often	sometimes	rarely/seldom never

Present continuous

We use the present continuous:

- for things happening at this moment
  I**'m writing** a letter.
- for things happening during this period
  We**'re doing** a project on dinosaurs.
- for future arrangements
  They**'re getting** married next month.
- for complaints (with *always*)
  Oliver **is always talking** about himself!
- with *at the moment, (right) now, temporarily*
  I can't talk to you because I'm cooking the dinner **right now**.

Be careful! Adverbs come in these positions in a sentence:

- after the verb *be*
  Tim is **usually** late.
- before all other main verbs
  I **never** use email.
- between the auxiliary verb and the main verb
  Olga is **now** living in Hungary.

State verbs

State verbs are not normally used in the present continuous tense. They can describe:

- feelings – *hate, like, love, need*
- thinking – *believe, know, think, understand*
- the senses – *hear, see, smell, sound, taste*
- appearance – *appear, look, seem*
- others – *be, belong, depend, have (got), own*

Some verbs have different meanings in the present simple and present continuous tenses.

	Present simple	Present continuous
be	Jeremy is my cousin.	You're being very annoying!
have	Ed has (got) a sister.	Kay is having a baby.
look	This exercise looks hard.	What is he looking at?
say	What does the letter say?	Shh! I can't hear what the teacher's saying.
see	We see terrible things on the news every day.	I'm seeing Shane tonight.
smell	That coffee smells delicious.	Why are you smelling the milk? It's fresh!
taste	This tastes like chicken.	I'm tasting the potatoes to see if they're ready.
think	I think you're wrong.	What are you thinking about?

Present perfect simple

We use the present perfect simple:

- for recently completed actions
  I**'ve** just **phoned** Sam.
- for actions that began in the past and continue into the present, mainly with state verbs
  She's **known** Keith for years.
- for actions that happened in the past, but we don't say when
  Sarah **has written** three novels.
- with *for* and *since*
  We've had this house **since** 1987.
  Tom's worked there **for** two years.
- with *ever, never, once, twice, three times,* etc
  I've **never** bought anything from a second hand shop.
  Have you **ever** been to the ballet?
  Dominic has been to Thailand **three times**.
- with *just, already* and *yet*
  She's **just** left work. (She left work a short while ago.)
  She's **already** left work. (She left work sometime before now, but we don't say when.)
  She hasn't left work **yet**. (She's still at work.)

Present perfect continuous

We use the present perfect continuous:
- for recent actions that are repeated or continued over a period of time
  I**'ve been planning** this holiday for weeks.
- with *for* and *since*
  I've been cooking **for** hours!
  We've been going out together **since** January.

Unit 2

Past simple

We use the past simple:
- for completed actions in the past
  She **bought** a pair of jeans and a top.
- for past states
  Harry **had** his own business.
- for past habits
  My best friend and I **went** shopping every Saturday.
- with *ago*
  Jeremy left five minutes **ago**.
  Pauline stopped working here a long time **ago**.

Past continuous

We use the past continuous:
- for an action in progress at a particular moment in the past
  At nine o'clock last night I **was waiting** for the bus.
- for an action in progress in the past that was interrupted by another event
  We **were driving** home when we saw the accident.
- for temporary situations in the past
  Gina **was working** as a waitress at the time.
- for an action in progress over a period of time
  Hector **was playing** basketball all morning yesterday.
- for annoying past habits
  When I was younger, my sister **was** always **picking** on me.
- for two actions in progress at the same time
  I **was reading** a novel while my brothers **were doing** their homework.
- to provide background information in a story
  The wind **was blowing** and the rain **was coming** down hard. I felt depressed as I sat by the window.
- with *when* and *while*
  While/When David **was digging** in the garden, he hurt his back.

used to + bare infinitive

- for past habits and regular actions (instead of the past simple)
  I **used to** cycle everywhere before I bought a car.
- for past states
  Our next-door neighbours **used to** have two big dogs.

Be careful! *Used to* is usually used to talk about things in the distant past.

Compare *used to* with *be used to* + *-ing* form which means 'to be in the habit of doing something':
I**'m not used to going** to bed at nine o'clock, so I couldn't sleep. (I don't normally go to bed at nine o'clock, so it was strange for me.)
He was from the UK, so he **wasn't used to driving** on the right side of the road. (He didn't usually drive on the right side of the road, so it was strange for him.)

would + bare infinitive

- for past habits and regular actions (instead of the past simple or *used to*)
  Dad **would catch** the eight o'clock bus every morning.

Be careful! We do **not** use *would* for past states.
~~Dad would live in a small village when he was a boy.~~

Past perfect simple

We use the past perfect simple:
- for a completed action that happened before another past event
  We **had** just **finished** our English lesson when the fire alarm went off.
- for a state that continued up to a point when something else happened
  Sal **had been** at secondary school for a couple of weeks before she met Fiona.

Past perfect continuous

We use the past perfect continuous:
- for an activity or situation which lasted for some time before another past event
  I **had been having** singing lessons for six months before I auditioned for the show.

Unit 3

Comparatives

- short adjectives
  My essay is **longer than** yours.
- long adjectives
  German is **more difficult than** English.
  English is **less difficult than** German.
- short adverbs
  I can run **faster than** you.
- long adverbs
  Mrs Hopkins explains things **more clearly than** Mrs Yates.

- as + adjective or adverb + as
  I am **as tall as** all my classmates. They are the same height as me.
  David's project is**n't** speak **as interesting as** Sarah's. Sarah's project is more interesting.
  Miss Hardy does**n't** speak **as clearly as** Mr Clements. Mr Clements speaks more clearly.

Superlatives

- short adjectives
  Ursula is **the nicest** person in the school.
- long adjectives
  This is **the most boring** poem I've ever read!
- short adverbs
  Who studied **the hardest** for the test?
- long adverbs
  Harry does his homework **the most quickly** of us all.

Irregular forms and patterns

Adjective	Comparative	Superlative
bad	worse	the worst
big	bigger	the biggest
far	further/farther	the furthest/the farthest
funny	funnier	the funniest
good	better	the best

Gradable adjectives

These adjectives are used to describe a quality.

- they can be used in comparative or superlative forms
  Anna is **helpful**. → She's **more helpful** than Maria.
  He's a **good** student. → He's **the best** student.
- they can be used with grading adverbs such as *very, extremely, rather, slightly* and *a bit* to show that a person or thing has more or less of a particular quality
  Don't call Julie, she's **very busy** right now.
  It's **extremely important** that you listen to me.
- they cannot be used with adverbs such as *completely, totally* and *absolutely*.
  It was a **very funny** story. → It was a **totally funny** story.

Non-gradable adjectives

These cannot be graded to show that there is more or less of a quality because they are 'extreme'.

- they do not occur in comparative and superlative forms
  Steve is an **excellent** driver. → He is **more excellent** than Andrew.

- they are not used with grading adverbs such as *very, extremely, rather, slightly* and *a bit*
  This author's books are **amazing**. → This author's books are **extremely amazing**.

However, they can be used with very 'strong' adverbs such as *absolutely, completely, totally*, etc.
  That film was **absolutely hilarious**!
  We were **completely exhausted** by the end of the day.

Question forms

In questions, the normal word order changes.
  He **is** a student. → **Is** he a student?

Yes/No questions

- be
  Are you tired?
  Were they surprised?
- Other verbs
  Do you **have** a headache?
  Did you **go** to the concert?

With *will* and modal verbs

- be
  Will you **be** back late?
  Can we **be** friends?
- Other verbs
  Will you **tell** me the answer?
  Can we **order** a pizza?

Wh- questions

- be
  Where **is** he?
  Why **are** they here?
  What **was** that?
- Other verbs
  Where **does** he **live**?
  How **do** they **know**?
  What **did** she **say**?

Be careful! Some Wh- questions can have two different patterns, depending on whether the question is about the subject or object of a sentence.

- Asking about the subject
  Who **likes** you? (Answer: **Theo** likes me.)
- Asking about the object
  Who **do** you **like**? (Answer: I like **Nigel**.)

Indirect questions

Indirect questions use normal word order and a phrase to introduce the question. Some end with a question mark, others with a full stop.
  Do you know if Dan is here?
  I wonder if you could help me.
  Could you tell me if this information is correct?
  I'd like to know if the course has already started.
  Do you know what/why/who/where/when/how ... ?
  Do you know who that girl is? (NOT: Do you know who is that girl?)

I wonder what/why/who, etc ...
   I wonder why they didn't invite me.
Could you tell me what/why/who, etc ...?
   Could you tell me where the post office is, please?
I'd like to know what/why/who, etc ...
   I'd like to know what you think of this book.

Question tags

We use tag questions at the end of statements to ask for agreement or to check that we are right.

The basic structure is:

- positive statement + negative question tag
  *You're enjoying university, **aren't** you?*
  *You've been studying for two years, **haven't** you?*
  *James **will** be here later, **won't** he?*
  *They **were** preparing for their exams, **weren't** they?*
  *Sally **could** help us, **couldn't** she?*
  *We **must** visit them, **mustn't** we?*

- negative statement + positive question tag
  *It **isn't** snowing, **is** it?*
  *You'd never met him before, **had** you?*
  *It **can't** be repaired, **can** it?*
  *Joe **wasn't** well today, **was** he?*
  *You **shouldn't** be playing that game, **should** you?*
  *Alice **doesn't** want to go to college, **does** she?*

Note: The pronouns and the modal verbs used in the main statement remain the same in the question tag.

There are some special cases.
   *I'm late, **aren't** I?*
   *We **have to** try harder, **don't** we?*
   ***Nobody** saw him, **did** they?*
   ***Nothing** is happening, **is** it?*
   ***Let's** phone her, **shall** we?*
   *You **had better** tell the truth, **hadn't** you?*

We often use question tags to ask for information or help, starting with a negative statement.
   *You **don't** know if there's a bank nearby, **do** you?*
   *You **wouldn't** be able to come straightaway, **would** you?*
   *You **couldn't** explain this to me, **could** you?*
   *You **haven't** got any time to fix my computer, **have** you?*

Question tags are used with imperatives for invitations and orders.
   *Have a piece of cake, **won't** you?* (polite)
   *Turn off that TV, **will** you?* (slightly annoyed)
   *Answer the door, **would** you?* (quite polite)
   *Come here, **will** you?* (less polite)
   *Don't forget, **will** you?* (only *will* is used with negative imperatives)

Unit 4

Infinitives and *-ing* forms

Verbs followed by the full infinitive: *agree, arrange, be able, choose, decide, expect, hope, manage, offer, prepare, promise, refuse, seem, want*
   *He decided **to spend** his time in prison usefully.*

Verbs followed by an object + the full infinitive: *advise, allow, ask, cause, convince, enable, encourage, expect, invite, like, persuade, remind, teach, tell, want, warn*
   *Owen persuaded **me to go** to the police.*

Verbs followed by either the bare infinitive or the full infinitive (with or without an object): *dare* and *help*
   *I didn't dare **(to) tell them** my mistake.*
   *I helped **Steve (to) fix** his motorbike.*

Verbs followed by an object + bare infinitive: *let* and *make*
   *Joe let **me use** his laptop.*
   *The traffic warden made **us move** the car.*

Verbs followed by the -ing form: *admit, avoid, consider, deny, enjoy, keep, mind, miss, recommend, risk, suggest*
   *He denied **taking** the money.*

Verbs followed by an object + the -ing form or the bare infinitive with a small change of meaning:

see
   *We saw **our team playing** football.* (see something which continues for some time)
   *We saw **our team play** a match against the other team.* (see a complete action)

hear
   *We heard **the dog barking** for hours during the night.* (hear something which continues for some time)
   *We heard **the dog bark** once and then silence fell.* (hear a sound which begins and then stops)

Verbs followed by either the -ing form or the full infinitive with the same meaning: *begin, continue, hate, like, prefer, start*
   *It started **snowing/to snow** on New Year's Eve.*

Verbs followed by the -ing form or the full infinitive with a change in meaning:

forget
   *I forgot **to switch** the oven off!* (not do something you were supposed to do)
   *I'll never forget **meeting** Britney Spears!* (not have a memory of)

need
   *We'll need **to leave** early tomorrow to avoid the traffic.* (have to do something)
   *The car needs **fixing**.* (passive meaning; we can also say, *The car needs to be fixed*.)

go on
   *Maggie started off as a lab assistant, but she went on **to become** a very successful scientist.* (stop one thing

and start another)
We went on **talking** until three o'clock in the morning. (continue doing something)

regret
I regret **to inform** you that your application was unsuccessful. (be sorry – formal)
David **regrets** buying an expensive car. (wish you hadn't done something)

remember
Remember **to unplug** the computer before you go on holiday. (to do something you are supposed to do)
Do you remember **seeing** this film at the cinema? (have a memory of)

stop
We stopped **to have** a drink because we were thirsty. (stop one thing in order to do something else)
Stop **talking** and finish your homework! (not do something any longer)

try
I tried **to fix** the tap, but it hasn't stopped dripping. (make an effort to do something)
Why don't you try **drinking** less coffee if you want to be healthier? (do something in order to solve a problem)

Prepositions are always followed by the *-ing* form.
Jenny is interested in **becoming** a social worker.
The police officer prevented me from **entering** the building.
I spend a lot of money on **going out**.

Future forms

will
We use *will* for:

- predictions (often with *I hope* or *I bet*)
  Mobile phones **will become** even smaller than they are now.
  I hope our team **will win** the match!
- spontaneous decisions (often with *I think*)
  I think I**'ll buy** a new laptop.
- offers and suggestions
  Shall I **help** you with the experiment? (**shall** is used instead of **will** in the first person question form)
  Shall we **stay** at home as it's raining?
- requests
  Will you **tell** me what you think of my biology project?

be going to
We use *be going to* for:

- intentions
  I've decided that I**'m going to study** law at university.
- predictions (based on evidence)
  Emily has always wanted a camera, so she**'s going to love** this digital one!

Present simple
We use the present simple for:

- arrangements, fixed events and timetables
  The exhibition **opens** at nine o'clock on Saturday.
  Jennifer **collects** the children at eight o'clock every morning.

Present continuous
We use the present continuous for:

- plans
  We**'re taking part** in a psychological experiment next week.
  Our cousins **are arriving** on December 23rd.

Future continuous (= *will* + *be* + present participle)
We use the future continuous for:

- predictions about something that will be in progress at a future time
  The world **will be running** out of oil soon.
  We **will be driving** to Grandma's house tomorrow at two o'clock.

Future perfect simple (= *will have* + past participle)
We use the future perfect simple for:

- a prediction about something that will be completed **before** a future time; the word *by* is often used with this tense
  The suspects **will have left** the country by tomorrow.
  She **will have received** the letter by next Monday.

Time clauses in the future

We use present tenses to refer to the future after the following words and phrases: *after, as soon as, before, by the time, in case, once, till/until, when, while*

- Present simple
  I'll take my mobile phone with me in case **I need** to call you.
- Present continuous (for an action in progress in the future)
  I'll make some sandwiches while you**'re having** a shower.
- Present perfect (for an action completed in the future)
  As soon as I**'ve received** your email, I'll call you.

Unit 5

Modal verbs

Modal verbs do not change form. We do not use *do* in the question and negative forms or add *-s* to the third person singular form. They are followed by a bare infinitive. The verbs *be able to, be allowed to, have to, let, need to* and *ought to* change their forms in the normal way but are often used to express similar meanings to modal verbs.

Obligation

We use *must* and *mustn't*:

- to talk about something which is necessary to do
  I **must** fix my bike. It's got a flat tyre.
- to tell somebody to do something or to talk about laws
  You **mustn't** touch that switch!
  You **must** drive on the right-hand side of the road.

We use *have to*:

- to talk about obligation in the future and the past
  I **(will) have to** get up early tomorrow morning.
  I **had to** work yesterday.
- to talk about something that we are obliged to do
  Ben **has to** make his bed every day.

We use *don't have to*, *needn't* or *don't need to*:

- to say that somebody is not obliged to do something
  Sarah **doesn't have to** go to work today.
  You **needn't** light the fire. It's not very cold today.
  You **don't need to** revise for the exam. It's been cancelled.

Be careful! *Mustn't* does not mean the same thing as *don't have to*.
  You **mustn't** drive the car. The brakes aren't working.
  You **don't have to** drive the car. I can drive if you want.

Ability

We use *can*:

- to talk about ability in the present
  Can your little brother ride a bicycle?

We use *could*:

- to talk about general ability in the past
  I **could** swim when I was four years old.

We use *be able to*:

- to talk about ability in the present, the past and the future
  Mr Chambers **is not able to** attend the meeting.
  Cindy **was able to** speak three languages.
  We'll **be able to** see the sea from our new house.
- to talk about the specific ability to do something in the past
  After several hours the firefighters **were able to** put out the fire.

Permission

We use *can*:

- to talk about something we have permission to do
  I **can** go to the party.

We use *be allowed to* or *let*:

- to talk about permission in the past and the future
  I **was allowed to** go to the party.
  They **let** me go to the party.
  I think I **will be allowed to** go to the party.

We use *can*, *could* or *may*:

- to ask for permission to do something
  Can/Could/May I come with you?
- *could* is more polite for requests
  Could you help me, please?

Advice

We use *should*:

- to give or to ask for advice
  You **should** leave now.
  What do you think I **should** do?

We use *ought to*:

- to give or to ask for advice
  You **ought to** leave now.
  What do you think I **ought to** do?

Prohibition

We use *mustn't*, *can't* or *not allowed to*:

- when we want to prohibit or stop someone from doing something
  You **mustn't/can't** go in there.
  You **are not allowed to** go in there.

so and *such*

So can be followed by an adjective, an adverb or by *much/many* + a noun.

It is often followed by a *that* clause to express a result.
  Your room is **so** dirty that you have to clean it now.
  Jimmy walked **so** slowly that he missed the bus.
  There are **so** many places to visit that I can't make up my mind where to go.

Such can be followed by a noun, an adjective + a noun or by *a lot of* + a noun.

It is often followed by a *that* clause to express a result.
  Your room is **such** a mess that you have to clean it now.
  Jimmy is **such** a slow walker that he missed the bus.
  There are **such** a lot of places to visit that I can't decide where to go.

too and *enough*

We use *too* to say that something is more than we would like it to be.
  It's **too** hot. (I can't play football.)
  You're walking **too** slowly. (We'll miss the bus.)

Too always comes before an adjective or an adverb
  We're **too** tired.
  Clare is **too** unhappy to smile.

It can be followed by a full infinitive, *for* + pronoun + full infinitive or by *much/many* + a noun.
  It's **too** hot to play football.
  It's **too** hot for me to play football.
  Our teacher gives us **too** much homework/**too** many exercises.

We use *enough* to say that something is just right (or not right).
*The box is big **enough** for the books.*

Enough usually comes after an adjective or an adverb.
*Yes, it's good **enough**.*
*You're not trying hard **enough**.*

It can be followed by a noun + full infinitive, *for* + pronoun or by a noun.
*I haven't got **enough** money to buy the ticket.*
*Yes, it's good **enough** for me.*
*There isn't **enough** sugar.*

Unit 6

Passive voice

We form the passive voice with the correct form of the verb *be* and the past participle of the main verb.

Active:

The cat **ate** the fish.
subject   object

Passive:

The fish **was eaten** by the cat.
(subject)   (agent)

We use the passive voice:

- when we don't know who carried out an action
  *A new factory **is being built** near my house.* (we don't know who is building it)
- when the action is more important than the person who carried it out
  *That book **was written** in 1948.* (we are not interested in who wrote the book)
- when it is clear or obvious who carried out the action
  *Three members of Greenpeace **have been arrested**.* (we know it was the police who arrested them)

Be careful! To talk about the person or thing responsible for an action we use an 'agent' with *by*.
*The forest was destroyed **by the fire**.*
*The car is being fixed **by my uncle**.*

Be careful! We never say 'by someone' or 'by people'.
The plants have been watered ~~by someone~~.
Centuries ago, it was thought ~~by people~~ that the Earth was flat.

We can use *with* to talk about what someone uses to do something.
*The field was planted **with corn** (by the farmer).*

Look at the difference between *by* and *with*:
*Harold was hit **with a branch**.* (someone hit him using a branch)
*Harold was hit **by a branch** during the storm.* (a branch broke off a tree during the storm)

Some verbs such as *give, offer, tell* and *show* can have two objects – a direct object and an indirect object.
The zoo-keeper gave the monkeys some bananas.
(active voice)

From this sentence, we can make two passive sentences.
*Some bananas **were given to** the monkeys (by the zoo-keeper).*
*The monkeys **were given** some bananas (by the zoo-keeper).*

Note: the passive is often used in formal language.

Present simple	Whales **are hunted** in some countries.
Present continuous	The tap water **is being tested** to see how clean it is.
Present perfect simple	I've **been stung** by a jellyfish!
Present perfect continuous	not used in the passive voice
Past simple	The park **was opened** in 1988.
Past continuous	The kitten **was being chased** by a dog when I saw it.
Past perfect simple	During their research, they discovered that the lake **had been polluted**.
Future simple	Ecological holidays **will be offered** by more travel companies in the future.
Modal verbs	The monkeys **mustn't be fed** by visitors.
Infinitive	Animals don't deserve **to be treated** so badly.
-ing form	You risk **being attacked** by a crocodile in that river!
Impersonal structure	**It is believed** that our planet is getting warmer.

Articles

A/An
We use *a* or *an*:

- with singular countable nouns, when we don't refer to something particular
  *Our summer house is near **a** beautiful beach.*
- to describe someone's job
  *Lucy is **an** environmental scientist.*

The
We use *the*:

- with singular, plural and uncountable nouns, when we refer to something specific
  ***The** bird that I saw was very unusual.*
  ***The** girls who go to my aerobics class are nice.*
  *Where do you keep **the** sugar?*

- with rivers, seas and mountain groups
  the River Thames, **the** Atlantic Ocean, **the** Alps
- with things there are only one of
  the world, **the** sun, **the** moon, **the** sky, **the** environment, **the** Earth
- with superlatives
  Mount Everest is **the** highest mountain in the world.
- with adjectives to describe a group of people
  The young are more interested in environmental issues than the **old**.
- with singular countable nouns when talking about things in general
  The tiger is in danger of extinction.
- with places of entertainment/leisure when talking generally
  I like going to **the** cinema/theatre/gym.
- with names of buildings
  the Houses of Parliament, **the** Natural History Museum
- with national groups.
  the English, **the** Spanish, **the** Japanese
- with some time expressions
  in **the** afternoon, in **the** 1980s

No article
We omit the article:
- with plural countable nouns when talking generally
  Donkeys are very gentle animals.
- with uncountable nouns when talking generally
  Katie loves milk.
- with countries
  India, France, Greece (but **the** United States of America, **the** United Kingdom)
- with meals
  We had lunch in a restaurant.
- with institutions (prison, school, hospital, etc) when someone goes there as a prisoner, pupil, patient, etc
  Lee was taken to hospital with a broken leg. (**but** Do you know where **the** children's hospital is?)
- with cities, continents, planets and mountains
  My aunt lives in London.
  I'd love to go to Africa.
  Human beings will visit Mars one day.
  Mount Fuji is in Japan.

Countable nouns

Countable nouns (eg *animal, house, forest, person, beach,* etc) can be singular or plural.
  This snake **is** poisonous.
  Some/Many animals **are** endangered.
  Are there any wolves left in Greece?
  There **aren't** any puppies left in the pet shop.
  There **are** a lot of rabbits in those fields.

Uncountable nouns

Uncountable nouns (eg *fruit, hair, work, advice, water, cheese, equipment,* etc) are singular.
  There**'s** some cheese in the fridge that smells horrible!
  Is there any milk left?
  There **isn't** any sugar for my cornflakes.
  There **isn't** much work to do today.
  Is there a lot of information on that website?

Be careful! News looks like a plural countable noun, but it is uncountable.
  What time **is** the news on?

Plural uncountable nouns

Plural uncountable nouns (eg *trousers, jeans, glasses,* etc.) don't have a singular form.
  These trousers **are** dirty. (**not** This trouser is dirty.)
  Joanna has got some new glasses. They**'re** really cool.
  Are there any scissors on your desk?
  There **are** a lot of jeans in the January sales.

We can use some nouns as countable or uncountable depending on the meaning.

cake
Uncountable: *Would you like some cake?*
             (part of a big cake)
Countable: *Would you like a cake?*
           (a small individual cake)

glass
Uncountable: *The roof is made of glass.*
             (the material)
Countable: *Do you want a glass of lemonade?*
           (something you drink out of)

wood
Uncountable: *We collected some wood to make a fire.*
             (pieces of wood/the material)
Countable: *There is a wood near my house.*
           (small forest)

paper
Uncountable: *I try to recycle all the paper I use.*
             (sheets of paper/the material)
Countable: *Can you buy me a paper when you go out?*
           (newspaper)

hair
Uncountable: *Mark has got very short hair.*
             (on one's head)
Countable: *Yuck! There's a hair in my soup!*
           (an individual hair or hairs)

room
Uncountable: *There isn't much room in here.*
             (space)
Countable: *This room has a lovely view.*
           (part of a building)

Unit 7
Conditionals

Conditionals with *if* contain two clauses – one expressing the condition (the *if* clause) and one explaining the result (often containing a modal verb).

When the *if* clause comes first, it has a comma after it:
*If you **come** to my house tonight, I **will give** you the books.*

When the *if* clause comes second, we don't use a comma:
*I **will give** you the books if you **come** to my house tonight.*

Zero conditional (*if* + present tense + present tense)
We use the zero conditional to talk about a situation that is generally true.
*If you **stay** in the sun too long, you **burn**.*

We can also use *whenever* to express something that is always true.
*Whenever Ian **gets** a haircut, he **thinks** it's too short.*

First conditional (*if* + present tense + *will/might/may/can/could*/etc + bare infinitive)
We use the first conditional to talk about a situation that is real or likely in the future.
*If you **give** me the CD, I **will copy** it for you.*
*If you **explain** the problem, I **can help** you.*

We use *if* + present tense + imperative to give instructions about present or future situations
*If you **see** Mary, **give** her my phone number.*

Second conditional (*if* + past simple or past continuous + *would/might/could* + bare infinitive)
We use the second conditional to talk about a situation that is impossible, unlikely or theoretical in the present/future.
*If I **was** rich, I **would buy** a big house.*
*If I **wasn't revising** for a test, I **could go out** and play football.*

Be careful!
We can say *If I were* ... instead of *If I was* ... :
*If I **were** rich, I would help the poor.*

We can also say *If I were you, ...* to give advice:
*If I **were you**, I **would work** a bit harder at school.*

We can also use *could* in the *if* clause:
*If you **could** go anywhere in the world, where would you go?*

Causative form

We use the causative to talk about things that other people do for us when we ask them to or when we pay them.

have/get + object + past participle
*I **have my hair cut** once a month.*

We can use the causative in any tense.
*I **am having my hair cut** now.*
*I **had my hair cut** last week.*
*I couldn't answer my mobile because I **was having my hair cut**.*

If we need to say *who* does it, we use *by*.
*I had the painting valued **by** an expert.*

We use *get* instead of *have* if the situation is less formal.
*You should **get** your jacket cleaned!*

We can also use the causative for unpleasant things that happen to us.
*I **had my favourite jacket stolen**.*
*He doesn't like **having his paintings criticized**.*

Two more causative structures which we can use are *have* + sb + bare infinitive and *get* + sb + full infinitive
I had my sister style my hair.
I got my sister to do it for me.

Unit 8
Defining relative clauses

We use defining relative clauses to define or identify a thing, person or animal. The following relative pronouns are used in them:

which	The tennis racket **which** Dad gave me is very good.
who	Mrs Smith is the woman **who** taught me to play the piano.
whom	To **whom** should I complain about the food?
whose	That's the girl **whose** brother is an actor.
where	The café **where** we used to meet has closed now.
when	I'll always remember the day **when** I met Ursula.
why	The reason **why** I started doing aerobics was to lose weight.

Be careful!
In defining relative clauses, *that* can replace *which*, *who*, *when*, *why* and *whom* (except after a preposition).
*Mrs Smith is the woman **who** taught me to play the piano.*
*Mrs Smith is the woman **that** taught me to play the piano.*

The following relative pronouns can be omitted when they refer to the object of a sentence.
*The rucksack (**which/that**) you lent me was in very bad condition.*
*That's the girl (**who/that**) Tim used to go out with.*
*I'll never forget the day (**when/that**) I met you!*
*Jack doesn't know the reason (**why/that**) I contacted him.*

Whom is used after prepositions, especially in formal English, to refer to a person who is the object of a relative clause.
*That's the man **to whom** I gave the money.*

Non-defining relative clauses

We use non-defining relative clauses to give extra information about something. They are separated from the rest of the sentence by commas. If the extra information is removed, the words that remain form a complete sentence. The following relative pronouns are used in them:

which	This chess set, **which** was a birthday present, was very expensive.
who	Mr Brown, **who** lives next door to us, is a pianist.
whom	The waiter, to **whom** we didn't give a tip, was very rude.
whose	That girl, **whose** dad is a film director, goes to my school.
where	That house, **where** I was born, is for sale.
when	In the 1980s, **when** I was a teenager, it was cheap to go to the cinema.

Be careful!

Which can also refer to a whole phrase.
   I can't swim, **which** is why I hate boats.

Where can sometimes be replaced by *in which* or *which ... in*.
   London is a city **where** you can do lots of things.
   London is a city **in which** you can do lots of things.
   London is a city **which** you can do lots of things **in**.

Unreal past

We use the past simple to talk about hypothetical situations in the present and future after certain expressions.
   I wish I **was** famous.
   If only we **didn't have** school today.
   Suppose you **won** a lot of money, what would you do?
   What if we **had** a party?
   It's (high/about) time we **started** enjoying life!
   I would rather you **didn't buy** another computer game.

We can also use the past continuous with *wish* and *if only* to talk about a hypothetical situation.
   I wish/If only I **was singing** in the concert. (Fact: I'm not singing in the concert.)

We use the past perfect with *wish* and *if only* to talk about something we regret doing or not doing in the past.
   I wish/If only we **had applied** to be contestants on Survivor. (Fact: We didn't apply.)
   He **wishes/If only** he **hadn't lied** to her! (Fact: He lied to her.)

We use *would* + bare infinitive with *wish* and *if only* when we want to criticize someone else's behaviour (but not our own).
   ~~I wish I wouldn't forget my keys all the time.~~
   I wish/If only George **wouldn't get** so angry.
   (Fact: George often gets angry.)

Third conditional

We use the third conditional to talk about things in the past that didn't actually happen. We can use either of these structures:

If + subject + past perfect tense, subject + *would(n't) have* + past participle

subject + *would(n't) have* + past participle *if* + subject + past perfect tense

   If Freddie had got up earlier, he **wouldn't have missed** the train.
   Freddie **wouldn't have missed** the train if he **had got up** earlier.
   If Freddie had got up earlier, **would** he **have missed** the train?
   Would Freddie have missed the train **if he had got up** earlier?
   (Fact: Freddie got up late and missed the train.)

Unit 9
Reported speech

We use reported speech when we want to say what someone said without using their exact words. We use a past tense reporting verb (eg *said*).

We usually change the tense of the direct speech:

   'I **don't go** to school.' ⟶ She said she **didn't go** to school.

   'I **didn't** eat it.' ⟶ He said he **hadn't eaten** it.

   'I **haven't seen** them.' ⟶ He said he **hadn't seen** them.

   'I'm **not coming**.' ⟶ She said she **wasn't coming**.

   'I **wasn't listening**.' ⟶ She said she **hadn't been listening**.

   'I **haven't been working**.' ⟶ He said he **hadn't been working**.

The past perfect simple and continuous do not change tense in reported speech:

   'I **hadn't finished**.' ⟶ He said he **hadn't finished**.

   'I **hadn't been waiting** long.' ⟶ She said she **hadn't been waiting** long.

With future forms we make the following changes:

   'I'**ll see** you soon.' ⟶ She said she **would see** me soon.

   'I'**m going to** buy a new TV.' ⟶ She said she **was going to** buy a new TV.

Modal verbs change in the following ways:

   'I **can** do it.' ⟶ She said she **could** do it.
   'I **must** go.' ⟶ She said she **had to** go.

Be careful! The modal verbs *may*, *might* and *could* do not change:
'I **may/might/could** go.' ⟶ She said she **may/might/could** go.

We also have to change references to time and place:
'I don't like it **here**.' ⟶ She said she didn't like it **there**.
'I'll see you **tomorrow**.' ⟶ She said she would see me **the next day/the following day**.
'It happened **yesterday/two days ago**.' ⟶ She said it had happened **the day before/the previous day/two days before/two days previously**.
'I'm going home **today/tonight**.' ⟶ She said she was going home **that day/that night**.
'I'm happy **now/at the moment**.' ⟶ She said she was happy **then/at that moment**.

Other changes include:
'**This** is ridiculous! I can't do **my** homework, I hate **these** lessons, and **those** exercises are too hard.' ⟶ She said **it** was ridiculous. She couldn't do **her** homework, she hated **the** lessons, and **the** exercises were too hard.

Other verbs can be used to report what somebody has said, but these follow different grammatical patterns:
Donna **offered to help** me.
Jim **denied that** he had done it.
Jim **denied doing** it.
Jim **denied having done** it.
They **suggested/recommended going** out.
They **suggested/recommended that we go** out.
She **agreed/refused to go**.
She **agreed that** it was a good idea.
Mike **claimed** that he knew the answer.
Mike **claimed to know** the answer.
I **stated/thought/doubted that** it was true.
He **told/warned me that** it was a trap.
He **told/ordered/warned/begged me to be** careful.
She **told me** the answer.
She **apologized** (**to** her mum) **for breaking** the window.

Reported questions

We use reported questions in a similar way to reported speech – when we say what someone *asked* without using their exact words. We make the same tense changes as in reported speech. Note that there are no question marks in reported questions and they follow the word order of statements, not questions.

When the direct speech question begins with a question word (eg *who, what, where, when, why, which, how*):
'**Why didn't you** say hello?' ⟶ He asked me **why I hadn't** said hello.
'**Where did you** go?' ⟶ She asked me **where I had** gone/been.
'**How did you** know?' ⟶ I asked her **how she had** known.

When the direct speech question doesn't begin with a question word, we use *if* or *whether*:
'**Is there** anything wrong?' ⟶ They asked me **if/whether there was** anything wrong.
'**Were you** OK yesterday?' ⟶ He asked her **if/whether she had been** OK the previous day.
'**Do you know** the answer?' ⟶ I asked James **if/whether he knew** the answer.
'**Are you going** to the party?' ⟶ She asked me **if/whether I was going** to the party.

Requests and commands
For requests and commands, we use the full infinitive:
'**Will/Can/Could** you help me with my computer?' ⟶ Paul **asked me to help him** with his computer.
'**Will** you come with me to the party?' ⟶ Maria **asked me to** go with her to the party.
'**Give me** the book.' ⟶ My teacher **told me to give** her the book.
'**Don't talk**!' ⟶ The man **told us not to** talk.

Unit 10

Modal verbs of probability

Certainty
We use *must* to talk about something we are certain of in the present or the future.
Chinese **must** be a difficult language. (=I'm sure that Chinese is a difficult language.)

We use *can't* as the opposite of *must* (not *mustn't*).
This map **can't** be right. (=I'm sure that this map isn't right.)

We use *will* to talk about something we are certain of in the present.
That **will** be John on the phone. (=I'm certain that it's John on the phone.)

We often use *bound to* + infinitive instead of a modal verb to talk about something we are certain will happen in the future.
It's **bound to** rain later. (=It will almost certainly rain later.)

We use *can't have* + past participle to talk about something we are certain of in the past.
It **can't have been** cheap to fly first class. (=I feel certain that it wasn't cheap to fly first class.)

We use *will have* + past participle to talk about something we are certain happened in the past.
You **will have seen** the Statue of Liberty in films. (=You have certainly seen the Statue of Liberty in films.)

Probability
We use *should/ought to* to talk about something which we think is probable in the present and the future.
  The journey **should/ought to** take about three hours.
  (=I believe the journey will take about three hours.)

We use *must have* + past participle to talk about something we believe to be probable in the past.
  Your trip to Argentina **must have been** interesting.
  (=Your trip to Argentina was probably interesting.)

Possibility
We use *may, might* and *could* to talk about something which is possible in the present or the future.
  That woman **may** be foreign. (=Maybe that woman is foreign.)
  This shop **might** sell stamps. (=Maybe this shop sells stamps.)
  It **could** be dangerous to go out at night. (=Maybe it's dangerous to go out at night.)

We use *should/ought* + *to have* + past participle to talk about possibility in the past.
  They **should/ought to have arrived** by now. (=I had expected them to arrive by now.)

We use *may/might/could* + *have* + past participle to talk about something which possibly happened in the past.
  This **may/might/could have been** the place where civilization began.

Be careful! *might/could* + *have* + past participle can also be used to complain about something.
  You **might/could have told** me you were going to be late! (=I'm annoyed that you didn't tell me you were going to be late.)

Be careful! *should have* + past participle can also be used to express obligation or criticism about the past.
  You **should have taken** your mobile phone with you.
  (= It was wrong of you not to take your mobile phone with you.)

Inversion

We use a different word order after some negative words and expressions, when they come at the beginning of a sentence. Inversions are usually used for emphasis in formal English.
  He had **never** seen a more beautiful place in his life! (normal word order)
  Never had he seen a more beautiful place in his life! (inverted word order = the same as word order in questions)

We use inversion after these words/expressions:

Hardly ... when
  Hardly had I got off the train **when** I realized it was the wrong station.

No sooner ... than
  No sooner had I got off the train **than** I realized it was the wrong station.

Rarely
  Rarely do you find such friendly people.

Not only ... but also ...
  Not only do I know that village, **but** I **also** lived there for a while.

Neither/Nor
  I don't speak Arabic. **Neither/Nor** does my friend.

Under no circumstances
  Under no circumstances must you go near the border.

Never
  Never have I eaten such delicious food!

At no time
  At no time did I feel in danger.

Only then
  Only then did I realize who the stranger was.

Only yesterday
  Only yesterday was I saying that we should buy a new car.

*Not until
  Not until we reached the hut **did we have** a rest.

  *the second verb, not the first, is inverted

Little
  Little did I know that I would never see Nell again.

Vocabulary file

Unit 1

Communication
attachment (n)
conference call (n)
email (n), (v)
fax (n), (v)
hands free (n)
hang up (phr v)
keep in touch (phr v)
letter (n)
online chat (n)
phone call (n)
SMS (Short Message Service) (n)
text message (n)
voicemail (n)
website (n)

Body language
frown (v)
nod (v)
raise your eyebrows (phr)
shake your head (phr)
sigh (v)
sniff (v)
wave (v)
yawn (v)

Phrasal verbs
bring up
come out with
get across
make up
stand for
talk someone into

Word patterns (say, tell, speak)
say a prayer
say sorry
say what you think
speak a language
speak up
speak your mind
tell a joke
tell a lie
tell a story
tell someone off
tell the time
tell the truth

Customs
anniversary (n)
best man (n)
bride (n)
ceremony (n)
get engaged (v phr)
get married (v phr)
groom (n)
honeymoon (n)
proposal (n)
reception (n)
toast (n)
wedding (n)

Character adjectives
chatty
dependable
impolite
on time
outgoing
punctual
quiet
reliable
rude
shy
sociable
sympathetic
talkative
understanding

Word patterns
best friend
brother-in-law
extended family
great grandmother
next-door neighbour
only child
single parent
twin sister

Negative prefixes

	Verb	Noun	Adjective
dis	able	ability	
	agree	agreement	
		satisfaction	satisfied
		belief	
im		politeness	polite
		possibility	possible
in		ability	
		capability	capable
		tolerance	tolerant
mis	treat	treatment	
	understand	understanding	
un			able
			believable
		certainty	certain
		suitability	suitable

Unit 2

Work
audition (n)
chef (n)
impress (v)
interpreter (n)
lucrative (adj)
official (adj)
salary (n)
schedule (n)
surgeon (n)
well-paid (adj)

accountant (n)
architect (n)
ballet dancer (n)
bank manager (n)
civil engineer (n)
construction (n)
finance (n)
holiday rep (n)
judge (n)
law (n)
medicine (n)
midwife (n)
reporter (n)
scriptwriter (n)
solicitor (n)
surgeon (n)
the arts (n)
the media (n)
tourism (n)
travel agent (n)
TV presenter (n)

be made redundant (v phr)
colleague (n)
company (n)
earn (v)
employer (n)
expenses (n)
freelance (adj)
friend (n)
full-time (adj)
get the sack (v phr)
income (n)
job (n)
manager (n)
nine-to-five (phr)
on strike (phr)
part-time (adj)
profession (n)
resign (v)
retire (v)
salary (n)
shift (n)
unemployed (adj)
wage (n)
win (v)

Shops and services
antiques shop (n)
art gallery (n)
charity shop (n)
chemist's (n)
department store (n)
estate agent's (n)
florist's (n)
garage (n)
hairdresser's (n)
internet café (n)
launderette (n)
library (n)
newsagent's (n)

Phrasal verbs
bring out
look round
run out of
sell out
set up
try on

Word patterns (*do, make*)
do (someone) a favour
do a job
do damage (to something)
do homework
do housework
do one's best
do the ironing
make a living
make an effort
make an offer
make dinner
make money
make the most of
make up one's mind

Adjectives
easygoing
energetic
exceptional
hard-working
optimistic
respectful
responsible
well presented

Using suffixes

	Adjective
adapt (v)	adaptable
ambition (n)	ambitious
care (n), (v)	careful
charm (n), (v)	charming
communicate (v)	communicative
create (v)	creative
determine (v)	determined
energy (n)	energetic
enthusiasm (n)	enthusiatic
like (v)	likable
organize (v)	organized
persuade (v)	persuasive
sympathy (n)	sympathetic
tact (n)	tactful

Unit 3

School subjects
art (n)
biology (n)
chemistry (n)
computer studies (n)
cookery (n)
English (n)
geography (n)
history (n)
maths (n)
PE (n)
physics (n)

School
detention (n)
junior school (n)
nursery school (n)
playing field (n)
private school (n)
public school (n)
register (n)
satchel (n)
secondary school (n)
sixth form college (n)
staff room (n)
state school (n)
timetable (n)
uniform (n)

Education and learning
academic (adj)
bachelor's (n)
campus (n)
compulsory (adj)
continuous assessment (n)
curriculum (n)
exams (n)
financial (adj)
graduate (n)
hall of residence (n)
journal (n)
laboratory (n)
lecture theatre (n)
library (n)
master's (n)
optional (adj)
practical (adj)
report (n)
research (n)
scholarship (n)
undergraduate (n)
university (n)

Easily confused words
certificate (n)
course (n)
degree (n)
instructor (n)
lesson (n)
pass (v)
professor (n)
pupil (n)
read (v)
revise (v)
student (n)
subject (n)
take (v)
tutor (n)

Phrasal verbs
drop out (of)
get into
get on with
pick up
point out
work out

Word patterns (get, take)
get (somewhere)
get a/the chance
get good marks
get homework
get on (my) nerves
take (someone) out
take a school subject
take care of
take the register

Word patterns (set)
be set in (film)
set (something/someone) on a surface
set a date
set an alarm clock
set homework

Noun suffixes

	Noun
able (adj)	ability
achieve (v)	achievement
attend (v)	attendance
depress (v)	depression
develop (v)	development
disappoint (v)	disappointment
enter (v)	entrance
entertain (v)	entertainment
fail (v)	failure
happy (adj)	happiness
improve (v)	improvement
perform (v)	performance
popular (adj)	popularity
populate (v)	population
press (v)	pressure
qualify (v)	qualification
real (adj)	reality
sad (adj)	sadness
willing (adj)	willingness

Unit 4

Crime
burgle (v)
cash machine (n)
crime rate (n)
gang (n)
hijack (v)
kidnap (v)
murder (v)
prevent (v)
prison sentence (n)
release (v)
rob (v)
speed limit (n)
steal (v)
stun gun (n)

Technology
access (n)
air conditioning (n)
button (n)
calculator (n)
click (on) (v)
download (v)
hack (v)
hard disk (n)
internet connection (n)
keyboard (n)
light bulb (n)
link (n)
log on/off (v)
mouse (n)
online (adj)
plug (n)
print (v)
radiator (n)
satellite dish (n)
scales (n)
scan (v)
screen (n)
socket (n)
switch (n)
switch on/off (v)
thermometer (n)
website address (n)
wire (n)

Collocations
carry out research
charge a battery
install software
service a car
turn on/off a tap

Prepositions
against the law
by chance
in danger of
in doubt about
on purpose
over eighteen
under (the) age (of eighteen)
under the circumstances
without delay

Phrasal verbs
break into
do away with
get away
give someone away
go up
look into

Unit 5

Transport
cabin (n)
car (n)
carriage (n)
check-in (v)
cruise (n)
deck (n)
engine (n)
flight (n)
gear (n)
handlebars (n)
minibike (n)
moped (n)
mountain bike (n)
pedals (n)
petrol (n)
platform (n)
scooter (n)
skateboard (n)
steering (n)
take off (v)
ticket (n)

Collocations – transport
board a ship
catch a train/bus/plane
drive a car/bus
get in/out of a car
get on/off a bus/train/plane
miss a bus/train/tram
ride a bike
take a bus/train/taxi/plane

Phrases with prepositions
at the port
drive off
get out of the car
go by car
go on a journey
go on foot
on board a ship
on the bus

Phrasal verbs
drop off
get back
make for
pick up
see off
set off
slow down
speed up
take off

Easily confused words
drive (n)
excursion (n)
journey (n)
travel (n)
trip (n)
voyage (n)

Travel
breathtaking (adj)
canyon (n)
fare (n)
guide (n)
highlight (n)
hike (n)
hire (v)
hitch-hiking (n)
holidaymaker (n)
itinerary (n)
package (n)
picturesque (adj)
resort (n)
scenic (adj)
sea voyage (n)
service (n)
site (n)
spectacular (adj)
trail (n)
trek (n)

Unit 6
Health and diet
bean (n)
beef (n)
biscuit (n)
cabbage (n)
cake (n)
calories (n)
carrot (n)
cereal (n)
cheese (n)
chips (n)
fat (n)
fattening (adj)
fish (n)
greasy (adj)
ham (n)
homemade (adj)
honey (n)
ice cream (n)
juicy (adj)
lettuce (n)
low-fat (adj)
melon (n)
nutritious (adj)
nuts (n)
olive oil (n)
pasta (n)
raw (adj)
rice (n)
sausage (n)
savoury (adj)
strawberry (n)
sweet (adj)
vitamin (n)
yoghurt (n)

Word partners
a bar of chocolate
a bottle of water
a bunch of grapes
a jar of jam
a loaf of bread
a packet of crisps
a slice of bread/cake
a tin of tuna

Phrasal verbs
cut down on
get over
give up
go off
put on
work out

Cooking and eating
bake (v)
boil (v)
chew (v)
fry (v)
grill (v)
lick (v)
melt (v)
roast (v)
sip (v)
suck (v)
swallow (v)
taste (v)

The natural world
blizzard (n)
damp (n)
flood (n)
fog (n)
forest fire (n)
harvest (n)
heatwave (n)
ice (n)
shower (n)
storm (n)
sunburn (n)

Prepositions before nouns
at fault
at risk
by mistake
for sale
in demand
in need

Prepositions after adjectives
afraid of
cruel to
different from
excited about
popular with
similar to

Prepositions after verbs
benefit from
care for/about
choose from/between
criticize for
pay for
refer to

Unit 7

Appearance and fashion
bleached hair (n)
casual look (n)
dark glasses (n)
fashion designer (n)
goatee beard (n)
hair gel (n)
high heels (n)
lip gloss (n)
make-up artist (n)
nose ring (n)
painted nails (n)
pierced lip (n)
pony tail (n)
skate shoes (n)

Phrasal verbs
catch on
keep up with
put on
roll up
take up

Word patterns
fit (v)
go with (v)
match (v)
suit (v)

Word formation
adolescence (n)
adolescent (n)
brave (adj)
bravery (n)
decoration (n)
decorative (adj)
except (prep)
exception (n)
face (n)
facial (adj)
identify (v)
identity (n)
mean (v)
meaning (n)
war (n)
warrior (n)

Paintings
abstract art (n)
canvas (n)
fantasy (n)
imagination (n)
landscape (n)
method (n)
portrait (n)
show (v)
still life (adj)
studio (n)
water colour (n)

Art

Noun (thing)	Noun (person)	Adjective	Verb
amazement	–	amazing, amazed	amaze
appreciation	–	appreciative	appreciate
art	artist	artistic	–
attraction	–	attractive	attract
beauty	–	beautiful	beautify
criticism	critic	critical	criticize
exhibit, exhibition	exhibitor	–	exhibit
paint, painting	painter	–	paint
sculpture	sculptor	–	sculpt
value	–	valuable, invaluable	value

Unit 8

Sports, hobbies and pastimes: *do*, *go* and *play*

do aerobics
do ballet
do karate
do weight training
go climbing
go cycling
go diving
go hiking
go horseback riding
go jogging
go sailing
go skiing
go swimming
play a musical instrument
play basketball
play chess
play table tennis
play tennis

Sports equipment

bat (n)
compass (n)
goggles (n)
helmet (n)
lifejacket (n)
racket (n)
rope (n)
rucksack (n)
saddle (n)
wetsuit (n)

Phrasal verbs

be into
put off
put on
take up
turn down/up
turn up (for/at)

Entertainment

audience (n)
author (n)
band (n)
best-seller (n)
chapter (n)
character (n)
composer (n)
concert (n)
fiction (n)
forecast (n)
hit (n)
novel (n)
opera (n)
orchestra (n)
page (n)
plot (n)
screen (n)
series (n)
singer (n)
stage (n)

Word patterns

front page (n)
lead singer (n)
live audience (n)
main character (n)
science fiction (n)
soap opera (n)
weather forecast (n)

Easily confused words

amateur (n)
DVD player (n)
DVD recorder (n)
fan (n)
game (n)
microphone (n)
opponent (n)
play (n)
professional (n)
speaker (n)
spectator (n)
stage (n)
studio (n)
supporter (n)
teammate (n)
viewer (n)

Unit 9

Reporting verbs
agree
apologize
beg
claim
deny
doubt
offer
order
recommend
refuse
state
suggest
warn

Radio and television
aerial (n)
broadcast (v)
commentary (n)
description (n)
DJ (disc jockey) (n)
documentary (n)
episode (n)
forecast (n)
horror film (n)
murder mystery (n)
news (n)
news bulletin (n)
newsflash (n)
newsreader (n)
reality show (n)
remake (n)
repeat (n), (v)
review (n)
romance (n)
satellite channel (n)
series (n)
signal (n)
sitcom (n)
station (radio) (n)
talk show (n)
TV channel (n)
TV set (n)
version (n)

Phrasal verbs
come out
flick through
pick up
tune in
turn off
turn over

Newspapers
caption (n)
editor (n)
gossip column (n)
headline (n)
horoscope (n)
journalist (n)
reporter (n)

Advertising
classified ads (n)
commercial (n)
jingle (n)
logo (n)
poster (n)
slogan (n)

Word formation

Noun (thing)	Noun (person)	Adjective	Verb
broadcast broadcasting	broadcaster	–	broadcast
edition editorial	editor	editorial	edit
excitement	–	(un)exciting excited	excite
photograph photography	photographer	photographic	photograph
presentation	presenter	–	present
product production	producer	–	produce
report	reporter report	reported reporting	report
view	viewer	–	view

Unit 10

Buildings
attic (n)
balcony (n)
block of flats (n)
bridge (n)
bungalow (n)
busy (adj)
cathedral (n)
cave (n)
ceiling (n)
cellar (n)
central (n)
corner (n)
corridor (n)
cottage (n)
cramped (adj)
damp (adj)
door (n)
dry (adj)
edge (n)
floor (n)
gate (n)
huge (adj)
hut (n)
inside (n)
landlord (n)
level (n)
lighthouse (n)
luxurious (adj)
modern (adj)
old-fashioned (adj)
owner (n)
quiet (adj)
simple (adj)
spacious (adj)
temple (n)
tiny (adj)
tunnel (n)
wall (n)

Places and prepositions
by a main road
by the sea
in a busy area
in a village
in the city centre
in the suburbs
on the coast
on the outskirts of …

Easily confused words
climate (n)
cost of living (n)
country (n)
countryside (n)
custom (n)
foreigner (n)
guest (n)
habit (n)
host (n)
local (adj)
regional (adj)
rural (adj)
standard of living (n)
stranger (n)
urban (adj)
weather (n)

Phrasal verbs
do up
fit in (with)
look down on
put up
put up with
take to

Writing bank

Writing: letter of application

Example question:
You have seen this advertisement in *The Globe* newspaper. You would like to apply for the job.
Write your letter of application.
Write 120–180 words.

> Part-time staff required for busy London store.
> Work Saturdays 9-6 only.
>
> **PAXON Electronics** are looking for a friendly, enthusiastic individual with good communication skills.
>
> The ideal candidate would have a good knowledge of computers, mobile phones and technical gadgets, and would be able to give customers good advice on new products.
> Foreign language an advantage but not essential.
>
> **Contact Rick Stein, Personnel Manager.**
> Why would you be suitable for the job and what will this job give you?

Model answer

Dear Mr Stein,

I am writing in response to the advertisement for part-time staff which appeared in *The Globe* on Monday. I am interested in applying for a position.

I would be interested in this job as I am hoping to go to university to study Information Technology in two years' time. I have a good knowledge of mobile phones and computers and I have had experience working in a similar shop with my uncle, who sells mobile phones. In addition, I am friendly, outgoing and I am good at dealing with people. I also speak French and a little German.

I feel I am suitable for this job as I am very keen on technical gadgets. I am currently working on an important school project about modern technology and working in your shop would provide invaluable help with this.

I hope you will consider me for this position. I will be available for an interview any afternoon after 4.30pm or Saturdays.

Yours sincerely,
Carla Simmons

Annotations:
- use appropriate opening and closing phrases
- say why you're writing and when and where you saw the advertisement
- say how the job would benefit you
- use set language chunks and useful phrases
- give some background information – interests, experience, etc
- say when you are free

Write successfully ...

- Take three minutes before you start writing to make a quick PLAN.
- You can MAKE IT UP – change your age, qualifications, experience and interests.
- Use the correct BEGINNINGS and ENDINGS, eg *Dear Mrs .../Dear Sir or Madam, Yours sincerely/faithfully*.
- Lay out your letter in short, clear PARAGRAPHS with an opening and closing.
- Use a FORMAL style of writing (avoid short forms like *I'm* and other chatty language).

Language chunks

Opening
Dear Sir/Madam;
Dear Mr ... / Mrs ...

Give a reason for writing
I am writing in response to ...
I am writing in connection with ...

Describe your skills, experience and qualities
I am interested in ...
I have a good knowledge of ...
I am good at ...

Say what you can offer and what you will get
I feel I am suitable for this position because ...
It would give me the opportunity/chance to ...

Closing
I am available from ... to ...
I hope you will consider ...
I look forward to hearing from you.
Yours sincerely;
Yours faithfully

Writing: story

Example question:
You have been asked to write a story for a competition. The story must begin with these words:
Sam knocked on the door and waited.
Write your story in 120–180 words.

Model answer

set the scene

use different past tenses to create time lines

comment on what happened and finish off the story – was it a good or a bad event?

Sam knocked on the door and waited. Sam was standing in the empty corridor outside the headmistress's office. Suddenly, the door opened.

Sam walked in and sat down nervously in front of the big desk. It had all started last Saturday when his headmistress had come into the newsagent's where Sam worked part-time. Sam was saving up to buy a computer. He wanted to start a school magazine. 'I didn't know you worked here, Sam' she had said. Sam had turned bright red. 'Come and see me in my office at break on Tuesday,' she had said and left the shop.

To his surprise, Miss Greenwich opened a drawer and pulled out a laptop. 'I think this will be very useful for the new school magazine,' said the headmistress. 'I used to have a part-time job when I was at school,' she said. 'I earned a bit of money, but it was hard work.' Sam breathed a sigh of relief. He wasn't in trouble after all, and now he could stop working at the newsagent's and concentrate on becoming a journalist.

create suspense

use adverbs and adjectives to make the story more interesting

describe the main event – why/how did it happen?

Write successfully...

- Think of an IDEA for your story before you start writing and make sure it fits in with the sentence you've been given.
- ORGANIZE your story. It should have a beginning, a middle and an end.
- Pay attention to verb TENSES. You will need to use mainly past tenses (past simple and continuous, past perfect simple and continuous, *used to*, *would*, etc) to tell your story.
- Use DIRECT SPEECH to make your story livelier.
- Use a VARIETY of words and expressions.

Language chunks

Setting the scene

The wind was blowing and it was pouring with rain.
I've never believed in ghosts, but …
He thought it was going to be a boring day because …

Describing the action

I couldn't believe my eyes!
She had a shock when …
To his surprise, …
We had no idea where/what/how …
I breathed a sigh of relief.
It had all started …

Commenting on events

Everything had turned out all right in the end.
Suddenly, things didn't seem so bad after all.
The funniest/best/most annoying thing was that …
It was the strangest/most frightening/most exciting experience I've ever had!

Writing: article

Example question:
You have been asked to write an article for the school magazine. The title of the article is:
How does school help us get a job?
Write your article in 120–180 words.

Model answer

How does school help us get a job?

Have you ever wondered whether school really helps? Although most students complain about school, they realize that the years they spend trying to pass exams are very important.

The fact is that school teaches skills for the future which do help. Firstly, students get an education. They take lots of different subjects which help with university entrance exams. In addition, at school students have to get on with each other and learn to be sociable. Lastly, school teaches us about punctuality and discipline, we have to arrive on time and meet deadlines.

However, as far as I'm concerned, school doesn't help students decide on a future profession. Most students are so stressed that they don't have a chance to think about what they really enjoy. In my opinion, schools should give career guidance so that students find it easier to decide.

To sum up, personally, I think it's true that school helps a lot, but students should have more time to develop hobbies and really understand what would make their future enjoyable.

Annotations:
- start with a question to get the reader's attention
- write a short, punchy introduction
- separate your ideas into paragraphs
- present both good points and bad points
- give your opinion
- include a short conclusion

Write successfully...

- Give your article a TITLE.
- Write about a subject that is RELEVANT to the question or title.
- Organize your article in PARAGRAPHS.
- Give REASONS and SUGGESTIONS related to the subject.
- Give your POINT OF VIEW.
- Check the LENGTH.

Language chunks

Questions to open your article
Do you ever wonder … ?
Have you ever … ?
What would happen if … ?
Do you think that … ?

Making a statement
The fact is …
It's true that …
Don't forget that …

Introducing ideas
Firstly, …
First of all, …
In addition, …
Secondly, …
Lastly, …
To sum up, …
In conclusion, …

Expressing your point of view
In my opinion, …
Personally, I (don't) think …
I believe that …
As far as I'm concerned, …

Writing: informal letter (transactional)

Example question:
You have received a letter from your friend. Read an extract from the letter and the notes you have made. Then write a letter to your friend using **all** your notes. Write your answer in 120–150 words.

> You won't believe what has happened. Our house was burgled and my new laptop was taken. I'm really annoyed. Have you ever lost anything really valuable?
>
> The problem is the email you sent about our camping trip was in there.
>
> Can you tell me about the meeting point - time and place? What equipment do I need to bring?
>
> Do you think it will be cold - what clothes should I bring?

Notes:
- Oh no! Ask if they took anything else?
- Yes! Left school bag on bus. Explain
- 11.00am at train station. Bring your GPS.
- make a suggestion

Model answer

use first names

Dear Arnold,

It was great to hear from you in a letter! You usually send emails.

Sorry about the burglary. Did they take anything else? Once, someone stole my iPod. That was valuable, but it was my fault. I left my school bag on the bus by accident. When I got it back my iPod wasn't inside.

I can't wait to go camping. The coach will be in front of the train station at 11.00am on Saturday the 3rd of July. How about bringing your GPS, as we'll be going walking. The team leader will bring all the sleeping equipment.

I think it will be cold in the evenings. I suggest you bring T-shirts and shorts for the day, and something warm to put on at night.

Shall I bring my laptop to play games? It's a bit heavy, but never mind!

Bye for now!

Samuel

use informal punctuation, eg exclamation marks

give reasons for your suggestions

include a little bit of extra information

Write successfully ...

- READ all the information carefully.
- Respond to all of the PROMPTS.
- ORGANIZE your answers in a logical order.
- Use clear PARAGRAPHS.
- Use an INFORMAL STYLE.
- Use a VARIETY of language.

Language chunks

Opening
How's it going?
Thanks for your letter.
It was great to hear from you!

Closing
I've got to go now because ...
Say hello to ... for me.
Give my love to ...
Bye for now!
Write soon!
Let me know how/what ...

Making suggestions
How about ... ?
What about ... ?
You could ...
Why don't you ... ?
One/Another idea is ...

Writing: essay

Example question:
Following a class discussion on transport and pollution in your town or city, your teacher has asked you to write an essay giving your opinion on the following statement.
Bicycle transport would make cities better places to live.
Write your essay. You can make suggestions if you want. Write your answer in 120–180 words.

Model answer

In many big cities getting around can be extremely problematic. Creating a transport system with bicycles could be the perfect solution.

Firstly, the city environment might improve. For example, air quality could get better as a result of fewer cars on the road and there might be less noise. In addition, due to a reduction in car numbers, roads may be safer.

Secondly, the public transport system would work more efficiently. For instance, if more people rode bicycles for short journeys, the public transport system might be less crowded. This would make travelling around the city by bus or metro more pleasant.

Thirdly, cycling is exercise. When people exercise they get healthier, happier and less stressed.

In conclusion, I think cities should do everything they can to encourage the use of bicycles. It would make life safer, healthier and more enjoyable for everybody.

give a general introduction

use a clear first sentence so the reader knows what you're aiming to say

use good linking words and formal language

support your arguments

give your opinion and a suggestion in the last paragraph

Write successfully...

- PLAN your answers.
- INTRODUCE and CONCLUDE your essay.
- Use clear PARAGRAPHS.
- Support your points with EXAMPLES and/or EXPLANATIONS.
- Stay on the TOPIC, and make sure it is RELEVANT.
- Use a variety of expressions to LINK or show CONTRAST.

Language chunks

Listing points
Firstly, …
Secondly, …
Thirdly, …
In addition, …
Also, …
Then, …
Another (reason /point/danger /etc) is …

Supporting one point of view
In the first place …
Furthermore …
Moreover …
A final point …

Giving explanations
because …
due to …
as a result of …
therefore …

Giving examples
for example, …
for instance, …
One example of this is …

Expressing contrast
On the other hand …
In contrast …
However …
Nevertheless …
Although …
While …

Making suggestions
I think we should …
We need to …
It would be a good idea to …
One suggestion is to …

Giving opinions
According to …
It is said that …
I am in favour of …
I agree that …
I think/believe that …
In my opinion …

Concluding
Overall …
To sum up …
In conclusion …
On the whole …

Writing: report

Example question:
The school canteen is going to be changed. Your teacher wants to know what changes should be made. You have been asked to write a report describing the canteen.

In your report, describe the food and environment in the canteen and make any recommendations for changes.

Write your answer in 120–180 words

Model answer

To: Miss Price
From: Kerry Ridgecroft
Subject: School canteen

Introduction
The aim of this report is to describe the school canteen and make recommendations for improvements.

Food
Although the food served in the canteen is very tasty, a healthy option is not always provided. Students are rarely offered fresh fruit or vegetables and most of the food is fried. Students should be offered a more nutritious menu.

Environment
The canteen staff are friendly and helpful, the seating area is attractive, and the walls are nice and bright. However, the canteen gets very crowded during the lunch break and it is difficult to find a table free.

Prices
The canteen is generally economical, but unfortunately, when healthier food is available it is more expensive and as a result students choose not to buy it.

Suggestions for improvements
I would recommend a change to the menu so that the canteen serves nutritious food at good prices. In order to solve the problem of seating, I recommend having two one-hour lunchtime shifts, at 12.00pm and 1.00pm. This will stop the overcrowding.

- say who the report is for and give it a title
- write the purpose of the report in the introduction
- use paragraph headings
- use linking words and formal language
- don't use contractions
- make your suggestions and recommendations in the conclusion

Write successfully...

- Write **To:** ... , **From:** ... and **Subject:** ... at the top of your report. MAKE UP names if necessary.
- Divide your report into short PARAGRAPHS.
- Give each paragraph a HEADING.
- Use FORMAL language.

Language chunks

Starting your report
The purpose/aim of this report is to ...
This report is about ...

Making recommendations
I would recommend ... because ...
I would particularly recommend ...
... is suitable for ... because ...

Concluding
On the whole, ...
Generally speaking, ...
To sum up, ...
In conclusion, ...

Writing: review

Example question:
You see this advertisement in your local newspaper.

> **Film critic needed**
> Do you think you have the talent to be a first class film critic? If the answer is yes, then write us a review based on any film you've seen recently and send it into the *The Daily Review* Newspaper. We are looking for someone to write a weekly cinema column. We will offer the post to the author of the best review.

Write your review. Write your answer in 120–180 words.

Model answer

- don't use contractions
- describe the setting of the film
- give a very brief summary of events
- give your opinion – either good or bad
- mention one special aspect of the film
- remember to give your recommendation whether it's good or bad

The Last King of Scotland

I am a big fan of films based on true events. I recently saw *The Last King of Scotland*, which combines both fact and fiction and was excellent.

The film is set in Uganda, and presents life during dictator Idi Amin's rule. The plot revolves around a fictional character, Scottish doctor Nicholas Garrigan, who moves to Uganda to work in a small clinic.

Idi Amin has just come to power and befriends him, asking him to become his personal doctor. At first Garrigan is impressed by Amin, but later realizes that he is leading a vicious and brutal political regime.

The plot is thrilling and Forest Whitaker is fantastic in his role as Amin. The shocking events depicted are very interesting for someone who knows nothing about Uganda.

What I really liked was the fact that although at the beginning of the film, Amin seems a fascinating character, by the end of the film he really shows his true colours, and you realize why the world turned against him.

I would definitely recommend this film. However, it does contain violent scenes, and is not suitable for children.

Write successfully ...

- Mention the TITLE or NAME of the book, play, film, programme or restaurant.
- DON'T waste too many words describing.
- You must give your own PERSONAL OPINION.
- Break your review up into different PARAGRAPHS.
- End with a RECOMMENDATION.
- Use a VARIETY of good vocabulary and structures.

Language chunks

Introducing the subject
I recently saw/read/watched …

What you liked about it
What I particularly liked about the … was …
I really liked …
The best thing about … was …

What it is about
The programme/film/book is about …
The film is set …
It begins …
In the beginning, …

Useful adjectives

Good	Bad	Neutral
amazing	dreadful	strange
impressive	uninteresting	mysterious
lively	poor	shocking
fascinating		
thrilling		
incredible		

Writing: email

Example question:
You and your English friend Jessica have arranged to stay at your uncle's house on an island during the summer holidays. Read her email and the notes you have made. Then write an email to Jessica using all your notes.
Write your email in 120–150 words.

From: Jessica Mitchell
Sent: 12th May
Subject: Summer holidays

Hello!
How are you? I can't wait for summer to come! I want to start planning my trip now and I've got a few questions.
First of all, where is it best to fly to? I know we're going to an island, but it might not be easy to get straight there. What do you recommend? ← *tell her*
Also, I was wondering if you could tell me a bit about your uncle's place. Is anyone else going to be there at the same time? I can't really remember much Greek. How will I communicate? ← *give a short description* / *explain who and how*
Although I love the sea, the doctor has told me I should avoid sitting in the sun for too long. Is there anything else to do apart from going to the beach? Perhaps I should bring lots of books! ← *make suggestions*

Write soon!
Jessica

Model answer

use first names / *use contractions and informal punctuation*

Hi Jessica,
I'm really excited about our holidays too!
In answer to your question about flights, I suggest you fly to Athens. We can travel to the island by boat, it's a great experience!
As for my uncle's house, it's a big villa by the sea. There's plenty of space and all my cousins will be there too. Don't worry, they are looking forward to meeting you and they all speak English.
You asked me about things to do other than going to the beach. Well, we never sit on the beach at midday and we always take an umbrella. How about doing a bit of sightseeing? There are lots of interesting ruins on the island, and plenty of nice cafés in a pretty little town. Why don't you look the island up online?
I have to go now, but write soon with your flight details.
Love,
Debbie

use informal language / *give reasons for your answers* / *use an appropriate closing phrase*

Write successfully ...

- ORGANIZE your information in a logical order.
- Use clear PARAGRAPHS.
- Cover all four points in the NOTES.
- Use an appropriate STYLE.
- CHECK for spelling, grammar and punctuation mistakes.

Language chunks

Openings
Dear Jessica,
Hi/Hello, Jessica
Thanks for your email.
It was great to hear from you.
I hope you're well.

Suggesting
Why don't you ...
I suggest ...
I think you should ...

Answering questions
You asked me about ...
As for ... ,

Closings
Hope to hear from you soon.
I have to go now.
Write soon.
Bye,
Take care,
Love,
Best wishes,

Speaking bank

Likes and dislikes
I like/don't like/love/hate + ...-ing
I prefer ...-ing to ...-ing
I'm keen on ...-ing
I'm very interested in ...

I'd like/love to ...
I wouldn't like to ...
I'd hate to ...
I'd prefer to .... than (to) ...

Talking about ambitions
I'm hoping to ...
I'm looking forward to ...
My dream is to ...
In the future, I'd like to ...

Comparing
X looks very ... whereas Y looks ...
X looks more/ ...-er ... than Y.
One thing they've got in common is that ...
Both X and Y seem ...
Compared with X, Y is ...

Making suggestions
What about + -ing ...?
How about + -ing ...?
What do you think about + -ing ...?
Why don't you ...?
Maybe/I think we should ...
It would be a good idea to ... because ...

Conversation fillers
I guess
I suppose
you know
I mean
you see
Well,

Describing people's feelings
She/He must be feeling ...
She/He might be feeling ...
She/He looks as if she/he ...
I get the impression she/he ...

Keeping the conversation going
And also ...
I think you're right, and ...
I see what you mean about ...
Wouldn't it be better to / if ... ?
I (don't) think I would ... but ...
That's a good point, but / and ...
Yes, but ...

Describing objects and places
It's something that you use to ...
It's for ...
It's a bit like a ...
It's a kind of ...
It's a place where ...